1895

Teacher Union Bargaining
Practice and Policy

Teacher Union Bargaining
Practice and Policy

Gene Geisert, Ph.D., and Myron Lieberman, Ph.D.

Precept Press
Division of Bonus Books, Inc., Chicago

98 97 96 95 94

Library of Congress Cataloging-in-Publication Data

Geisert, Gene.
    Teacher union bargaining : practice and policy / Gene Geisert and
Myron Lieberman.
        p.   cm.
    Includes bibliographical references and index.
    ISBN 0–944496–43–1
    1. Collective bargaining—Teachers—United States. 2. Teachers'
unions—United States. I. Lieberman, Myron. 1919-   II. Title.
LB2844.59.U6G45   1994
331.89'0413711'00973—dc20   94–23092
                                           CIP

5 4 3 2 1

Precept Press
160 East Illinois Street
Chicago, Illinois 60611

Cover design by Shane R. McCall
Composition by Point West, Inc., Carol Stream, IL

Printed in the United States of America

CONTENTS

PREFACE

Collective bargaining is by nature adversarial. When boards understand this fact and adequately prepare themselves accordingly, they will be better able to deal with the realities of bargaining and the threats to their integrity. Divisions within the board or between board members and administrators weaken management and foster excessive union demands. A strong, united, and knowledgeable board has many advantages and normally will be able to defend itself adequately. The consequences of not being prepared are loss of management prerogatives, loss of flexibility, increased public dissatisfaction, greater uniformity, and excessive operating costs.

As long as boards are legally required to bargain collectively, they must remain skeptical of bargaining strategies that assume away basic conflicts of interest. Three decades of school district bargaining have not resulted in substantial improvements in American education. It seems unlikely that further restrictions on management will achieve the improvements in the nation's schools that reform efforts seek to accomplish.

This book combines the practical with the conceptual and policy dimensions of teacher bargaining. Initially, we analyze face-to-face bargaining; that is, issues of immediate practical concern to school board members and practitioners who may be unaware of or indifferent to the larger conceptual issues. Subsequently, issues that involve broader policy considerations will be examined. These issues may or may not surface during bargaining sessions. For example, the question of whether individual teachers should be forced to pay for representational services they do not want frequently surfaces during negotiations, but this question involves constitutional, statutory, political, and civil rights issues as well as those related to bargaining. Nor are the answers to such questions clear from the conceptual foundations of teacher bargaining; the latter are often silent or inconsistent on the issue as it emerges in bargaining sessions and in legislative forums.

The objective of part 1 of this book is to assist persons who must engage directly in the negotiating process or who have ongoing responsibilities for what happens in bargaining meetings. Someone who is drowning does not need a dissertation on the navigational problems that led up to their plight, but it is essential to view the immediate problems in context and from a perspective that goes beyond resolution of the immediate bargaining problem. For this reason, broad policy issues are addressed as well as those that must be resolved at the bargaining table. Because it was not feasible to discuss all of the broad policy issues, we have emphasized the ones most likely to affect across-the-table bargaining.

Part 2 raises various policy issues arising out of teacher bargaining. Here, the focus is not on how to cope with the process of bargaining, but rather on whether and how the process might or should be changed as a matter of public policy. Part 2 is analogous to a discussion of the desirability of a tax that must be paid. Although we cannot avoid paying the tax, we may also wish to discuss various features of it, to see whether the tax should be maintained or changed in some way. Thus, even though it recognizes that school management in most states has no immediate alternative to bargaining, part 2 presents policy alternatives, both to the entire process and to specific features of it.

The first four chapters in part 2 challenge the public policy rationale for teacher bargaining and/or the rationale for public sector bargaining generally. The remaining chapters discuss specific features of teacher bargaining without necessarily challenging the process *in toto*; however, if valid, some of the specific criticisms of teacher bargaining would require basic changes in it. In addition, several chapters in part 2 have implications for bargaining at the table. For example, the treatment of binding arbitration in bargaining sessions may be affected by how school boards assess the policy issues discussed in part 2. In this sense, part 2 is to some extent a continuation of the discussion in part 1.

The authors wish to express their gratitude to Robert S. Summers for permission to present his essay, "Public Sector Collective Bargaining Substantially Diminishes Democracy," as chapter 9 of this book. It originally appeared in *Government Review*, as also did articles from which chapters 10 and 15 are adapted. Chapter 16 appeared in substantially similar form in *Public Interest*. Some sections of chapter 11 first appeared in the *Phi Delta Kappan*.

Some other sections of this book are taken from a previously published volume on the teacher bargaining by one of the authors.* This book is a greatly expanded version of that volume, undertaken because a simple revision could not do justice to new issues that have emerged since 1979. Most of the sections taken from the previous book relate to procedures and techniques for use in bargaining sessions; as practitioners on both sides will attest, these do not change very much, even over long periods. Partly for this reason, the practical "how-to-do-it" sections should be useful regardless of the extent to which readers pursue the theoretical and conceptual dimensions of bargaining with teachers that are discussed in part 2.

GENE GEISERT, PH.D.
MYRON LIEBERMAN, PH.D.

---

* Lieberman, Myron, *Before, during, and after bargaining* (Chicago: Teach 'Em Inc., 1979).

ABOUT THE AUTHORS

Gene Geisert, Ph.D., is chairman of the Division of Instructional Leadership of St. John's University, New York City, N.Y. Prior to this affiliation, Dr. Geisert held a number of positions in the educational field, including those of superintendent of New Orleans Public Schools, Wilmington (Del.) Public Schools, and Alpena (Mich.) Public Schools. He is also president of Think Networks Inc., a producer of computer-based educational materials. He has served as an educational consultant to the governments of China, France, and Germany, was given a meritorious service award as chairperson of National Assessment of Education Progress, and was named an educational leader of the century by the American Association of School Administrators.

Dr. Geisert is the author or coauthor of seven books and manuals in the educational field, including *Simulation Exercise for Collective Bargaining*, has authored numerous articles in professional journals serving the field, and makes frequent appearances on lecture platforms at gatherings of educators both in this country and abroad. He earned his doctoral degree in education administration at the University of Michigan and master's and bachelor degrees at the University of Toledo. Dr. Geisert has held leadership positions in various organizations in the educational field, including the American Association of School Administrators and the Association of Superintendents of Large City Schools.

Myron Lieberman, Ph.D., is senior research scholar at The Social Philosophy and Policy Center, Bowling Green (Ohio) State University. Previous positions he has held include professorships in education at the University of Pennsylvania, Ohio University, University of Southern California, City University of New York, Hofstra University, and Rhode Island College.

Dr. Lieberman's experience in school district collective bargaining includes service as chief negotiator in over 200 contracts in seven states. In addition, he has served as a consultant on collective bargaining for scores of state and national educational organizations, including the National Education Association, the American Federation of Teachers, the National School Boards Association and the American Association of School Administrators. As employment relations consultant for the latter organization (1974-77), he was also responsible for collective bargaining publications, training, legislation, and research. Dr. Lieberman has served as director or staff member for six national institutes on collective bargaining sponsored by Phi Delta Kappa.

In addition to being a Fellow of the Public Service Research Council, Dr. Lieberman has received a distinguished professorship from the Virginia Consortium on Higher Education, and a distinguished alumnus award from the University of Illinois. He is the author or coauthor of 15 books on education subjects and numerous monographs, special reports, and articles that have appeared in both professional journals and in the lay press. He has been a guest speaker at conventions of virtually every major national education organization and an invited lecturer at some 100 colleges and universities in the United States, Australia, and Canada. Dr. Lieberman received his graduate degrees from the University of Illinois. He also holds undergraduate degrees in science and law from the University of Minnesota.

PART I
STRATEGIES FOR SUCCESS IN NEGOTIATIONS

1. MUST SCHOOL BOARDS BARGAIN?

The first policy issue some boards face in bargaining is whether to bargain collectively at all. Although this option no longer exists for most boards, it is a useful point of departure, because it helps to clarify several broad policy issues related to bargaining. In the private sector, where unionism began, about one worker in eight carries a union card. Private employers oppose unionization more frequently and effectively than public employers, such as school boards. Indeed, private sector management often conducts a strong no-representation campaign the moment a union organizer arrives on the premises. The employer's objective is to convince employees that they are better off if they do not unionize and bargain. In fact, many companies don't wait for union organizers to appear before conducting campaigns intended to discourage unionization.

These no-representation campaigns are often effective. Sometimes they are so successful that unions can't muster the employee support necessary to initiate a representation election, let alone win one. Should school management try to remain free of union involvement? After all, as in the private sector, unionization increases costs and decreases managerial control over district operations. From school management's point of view, a union can do nothing for employees that cannot be done voluntarily and without unionization at less cost. At the same time, many disadvantages can be avoided when employees are not unionized. In practice, school boards usually accept unionization without opposition. One reason is that the idea of conducting a no-representation campaign simply has never occurred to most school officials. Another reason is that opposition seems hopeless. Nevertheless, in view of the fact that many employers in the private sector successfully opposed unionization, the absence of opposition to it in public education calls for an explanation.

In considering their options, school boards and school administrators must take the long view. It is hardly worthwhile to oppose unionization if such opposition will be successful for only a year or two. Such short-lived opposition may serve only to antagonize a successful union, inflame its militancy, and intensify its antimanagement attitude. Furthermore, unionization differs in the public and private sectors, and the differences make it more difficult to oppose the unionization of public employees. For instance, local teacher organizations were established in school districts long before there were efforts to bargain collectively. Similarly, so were the civil service organizations that represent many noncertified personnel. In contrast, when organizers from a private sector union first attempt to solicit support among workers, they are rarely greeted by dues-paying union members from that union.

Private sector unions usually lack dues-paying members until the union achieves recognition as the bargaining agent. Furthermore, public sector employee organizations often have the right to represent their members, even if the organizations do not have collective bargaining rights. This means that school boards often must deal with an employee organization regardless of whether it represents a majority of employees in an appropriate bargaining unit.

Union influence, then, is pervasive throughout public education, whether or not school districts are legally obligated to bargain collectively with employee unions; affiliates of the National Education Association (NEA) and the American Federation of Teachers (AFT) have been a presence in school districts for decades. Consequently, teacher organizations are usually perceived by school administrators as familiar forces. NEA and AFT field representatives typically are given a less hostile reception from school administrators than union organizers receive from managers in private industry.

Another difference between the public and private sectors relates to the time that must elapse between union organizing drives. Clearly, it would be unfair to the employer to allow unions to seek another election for recognition immediately after employees have voted to reject it. Likewise, it would be unfair if a vote against union representation were to bind employees permanently. From a management point of view, the longer the time span between representation elections the better, because less disruption will occur. Several states, however, require only a one-year waiting period after an unsuccessful representation election. This relatively brief period tends to discourage school management from campaigning against union representation. The extent of support the union receives from teachers, the depth of the union's involvement in district affairs, and the time limit imposed on organizing efforts are three of the crucial elements to consider before launching a no-representation campaign. Another factor is whether supervisors, principals, or both have the right to bargain collectively. In districts where they do, top management is less likely to receive their support in a no-representation campaign.

One recurring problem is that material that employees read and hear on collective bargaining tends to come from the union. In fact, some school administrators mistakenly believe that it is illegal to urge school employees to vote against union representation. School officials do have the right to urge their employees to reject unionization and collective bargaining, but how that right is exercised is another matter.

Management cannot tell teachers that they will be fired, transferred, or deprived of any benefits because of their support for the union. In addition, management cannot interrogate employees about their views on unionization. Although management can express its opposition to collective bargaining, such expression must not be coercive or promise a benefit in exchange for an employee vote against unionization. Management must observe these restrictions if it conducts a campaign against union representation. Nothing is achieved if employees vote to reject union representation only to have the vote set aside because of illegal employer conduct.

Precisely what management can say and do to discourage unionization varies somewhat from state to state. Usually, school management can urge its employees to reject a union's attempt to call a representation election. In its rationale, a board can point to the costs of union dues and assessments and to the possibility that these fees will increase. School officials are free to quote NEA or AFT contracts that require union membership or payment of service fees as conditions of employment. They can make it clear that if the union wins recognition, employees may then be required to bring their problems to the union instead of to their supervisors. It is also appropriate to tell employees that neither the board nor the administration wants or needs the union, and that employee benefits in the district compare favorably with salary and other benefits in unionized districts.

Finally, school management can emphasize that although the union can always out-promise management, it cannot deliver a single benefit that is not agreed to by the administration and the board. This point can be persuasive because most bargaining laws assert specifically that neither party is required to agree on any proposal or make any concession during bargaining.

Of course, every school district is different, and the variables render it impossible to prescribe a detailed no-representation strategy suitable for every district. In general, however, boards should avoid extreme positions that are not based on objective assessments of district strengths and weaknesses. As a practical matter, opposition to union representation may not be worthwhile; nonetheless, boards should not assume that opposition is prohibited as a matter of law. If a no-representation campaign is appropriate, it is essential to avoid actions that will legally jeopardize a teacher vote against union representation. Practically, this means that boards should employ experienced labor counsel before embarking upon a no-representation campaign. Otherwise, they probably will need to employ such counsel anyway in order to litigate the problems they have created in trying to avoid union representation.

School boards typically underestimate employee support for collective bargaining, and relatively few board campaigns against it have been successful. Indeed, such campaigns seem to be successful only in rural or high-salary districts; they are rarely successful in other districts, especially on a long-range basis. Also, efforts to disestablish an incumbent union must be distinguished from efforts to forestall unionization in the first place. Campaigns to disestablish an incumbent union are virtually always the outcome of an employee—not a management—initiative. Furthermore, the reasons for them are likely to stem from union failure to achieve an expected level of benefits or to avoid employer "take-backs." Thus, employee dissatisfaction with an incumbent union is not necessarily a positive development from management's point of view.

2. ORGANIZING FOR COLLECTIVE BARGAINING

Introduction

School boards and superintendents who carefully prepare themselves for bargaining are much less likely to negotiate away their rights to manage the district. A school board that naively sits down to bargain with professional labor leaders without clear goals is likely to accept important provisions that restrict its ability to provide competent management. Even with preparation, the pressures that develop during bargaining sessions can cause rifts between board members and administrators that seriously weaken management's collective resolve. Under normal conditions, a well-organized management team has the advantage in bargaining. Conversely, the lack of positive direction and/or internal bickering frequently will cause management to lose this advantage. Recently, various movements that approach bargaining as a cooperative venture have been heralded for their "vision." Because bargaining is clearly an adversarial relationship, board members should be wary of such approaches.

During the past few years, there has been considerable discussion of "the administrative team" or "the management team" in education. Conceptually, the administrative team is a districtwide group responsible for districtwide operations. Understandably, the concept has received increasing attention as teacher bargaining has increased. Successful bargaining requires unity, and the administrative team is perceived as a way to achieve and maintain such unity. This chapter presents two contrasting views of the concept.

Rationale for the Administrative Team

According to its proponents, the "administrative team" is a thoroughly practical technique that deserves immediate and widespread application.

Here is how and why the administrative team is supposed to work:

Initially, the team approach is written into board policy. The superintendent must choose team members carefully, including a representative from each administrator group in the district (both certified and classified). The board should develop a team job description that outlines the relationships among team members. The board also needs to define the duties the team is to accomplish, the cooperative ventures to be undertaken, and the responsibility and authority of team members. For example:

- The team should be the officially designated leadership unit for developing, recommending, implementing, and monitoring board policy and administrative regulations.
- The team must be recognized by the board as a storehouse of seasoned counsel that operates on the scene where the action is; this reservoir should be tapped regularly and consistently for information and advice.
- The team functions through the superintendent.
- The members of the team must be respected. The board must recognize that its team members need protection from unwarranted attack and from having the team's actions and decisions reversed by higher authorities. (Nevertheless, agreed-to procedures should be open to review and reversal at a higher level, but such arrangements must be understood and condoned before an incident occurs that could cause reversal.)
- Team members are compensated through a process that guarantees members fair and just reward for the time they work and the responsibility and skill they must exercise in their tasks.

To help assure that the team makes sound decisions from the outset, the board of education should allow management team members to have input into decisions that affect the operation of the school district before any new policies are adopted. This amounts to a "debugging" device before final action is taken by the board. The procedure requires that each member of the team review proposed policies and file with the superintendent an Educational Impact Statement, which essentially is a statement that sets forth the likely consequences of any given management decision in terms of its effect on an individual program and if appropriate, the operation of the school district. The justification for this process is twofold. First, it assures that members have both the opportunity and responsibility to analyze proposed policies from their own point of view; they can assess proposals on the basis of their individual sphere of operation and offer observations concerning the administrative consequences if given policies were adopted and implemented. Second, the process requires responsible and continuing participation by each member of the team.

As one might expect, leadership qualities exhibited by the superintendent cast long reflections over the team. Superintendents must recognize and comport themselves as leaders in a power-sharing situation.

Superintendents who are seen as effective team leaders carrying out the will of the board while functioning as members of their teams will be more powerful than superintendents who act unilaterally without concern for middle managers. It is reasonable to assume that these managers will support the team-oriented superintendent more consistently than a superintendent who usually ignores those at the central office or building level.

- Total commitment to the team concept must be felt and demonstrated by the superintendent. He or she should not structure the group so that there is only one-way communication and power emanating from the superintendent.
- A mechanism must be developed whereby team members have representation. If the school district is small, such representation can be direct; in a large district, representation from various levels of middle management might work best. Area representation functions nicely in some districts. In other districts, position representation does the job as individuals from various positions established within the district organizational chart are selected for their expertise.
- All administrators should be active participants in team activities both at a personnel level of responsibility as well as in districtwide matters. They must perform individually as well as collectively.
- Job descriptions should be written that include responsibilities, duties, and authority.
- The team must have adequate time for decisionmaking. Board agenda should be distributed to the team at the same time such documents are given to board members; in like manner, the team must receive copies of

proposed board minutes, followed by adopted minutes, after each set has been prepared for distribution.

- The board of education should endorse the Educational Impact Statement system of policy development and arrange to have statements and accompanying recommendations submitted to the board before any policies are adopted.
- Communication is the key to success in team management. Individually and collectively, team members must analyze their responses to proposed policies and take time to develop a consensus on any controversies that arise.

It is reasonable to assume that team members sometimes will disagree with the superintendent's position on an issue. To prepare in advance for these situations, a method for coping with them must be established when the team *first begins its work*. These procedures should then be written into the policy statement that governs the team's activity.

In dealing with disagreements, some superintendents will go no further than allowing the team to have input. If the team and the superintendent do not agree, the superintendent attempts to explain his own position, but then makes a recommendation to the board for consideration.

To reiterate, a policy governing the emergence of basic disagreements must be developed and agreed upon *before* the first dispute occurs. There should be a genuine two-way flow of frequent and candid information within the group. In none of the approaches noted above does management abdicate its responsibility for making decisions. If there is no group consensus on the best way to proceed, the superintendent makes the decision, confident that group members have unearthed all of the relevant facts. The question of accountability remains clearly in the hands of those appointed by the board as legitimate caretakers of responsibility.

The marked increase in collective bargaining activities within a school district is ample proof that boards of education and superintendents should look at the team management idea very seriously. It stands to reason that subordinate administrators who are not involved substantially in both the development and administration of school district policy may decide that the only way to put muscle into their convictions is to sit across from top management at the bargaining table. On the other hand, if middle managers are viewed as team members by the board and superintendent, they will develop loyalty to the upper echelons and help the school district improve its bargaining position.

The Case Against the Administrative Team Concept

The administrative team concept has elements of plausibility, even logic. In practice, however, the concept creates a number of problems. Let us see why the concept has initial appeal, as well as why its practical value isn't as convincing.

First, the meaning of *administrative team* is neither clear nor commonly understood. Although fuzziness surrounds the concept, this much is evident: Collective bargaining requires unity on management's side. In a bargaining session, a school district must present a solid front, regardless of differences that exist within the management negotiating team. A district cannot afford to let the union exploit its management conflicts

The difficulties arise when top management must demonstrate its support of middle management. To achieve this objective, the district may offer long-term contracts for middle management. The assumption is that such contracts are one way for the board to ensure the support and loyalty of its middle managers.

In this connection, the National Football League shows a more sensi ble approach to accountability and responsibility than most school districts. In the NFL, head coaches typically hire and fire the assistant coaches; it is contrary to common practice to give assistant coaches contracts that extend beyond the contract of the head coach. As a result, the fortunes of the assistant coaches are clearly related to those of the head coach. In contrast, school districts typically employ superintendents who are not allowed to employ assistants of their own choosing, except perhaps over a long period. It is difficult to understand why coaches, but not superintendents, should have the authority to hire and fire their subordinates. The management team concept should not be used to weaken the authority of top-level district managers over the middle-level managers.

Another unfortunate outcome of administrative team jargon is the tendency to treat management personnel as a quasi-legislative body. The usual reaction of appointees to the management team runs like this: "If we are in this together, we must have something to say about policies that are adopted." Before very long, team members begin to regard their advisory role as a legislative one. To illustrate: Suppose a superintendent solicits the advice of principals on smoking rules. For various reasons, their opinions may be contrary to policies ultimately adopted by top management. Of course, the principals will eventually learn that their opinions ran

11

counter to the policy adopted. When this happens, many will conclude that being on the administrative team is a sham. Board members and superintendents compound the confusion by treating middle management participation in policymaking as a criterion of "democratic governance." One might just as well criticize football coaches or quarterbacks for being "undemocratic" because they do not poll team members on what plays to call, or follow their recommendations when they do.

Fundamentally, the administrative team concept is an outgrowth of the same fallacy that often underlies the rationale for teacher bargaining. The fallacy is that a democratic school system is one that maximizes employee participation in management, regardless of circumstances. Employee participation in the policymaking process is a means, not an end. Like any other means, it has limits and conditions that should be subject to management discretion. Whether such discretion is exercised "democratically" depends more on its relationship to the community than to its acceptability to middle management.

The Board's Negotiating Team

The size and composition of the administration's negotiating team are issues that need to be faced. Should the superintendent negotiate? How many members should be on the team? Should the board employ an outside negotiator? Questions such as these crop up whenever district negotiations are discussed. Even administrators who have been through the process are not always sure of the "right" answers to these questions.

Let us first consider the size of the negotiating team, since this question affects composition of the team. Because there is no magic in any particular figure, the optimum size will be a compromise among several factors. First, the smaller the team, the easier it is to reach agreement, both within the team and with the union team. There are several reasons for this. Less time is needed to caucus. It is easier to maintain an atmosphere of informality with small negotiating teams. Larger teams on either side increase the need for formal procedures to govern negotiations. Furthermore, interruptions of regular duty assignments can be minimized. Negotiations can take a long time, perhaps much of it devoted to waiting for the union to respond.

On the other hand, the smaller the team, the greater the danger of a major mistake in negotiations. Even the most knowledgeable administrators may be unaware of unique school situations that should affect their response to union proposals. For example, consider a clause stating the board's right to require teacher attendance at evening meetings. There may be considerable variation among elementary schools in the district. An elementary principal on the negotiating team who is not aware of all the variations may respond in terms of the practice in particular schools that require only three evening meetings per year. This may undermine programs in schools where teachers are required to attend five evening meetings per year.

Obviously, every principal can't be on the negotiating team. Yet, again and again, one finds variations from school to school in the lunch program, bus duty, attendance after class, or on other items being negotiated. Sometimes, the variations are unjust and should be negotiated out of existence. Sometimes, however, they are justified and may be inadvertently negotiated away because the administration negotiating team was unaware of them.

Two procedures should be used to minimize these problems. First, the negotiating team should explore all proposals carefully with the entire staff, so that any unusual situations are recognized. Second, the negotiation agenda should be structured so that particular experts are available when their expertise is needed. Thus, payroll and computer personnel need to be available only when specific items, such as the number of separate deductions or duration of pay periods, are being negotiated. To provide needed insight, the board and superintendent must select representatives who use expertise effectively. In the private sector, the management team is conversant with every school plant involved in negotiations. Yet, boards often select negotiating teams that lack representation from school plants. Ideally, the negotiating team would include representation from every school and administrative agency likely to be affected by the negotiated agreement. Such a team would include several individuals whose presence is necessary only when items relating to their expertise are being negotiated.

Continuity in negotiations and contract administration is also essential. When a successor agreement is negotiated, the board should not be represented by a completely new team. Generally speaking, five team members should be enough for school systems employing up to 1,000 teachers; negotiations in some districts employing more than 3,000 teachers have been conducted successfully by three-member teams. Board teams need not be very large if there is adequate communication with the entire staff and effective use of ad hoc team members. A key concept in developing the board negotiation team is to include members who collectively are knowledgeable about all aspects of school management affected by negotiations.

It is highly undesirable to permit the administrative staff or any subunit thereof to select members of the administration negotiating team. For instance, the superintendent should not permit the principals to select a principal to be on the team. The person so selected may be the most popular principal, or the least busy one, or anything but the most effective negotiator.

It is also a mistake to assign staff members to the negotiating team merely because they hold certain positions in the system. Superintendents naturally prefer to have the business manager or director of personnel on the administration team. However, subordinates may be more effective members of a negotiating team than their superiors; for example, an assistant principal may be a more effective negotiator than a principal. Even so, it may be politically desirable also to include a representative from among the principals.

A board should never allow the union to dictate the composition of its negotiating team. Some administrators are afraid to say no to anything for fear of jeopardizing their real or assumed popularity with teachers. Staff members seeking popularity do not belong on board negotiating teams.

Except in districts with only a few hundred (or fewer) teachers, the superintendent should not be on the negotiating team. The superintendent should be kept aware of the progress of the negotiations and should periodically provide direction to the team based on guidelines set by the board. However, the superintendent should not be present continuously as a member of the negotiating team; to do so runs the risk of having to wait endlessly while teachers caucus, or having the performance of board business continuously disrupted because of the uncertain course of negotiations. The teachers are required to negotiate with the board's representative, whoever it may be. For this reason, neither the union nor the superintendent should be upset because the superintendent is not a member of the board negotiating team.

The Chief Negotiator

Perhaps the most important negotiating decision boards make is to designate their chief negotiator. Teachers unions have been drafting contract language for several decades. They have sophisticated computer operations to analyze salary schedules, fringe benefits, and contract clauses. Unions employ highly trained negotiators and labor attorneys with decades of experience. In contrast, a local school district usually has a board whose members seldom understand the rudiments of collective bargaining or the implications of proposals made by the union. Given this mismatch, it is not surprising that school boards frequently negotiate away rights that are needed to operate the school district effectively. To avoid this outcome, many school boards use an outside consultant to serve as their chief negotiator. The potential advantages of using an outside consultant are:

- The outside consultant is usually a specialist in negotiations and related services. An individual who negotiates 25 contracts a year will tend to be more knowledgeable about all aspects of negotiations than a district employee who negotiates one or two, perhaps every other year.
- District officials may prefer to have criticisms of their negotiating positions directed at outsiders instead of school board members and district administrators.
- The outside consultant is more likely to be knowledgeable about agreements reached and the status of negotiations in nearby districts; such knowledge can be very important in the negotiations.
- Typically, outside consultants can be more candid with the school board and district management than can district employees. The fear of losing one of several clients is not as great as the fear of losing one's full-time position. Furthermore, relationships between district employees and the school board are more likely to be affected by issues that are not germane to negotiations.
- The real cost of employing an outside negotiator may be less than the costs of using a district employee as the chief negotiator. For example, the consultant's costs for information services related to negotiation are shared by several districts, whereas boards that employ their own employee as chief negotiator must usually absorb all of these costs.
- It is easier to terminate the services of an outside consultant than the services of a district employee.

The disadvantages of using outside negotiators:

- A district employee is more likely to be available when needed, especially in the closing stages of negotiations.
- A district employee is likely to be more knowledgeable about district developments affecting negotiations. Also, a district employee is more

likely to be aware of past negotiations and their implications for the current situation.

- Inasmuch as the district must administer as well as negotiate contracts, it is desirable to have the contracts negotiated by district employees who will administer them.

It must be emphasized that the foregoing advantages and disadvantages are central tendencies that do not necessarily apply to every situation. For instance, an outside negotiator employed by a district for several years may be more knowledgeable about the district than a newly appointed superintendent or principal. Outside negotiators are often desirable—even essential—but the more skilled ones try to reduce, rather than increase, the board's dependence on them.

The rates for outside negotiators vary widely. Many are labor attorneys who bill the school district at their usual hourly rate, perhaps with some modifications for all-night or other extended meetings. Both hourly rates and fixed fees have dangers of their own. If the fee is fixed, the outside negotiator may be tempted to conclude the negotiations by conceding too much, too soon. After all, the negotiator is, in effect, working for nothing if the fee is fixed and negotiations are lengthy. Realistically, the hourly rate is more equitable and safer, because it is virtually impossible to know how much time will be required.

Unfair labor practice charges, for example, can require weeks of hard work, including appearances before hearing officers and state labor relations agencies. Although unions may file frivolous charges as a negotiating ploy, the charges must be answered. Internal union politics may make it impossible to negotiate an agreement expeditiously. In general, boards and school administrators underestimate the time negotiations take, a tendency that leads to some unpleasant surprises when the bills come due.

In considering employment of an outside negotiator, boards should consult board members and superintendents in districts where the negotiator has previously worked. One should be skeptical of consultants who agree with everything the board wants to do; such agreement frequently suggests an overwhelming desire to get the business rather than sound professional judgment. Boards should not, however, automatically exclude consultants who formerly represented unions in negotiations. Just as in private employment, some of the best negotiators started out as union representatives and were subsequently recruited by management.

Frequently, boards of education are predisposed to seek an attorney to serve as their chief negotiator. Many labor attorneys are experts in the field of collective bargaining and are quite capable of negotiating a good contract. However, attorneys skilled in labor negotiations are not always available to local school boards. Most boards of education represent small communities not particularly attractive to labor relations lawyers. As a result, boards are often tempted to employ school attorneys who have been retained by the board for general school-related legal matters. This person may be a good school attorney but may lack the qualifications of a successful negotiator. School board attorneys are employed to provide written opinions on bargaining issues or on technical school law matters. Labor agreements, based upon the relationship between the parties, are likely to be adjudicated by an arbitrator, not the courts. Of course, attorneys who specialize in labor relations can often conduct negotiations in a very competent way. The critical consideration is not whether the negotiator is an attorney but whether the negotiator is thoroughly familiar with collective bargaining by unions representing school district employees.

Board/Administrator Relations In Bargaining

Bargaining often leads to strained relations between school boards and superintendents. To minimize the possibility, both board members and superintendents must be sensitive to pressures they will face in the negotiation process.

Intimidation often works, and teachers unions know it. Assaults on administrators' job security often weaken their opposition to union demands. Staging and publicizing a "no confidence" vote on the superintendent is a frequent example of this tactic, which works equally well on school board members and principals, although for somewhat different reasons in each case.

Teachers unions can often intimidate board members wherever the unions play a significant role in school board elections or appointments. Most board members naturally want teacher support. Failing that, they at least want to avoid teacher opposition. If the board is faced with controversial decisions on integration or new bus routes or sex education, members facing reelection may be especially reluctant to oppose union demands in bargaining. Board members who previously opposed teacher demands often demonstrate surprising flexibility as election day nears.

Suddenly they find merit in proposals that would have been rejected out of hand earlier in the year. If a school board member would rather be right than reelected, the teachers union can usually find a candidate who prefers being elected to being right. A host of challengers may even be waiting in the wings, lacking nothing but a campaign organization or issue. Teachers unions can provide both. Needless to say, union-backed winners are more inclined to support union demands made during bargaining.

The election calculus varies widely among school districts. In some communities, teachers union support would have a negative effect on a candidate's prospects for election. In such communities, school board members are not subject to union intimidation, but in many school districts, especially larger ones, union support can be decisive, and school board behavior in bargaining shows it.

This reality is often overlooked because the pressures on school board members differ from the pressures on management in the private sector. It is difficult to intimidate board members economically, but they can often be intimidated politically. In the real world, alternatives open to board members may be to make concessions and remain a school board member, or to reject union demands and lose or risk losing one's seat on the board.

Similarly, unions know that criticizing the superintendent—especially one who is insecure—can be very effective. Thus, the union may focus on the superintendent's expense account or take a "no confidence" vote. The effectiveness of such tactics depends upon whether voters realize that the tactics are intended to gain concessions in matters that have nothing to do with the superintendent's integrity or competence; in fact, the actions triggering the "no confidence" vote are sometimes the best reasons to support a superintendent.

In any case, a popularity contest among employees is not an appropriate criterion for evaluating the superintendent's effectiveness. It should not be necessary to explain that the superintendent is being characterized as a plantation overseer for tactical purposes. Nevertheless, the school board that allows teachers to control the destiny of the superintendent has lost control of the district. The superintendent will naturally be more concerned about popularity with teachers than the effectiveness of the school system.

It is futile to expect superintendents to act as if union attacks on their performance will have no effect on negotiations. Many a bargaining session Waterloo has been preceded by the erosion of administrator confidence in the board. Lacking confidence in the board's ability to recognize intimidation as a bargaining tactic, some superintendents make harmful concessions to the union. Some superintendents need not be intimidated: They personally seek teachers union support for philosophical and/or political reasons and frequently recommend bargaining positions that are harmful to management in general.

Potent as intimidation can be when applied to board members and superintendents, it often manifests its most pernicious effects at the building level. Suppose teachers file a large number of grievances against a principal who enforces an unpopular board policy. The principal may begin to worry: "If more grievances pile up in my school than in the others, I'm going to look bad." Understandably, the principal may begin to overlook teacher conduct that merits disciplinary action. In effect, the principal has become intimidated because the board and superintendent have not demonstrated awareness that the grievances are being filed for tactical reasons.

All this is not to say that teacher views are irrelevant and that school administrators are always right. Board members should be skeptical of criticisms publicized during negotiations, especially if the criticisms could have been but were not raised before negotiations.

Teachers often submit proposals allegedly intended to provide "due process" for teachers suffering from administrative abuse. When school board negotiators demand specifics, union negotiators often demur and plead the need for anonymity to protect the teachers involved. This is a good time for the board to express its support of the administrator being criticized. Frequently, the contrast between alleged union concern for due process and its willingness to engage in anonymous attacks upon administrators is difficult for even veteran union negotiators to overlook.

Teachers unions attack board negotiators for many reasons. For example, by criticizing the funds spent to hire an experienced negotiator, the union hopes to intimidate the board into doing away with competent opposition. Alleging that the negotiator is holding up an agreement is another strategy intended to achieve the same objective.

Board Mistakes In Bargaining

What are some of the costly mistakes boards often make in bargaining? We can readily identify seven that experienced board negotiators frequently cite.

1. Importance of Expertise at the Outset

School boards make more costly mistakes in their initial reactions to negotiations than at any other time. When board members are not aware of the consequences of a seemingly sensible, innocent action, the entire course of negotiations can be altered.

Example: One of the authors was employed as a negotiator by a board that had previously insisted upon opening negotiating sessions to the general public, a stance that had led to procedural problems making effective negotiations all but impossible. When the negotiator recommended discontinuation of open negotiating sessions, the board said in effect: "We agree that these sessions have proved to be undesirable, but we made such a public issue of having open sessions that we'd look foolish if we were forced to change our position."

The board's reaction is a good example of why the board should not have advocated open negotiating sessions in the first place. It is always more difficult to change a position advocated publicly than one advocated only in negotiations with the union. The main point is that the board adopted its initial position before seeking advice from someone with a practical background in negotiations. Any experienced negotiator would have told the board that the teachers union would pack the audience with union supporters who would applaud every union statement and jeer every management one.

In another district, the same author was employed as negotiator by a board that had agreed to negotiate with teacher organization A over the protests of teacher organization B. Unfortunately, B's protests were justified, so the negotiator recommended that the board suspend negotiations until the issue was resolved by a representation election. The board, however, felt that it could not retreat from its recognition of organization A. As a result, the board's negotiating team spent fruitless months negotiating with A, only to have B win a representation election ordered by the state labor relations agency. Had the board consulted an experienced negotiator before its unwarranted recognition of A, it would have avoided months of expensive and time-consuming negotiations.

2. Board Members at Negotiating Sessions

One of the most common board blunders is to allow board members to negotiate or to be on the negotiating team. This blunder is often aided and abetted by superintendents who prefer to avoid assuming responsibility for the outcome of negotiations. In the superintendents' view, if the board negotiates effectively, there is no problem. If the board botches negotiations, administration can blame the board. Nevertheless, it is usually a major mistake for any board members to be present at negotiating sessions. Exceptions are sometimes justified, especially in small districts when the teachers are not represented by full-time union negotiators, but the exceptions are not as frequent as many boards assume.

Board members do not teach. They do not drive buses, cook in the school cafeteria, or coach the athletic teams. By the same token, they should not attempt to negotiate an agreement with teachers. That task, like the others mentioned, should be delegated, through the superintendent, to competent personnel. If the superintendent cannot recruit such personnel, the board should not attempt to perform these roles. It should recruit a new superintendent.

Board members should avoid negotiating sessions because they may require enormous amounts of time. Their most crucial task is policymaking. Anything else that takes up a lot of time weakens their ability to perform their most important task. Negotiations can be extremely time-consuming, especially if impasse procedures come into play. Inasmuch as irregular attendance at negotiating sessions leads to highly undesirable consequences, the problems are best avoided by nonattendance by board member at negotiating sessions.

Negotiations require a certain degree of skill and knowledge. Certainly, some board members can acquire these qualities. However, treating negotiations as an exercise in adult education for board members can be a very costly way to teach them that the task is better left to qualified personnel. Equally important, many board members do not have the personality traits required for effective negotiations. (This, incidentally, is as much a compliment as a criticism.)

Most important, having board members negotiate places the board at a crucial strategic disadvantage. Board members cannot ethically—and in some states, legally—oppose ratification of an agreement they have personally negotiated. Many agreements are consummated in the early morning hours, as deadlines near, and the parties are fatigued. The board member who negotiates virtually forfeits the right to consider ratification in a deliberate, noncrisis atmosphere, away from the pressure of a deadline. Furthermore, the union is likely to assume that board members at the table accurately reflect the thinking of all board members even when this is not the case.

The board should operate as a unit and not become fragmented. Board members at the negotiating table are viewed as holding the views of the entire board. When board members are present at negotiations, every word they utter and every concession they accept is regarded as an authoritative expression of the views of the entire board. In any event, board members participating in negotiations should never comprise a majority of the board. It is imperative to leave the option of having to go to the full board for approval.

3. Authority to Negotiate

Some school boards recognize the need to stay out of the negotiating process. They establish a negotiating team, but then fail to give it sufficient authority to negotiate. Consequently, the negotiating team must refer every issue to the board. This is unwise for several reasons. A board should retain the right to ratify an agreement, especially if the members of the teachers union must also ratify the agreement. On the other hand, the board must not regard negotiating team members as mere messengers who carry messages to and from the board to the teachers. Under such circumstances, union negotiators will ridicule the board's messenger service or even charge the board for committing an unfair practice—being represented by negotiators lacking the authority to negotiate.

Many boards fear that the delegation of authority to negotiate constitutes abdication of their decision-making authority. This will not happen if the board knows what to delegate and to whom. If items involve board policy, the board's negotiators should thoroughly explore these items with the board. If this is done, the board negotiator will not agree to anything that might be rejected by the board, and consequently, the board will not be forced to reject an agreement.

Many items involve administrative matters rather than board policy. On these items, the board should normally accept the views of its administrative staff. If the administration says it can administer the schools effectively, pursuant to an administrative policy that is also acceptable to the union, the board should be cautious in rejecting such a policy.

It is obviously important to avoid confusion over what is "administrative" and what is "board policy." Ideally, the superintendent should make the decisions as to whether it is necessary to discuss an item with the board before the negotiating team discusses it with the union. It is to be hoped that the superintendent knows the board well enough to make the right decisions on such issues. At the same time, the superintendent should give the board a complete list of the union's demands, making it clear that any board member should feel free to raise any question about any item.

From a practical point of view, the ultimate decision as to whether an item involves board policy or administrative policy must lie with the board. True, the board may unwisely decide many things that should have been left to administrative discretion, but that is its prerogative.

4. Importance of Financial Clarity

Whenever possible, the board should give its negotiating team a realistic estimate of the funds that will be available for the next school year. If negotiators do not have this figure, they will either be afraid to make any concessions (for fear the total package will exceed what the board is willing to pay) or they will find that they have agreed to items costing more than the board's "final" figure.

Ideally, school boards should provide their negotiating teams with the board's actual dollar limit. Some boards, however, fear that their negotiators will invariably commit funds to the limit of their authorization, even if an agreement can be reached at a lower cost to the board. Consequently, boards sometimes deliberately understate their spending limit.

In the long run, this practice destroys the credibility of final offers or limits established by the board. A board that cannot trust its chief negotiator with the board's bottom line positions should change either its attitude or its chief negotiator.

5. Timing of Concessions

Some boards come in with a final offer very early, very sure within themselves that they will make no further concessions. Meanwhile, neighboring school districts are settling for more than this "final" figure. By holding back too long and too much from its "final" offer, a board may exacerbate teacher militancy. Such boards end up offering an amount that would have brought about an earlier agreement that would have avoided a strike but is now insufficient to bring about an agreement.

The point here is that timing is crucial in negotiations. A board may decide upon the overall parameters of its settlement in, say, November, but in the ensuing months, inflation may increase significantly, other public employee groups may achieve unanticipated benefits, or state aid may increase. For these and other reasons, the amount that appeared quite generous in November may be inadequate when the contract expires in June.

Boards must avoid setting a minimal "final figure" under no pressure and then increasing it as soon as the teachers strike or threaten to do so. The mistake here is not necessarily the upward adjustment but the premature final offer. The teachers rarely regard any offer made in the early stages of bargaining as "final." After all, a board is not likely to lower an offer once it has been made, so why not try to persuade the board to raise its offer? In other words, boards do not speed things along by offering all they can immediately. It rarely works out that way.

As noted earlier, board members should refrain from involving themselves in making salary offers. One of the authors recalls an episode with a board president who insisted on attending all negotiating sessions. After weeks of hard bargaining, it became clear to the professional negotiators for the union and for management that a settlement could not be reached and that an impasse existed. Personal concerns on the part of the local National Education Association (NEA) teacher president stood in the way of a fair and equitable settlement. Negotiators on both sides were about to recommend standard impasse procedures when the school board president protested, saying, "These teachers are reasonable people; when they hear our final settlement figure, they will back down from their unreasonable demands and accept our offer." In spite of a consultant's recommendation not to do so, the board president called other members of the board at 2 a.m. and asked each for a personal commitment to let him offer the total board salary package. Upon receiving their approval, the board president proceeded to make the offer. After a brief caucus, the union team returned without making any significant movement toward settlement. An impasse was declared and fact-finding initiated. By this time, the board president was aware of what he had done. "What should I do?" he asked, having just cost the school district several hundred thousand dollars. About all that could be done was to learn from the experience.

6. **Concessions as a precondition to negotiations**

Boards sometimes agree to negotiate only if the union meets some board demand, such as that negotiations be conducted at the central office of the board. In most states, such demands are illegal, since they require the union to make concessions in order to exercise its legal rights. Of course, a board has the right, even the duty, to make sure that it negotiates only with an appropriate organization and under appropriate circumstances. Nevertheless, some boards erroneously believe they can dictate negotiating procedures as a precondition to negotiating with the union.

Boards should negotiate with whomever the teachers have duly chosen. Perhaps the teachers have not chosen well, but board statements to this effect usually do more harm than good. Boards don't always choose their representatives so well either, but a board should not change its negotiator simply because the union objects to the board's negotiator. For better or for worse, both sides should choose their own representatives and then go forward as best they can.

Sometimes the board's position is that it will meet with the teachers but not with "outsiders," such as field representatives of NEA or American Federation of Teachers (AFT). Any such refusal is usually considered an unfair labor practice, as it should be. Boards should accept the right of teachers to choose their own representative. No self-respecting teachers union would—or should—accept a board's veto power over its right to designate its negotiators. Instead of making an issue over this, a board should focus on designating the strongest possible negotiating team for itself.

7. **Procedural mistakes**

Negotiating schedules and procedures should be agreed upon. Each side is required to make reasonable accommodations to procedural proposals made by the other party. Such proposals relate to the days and times set aside for negotiations, the site(s) for negotiations, size of the negotiating teams, order of items to be negotiated, procedures governing press communications on the progress of negotiations, and other items of this nature.

Inexperienced negotiators sometimes propose a negotiating schedule months in advance, including specific times, places, and agendas. The board's negotiators may not be able to avoid a major confrontation if the union negotiators are foolish enough to insist upon such a blueprint. In practice, detailed and rigid procedural arrangements are invariably impractical. Negotiating schedules or agendas may need to be changed due to illness of key persons, nonbargaining emergencies, time required to get relevant information, the necessity to wait for resolution of state aid or legal issues, and other unforeseen reasons of this nature. Tentative working arrangements that allow the parties to plan their work schedules effectively are essential, but the further into the future these arrangements are projected, the less useful they are likely to be.

'Win-Win' Bargaining

"Win-win" bargaining is still another attempt to bring civility to teacher bargaining. Using a sensitivity training approach, the "trainer" attempts to get the parties to rise to a higher level of understanding and accord. There is no harm in the parties getting to know each other better as long as school management understands the adversarial nature of collective bargaining and avoids acceptance of contract language that restricts its ability to manage district operations. The union agenda is clear: It intends to foster teacher empowerment and win concessions from the board. All too often, win-win bargaining is an excellent means of accomplishing those goals. The question is whether school boards and school administrators will bargain away the right to manage their districts for the sake of a more collaborative relationship with teachers unions. In several instances, that has happened.

A good example of what not to do is a Cincinnati agreement.[1] The contract provided for class size limitations, grading/promotion standards, peer-appraisal programs, and joint committees made up of board members and union teachers, with the union leadership having responsibility for appointing the teacher members. Through win-win bargaining, additional language resulted in a decrease in teacher work load, the establishment of the lead teacher concept, and the founding of a joint committee to oversee the use of a new professional development fund. These "reforms" did not evolve from amicable negotiations, but rather from adversarial negotiations that had been preceded by a lengthy, well-crafted campaign by the union to persuade the public that the union was better suited and more interested than the board of education in improving education in Cincinnati. The result was tremendous public pressure on the school board to accept changes that they were not prepared to make. Fearful of a strike and further erosion of public support, the board negotiated away much of its right to manage the schools and control district policy. The Harvard Negotiation Project, which managed the process, calls their approach "win-win," but the union side did all the winning.

Win-win approaches to negotiations need critical analysis if school boards and administrators are to fully understand the consequences of negotiating educational reforms as part of bargaining. Unfortunately, districts seeking a way to meet employee concerns in a less adversarial manner all too often need protection from themselves. Win-win negotiations purport to leave everyone living happily ever after, but a careful reading of contracts negotiated under this procedure suggests that any decline in adversarial conduct is accompanied by a decline in board authority to manage district operations.

---

[1]Teacher bargaining contract between the Cincinnati Board of Education and the Cincinnati Teachers Association, 1985-87.

3. TACTICS IN NEGOTIATING WITH TEACHERS UNIONS

Introduction

One of the critical differences between collective bargaining and other kinds of negotiations is that an elaborate legal structure regulates labor negotiations. This structure is the most important single determinant of negotiating strategy and tactics in collective bargaining.

The statutory basis for the legal regulation of collective bargaining by public school employees is usually a law forbidding a public school employer to "refuse or fail to meet and negotiate in good faith with an exclusive representative." It is also an unfair practice for an employer to "refuse to participate in good faith" in the statutory impasse procedures. Most state public employee bargaining laws impose similar obligations upon employee organizations representing public school employees. Despite differences in language, these provisions are frequently the same in substance as section 8(a)(5) of the National Labor Relations Act (NLRA), which requires private sector employers to bargain in good faith. Indeed, many state laws define "meeting and negotiating" in terms that would be equally applicable to the duty to bargain in the private sector. The California statute, for example, states that:

> Meeting and negotiating means meeting, conferring, negotiating, and discussing by the exclusive representative and the public school employer in a good faith effort to reach agreement on matters within the scope of representation and the execution, if requested by either party, of a written document incorporating any agreements reached.

Although the California definition is helpful, it does not address many important questions. First, it does not deal with the selection of the parties' representatives. However, section 3543 of the California statute guarantees to public school employees the right "to form, join, and participate in the activities of employee organizations of their own choosing." Similar language in other public sector statutes has been interpreted to mean that the union has the right to select the individuals who will negotiate with representatives of the employer and that interference with this right by an employer is an unfair labor practice. The fact that an employer finds one or more of the union's representatives personally objectionable does not ordinarily justify an employer's refusal to negotiate. In this connection, the Wisconsin Employment Relations Commission made the following comment:

> Personal differences arising between the representatives of the parties engaged in negotiations with respect to wages, hours and working conditions of municipal employees do not constitute a valid reason for refusing to bargain in good faith. Both municipal employers and representatives of their employees have the right to designate whomever they choose to represent them at the bargaining table. To allow either or both parties to refuse to bargain with each other because of alleged or actual conflicts between their representatives would be contrary to the intent and purpose of the (act). (City of Superior, WERC Decision no. 8325 [1967])

Although both parties thus have broad rights in terms of selecting their bargaining representatives, the selected representatives must have sufficient authority to engage in meaningful negotiations. The designation of representatives who do not have power to agree and who must continually check back with their principals constitutes bad faith bargaining. This does not mean, however, that a party's representatives must have authority to reach binding agreement without any need for ratification. To the contrary, both parties in the public sector typically submit a tentative agreement to their principals for ratification.

Another dimension of the employer's duty to negotiate is the duty to furnish relevant information to the union. The courts and the various labor boards have consistently held that employers are required upon request to provide unions with sufficient data with respect to wage rates, job classifications, and similar matters to permit the union to bargain intelligently, administer the contract, and prepare for negotiations.

In this regard, the union is not required to justify its request for data unless the data appear to be clearly irrelevant. Rather, the burden is on the employer to show that the requested data are not relevant. An employer is not required to supply the information in the form requested as long as it is submitted in a manner that is not unreasonably burdensome to interpret.

The duty to bargain in good faith also includes the requirement that an employer not make unilateral changes in wages, hours, or working conditions that are subject to negotiation without first negotiating with the union. Thus, the Connecticut State Board of Labor Relations observed that "It is well recognized that unilateral employer action upon a matter which is the subject of current collective bargaining between parties constitutes a failure and refusal to bargain in good faith upon the issue in question." In one case, for example, the Connecticut board held that an employer acted improperly when it unilaterally adopted a new classification plan while negotiations were in progress. However, once an employer has given the union an opportunity to negotiate over a given proposal and it appears that the parties are at impasse, the employer is permitted to implement such proposal unilaterally.

Although courts and labor boards may not pass judgment on the results of negotiations, they review negotiations to determine whether the parties have negotiated in good faith. What constitutes good faith bargaining has been defined in various ways. The Connecticut Supreme Court summarized it this way:

> The duty to negotiate in good faith generally has been defined as an obligation to participate actively in deliberations so as to indicate a present intention to find a basis for agreement.... Not only must the employer have an open mind and a sincere desire to reach an agreement, but a sincere effort must be made to reach a common ground.

In determining whether there has been good faith bargaining, the courts and labor boards consider the *totality* of the parties' conduct throughout the negotiations. Thus, although an employer has the right to insist upon a management right clause, an employer's good faith is suspect if the employer insists on retaining unilateral control over wages, hours, and working conditions if such control would require the union to waive practically all of its statutory rights.

Finally, it should be noted that it is not illegal for an employer to advise its employees of what is occurring in bargaining sessions. One court noted the following in construing a public sector labor relations law:

> The act does not prohibit an employer from communicating in non-coercive terms with his employees while collective negotiations are in progress.... The element of negotiation is critical. Another crucial factor in these cases is whether or not the communication is designed to undermine and denigrate the union.

Nine Guidelines in Applying Negotiation Law

There are many refinements to these legal principles, but taken as a whole, they suggest nine general guidelines that may be helpful in applying the law to the actual conduct of negotiations:

1. Select negotiators with meaningful authority to engage in the give-and-take of negotiations.

2. Upon request, provide relevant information in a timely fashion.

3. Don't take unilateral action on matters that are subject to negotiation unless and until such matters have been presented to the union's bargaining team and the parties are at impasse on said matters. This prohibition does not apply during the term of an existing collective bargaining agreement under which the employer has specifically or implicitly retained the right to take the action in question.

4. Don't make proposals on a take-it-or-leave-it basis. After a reasonable period of negotiations, however, an employer can and should state its final position.

5. Don't communicate proposals to employees until after they have been presented to the union's bargaining team.

6. Avoid categorical statements such as, "We will never sign a contract."

7. Take good notes at bargaining sessions. Good notes serve three purposes: First, they provide a good means for informing board mem-

bers about what is going on in the negotiations. Second, they are helpful in reconstructing what actually occurred in negotiations if it ever becomes necessary to defend against a charge of refusing to negotiate in good faith. Third, negotiating notes are often useful in ascertaining the intent of parties in agreeing to given provisions in the contract. As such, they can be extremely useful in administering the contract and in presenting evidence of the parties' intent in arbitration proceedings. (It is generally indicative of bad faith bargaining for one party to insist that there be a verbatim transcript of negotiations or that negotiations be tape recorded. As the National Labor Relations Board (NLRB) states, "...many authorities and practitioners in the field are of the opinion that the presence of a stenographer at (bargaining) meetings has an inhibiting effect. The use of a stenographer or mechanical recorder to create a verbatim transcript does tend to encourage negotiators to concentrate upon and speak for the purpose of making a record rather than directing their efforts toward a solution of the issues before them." However, nothing prohibits both parties from agreeing to have a verbatim transcript of negotiations.)

8. Make proposals and counterproposals of your own. Although the law does not require that either party agree to a proposal or make a concession, proposals and counterproposals are common practice in collective bargaining, and the willingness to make them is evidence of good faith.

9. Don't delay unnecessarily the start of negotiations. State laws frequently tie negotiations to the district budgetary process. For example, in California negotiations must begin sufficiently before the adoption of the final budget for the ensuing year "so that there is adequate time for agreement to be reached or for the resolution of an impasse."

Choosing an Appropriate Negotiating Strategy

As to strategy, there is no single, right way to negotiate. Experienced negotiators use a variety of approaches and styles. A successful negotiator must use an approach consistent with his or her own personality, experience, and background. Some highly successful negotiators are aggressive table-pounders, while others are quiet and reserved; however, no negotiator should try to copy the technique of someone whose personality is completely different.

When the negotiator and negotiating team members have been selected, they should begin preparing for negotiations. It is a cliché among trial lawyers that preparation is 99 percent of trial technique. No good trial lawyer would attempt to present a case in court without full knowledge of the strengths and weaknesses of his case, the facts he intended to prove, the arguments of the other side, the facts with which to counter those arguments, and a thorough knowledge of the law involved. The same is true of collective bargaining. Contrary to popular belief, rhetoric is not the central ingredient of hard bargaining. Hard bargaining requires having the facts with which one can convince the union (and later, perhaps, a fact-finder or the faculty) of the validity of a position. The effect of showing a union negotiator who has been decrying the poor salary scale in a district that district salaries in fact rank high in the area can be devastating. Moreover, when the union recognizes that the management team is well informed, it is less likely to continue with exorbitant demands and more likely to adopt a reasonable position earlier in the negotiations

Preparation for negotiations should begin by thoroughly reviewing existing personnel policies, both written and unwritten, and existing methods of operation. This review should include contacting each administrator and supervisor about any problems they have encountered in the day-to-day administration of present policies. Comments about such problems should be submitted to the negotiator in writing, so that the latter can substantiate any arguments made during bargaining. Management proposals should be keyed to its policy manual.

Preparation also includes an effort to anticipate the union's demands. In many cases, this should be easy, since the unions will have a standard initial proposal. Nevertheless, anticipated union demands should be evaluated from the standpoint of cost and their impact on the district's ability to fulfill its responsibilities.

Labor negotiations can be viewed as a process of bringing the union and the employees it represents down to earth. The way to facilitate this process is to get the union to set priorities on its demands, a continuous process throughout negotiations. Management initiates the process by getting the union to submit its proposal first. This establishes a ceiling for the union and requires it to make some preliminary judgment as to its priorities. Of course, the union's initial demands will be extravagant, but forcing the union to submit all of its demands in writing usually has some restraining effect. On occasion, a union will try to avoid this restraint by holding back some of its demands. For example, the union might present a complete proposal on all items except salaries, simply stating that it wants a "substantial" salary increase, and leaving the definition of "substantial" to some future time. Because not having the total union package places the board in an impossible negotiating position, the board team should at some point refuse to continue negotiating until the complete list of union demands has been submitted.

Analyzing the Union's Proposal

When the union presents its proposal, the management team should go through it carefully, first with the union and then on its own. The union should be asked to explain the reason for each provision, because much of the language probably will be "boilerplate"—standard language the union is using in all districts. The language may have nothing to do with the situation in a particular district, and the union negotiators may not fully understand the purpose of it. Where the union's proposal would change existing practice, the union negotiators should be asked: "What's wrong with our present way of operating?" "What actual problems has our present practice caused the employees?" In many cases, the justification given by the union for its demands will be much narrower in scope than the provision. This helps management begin the process of separating the wheat from the chaff and assigning priorities to the union's demands. It also provides a basis for counterproposing a more limited provision that will meet the asserted justification without the cost of the union's original proposal. The actual problem that gives rise to a proposal is frequently very different from the problems addressed by the proposal. In addition, questioning clarifies the meaning the union gives to the language and thus provides information necessary to draft a counterproposal.

What if management is adamantly opposed to any concessions, however watered down, to a particular proposal? Some negotiators do not even probe the proposal with questions, on the theory that such questions will dignify the proposal. This argument is fallacious. Few union representatives are that unsophisticated. Moreover, it is too early for the negotiator to be certain that nothing related to the item will be included in the contract. It is not unusual for clauses without a bargaining history to be accepted in the contract after a strike. Negotiators should refrain from overreacting to proposals that are ludicrous on their face and should resist the temptation to display superior wit or engage in ridicule.

After reviewing the union's proposal with the union, the board's bargaining team should make sure it fully understands the proposal and has not overlooked anything. This process should clarify points that were missed or obscured in the first review. Reviewing the union's proposal may take several sessions, but it can be the most important part of the negotiations, inasmuch as it pinpoints the real issues and helps to set up the trade-offs that may be necessary to reach an agreement later on. Also, the review demonstrates to the union that the board team is taking the union proposal seriously. This does not mean, however, that the board team should try to counter every item or subject covered in the union's proposal. Instead, it should omit proposals on subjects on which its objective is to avoid any provision relating to that subject. Furthermore, issues covered by the union's proposal may be outside the scope of negotiations. Subsequently, some subjects encompassed by the board's counterproposal might be omitted from the union's next proposal.

Both sides have the right to submit proposals. The board team should avoid responses that are limited defensively to what the union has proposed. The board team should take the initiative in those areas in which it is obliged to do so. For example, the union's proposal is unlikely to include a management rights or no-strike clause, subjects the board team might wish to include in the contract. Certain fringe benefits may have gotten out of control or become subject to abuse. If so, the board team should propose changes to remedy the problem. Finally—and of great importance—if negotiations lead to an impasse, it will be very helpful to have some board proposals on the table so that the impasse procedures are not a one-way street, with the union having everything to gain and nothing to lose.

Developing a Counterproposal

After reviewing and analyzing the union's initial proposal, it is usually desirable to develop a complete counterproposal that covers all items in the final contract, from the preamble to the termination clause. To a large extent, the board's initial proposal may be a restatement, in contractual language, of the district's existing policies. In the counterproposal, however, the board negotiator should try to include agreement on a few union proposals. These should be minor items, such as a saving or a termination clause. Action on major items should be reserved until the union is ready to demonstrate corresponding movement on its side. By agreeing to a few items, the board team hopes to generate some momentum toward agreement and to establish a climate of reasonableness. If the union perceives the board as being completely inflexible and unreasonable, it won't have any incentive to change its position; for this reason, the board team should hold out the carrot of possible movement from the beginning.

The board's initial counterproposal should be limited to matters not relating directly to wages or fringe benefits. This is consistent with the general practice in labor negotiations of trying to reach agreement on all noneconomic items before discussing economic matters. This procedure is usually advantageous to management because the union frequently will make concessions in the later stages of negotiations in order to proceed to the economic issues. Nevertheless, it is sometimes impossible to adhere completely to this procedure if the union is holding firm on a few noneconomic items, and the best (if not the only) strategy to get it to move is to "buy" movement through the board's economic proposals. Also, economic and noneconomic issues can be so intertwined that discussions of both must begin early in negotiations.

As negotiations continue and agreement is reached upon some items, it is customary to mark these items as tentatively approved (TOK) and to initial and date the language. In reaching these agreements it is important to agree upon specific language; agreements "in principle" have a way of evaporating when it comes time to approve specific language. When the parties cannot agree on an item, it is marked "pass" or "hold" and discussed again in later sessions.

The objective in submitting a complete management counterproposal is to get the union to move from its initial proposal. This is a gradual process. The union bargaining team should have an opportunity to articulate all of their concerns; then management should focus subsequent discussion of its counterproposal. As negotiations proceed, agreements on particular items should be incorporated in subsequent redrafts of management's counterproposal; the redrafts should note that a particular item has been agreed to and the date of such agreement. This is a continuous process. After each negotiating session, the counterproposals should be updated and all items agreed to at the previous session noted. Eventually, both sides will be working from a management document. By structuring the negotiations in this way, management gains control of drafting the agreement. Some union representatives are happy to have management negotiators assume this responsibility, which they dismiss as mere paperwork, but control of drafting means control of substance and outcome as well as process.

This constant redrafting serves two functions. First, it keeps the parties informed about where they stand and what agreements have been reached. Second, it constantly resubmits and keeps management proposals on the table. What about the big stack of proposals that the union originally submitted? Management should not refer to them. If the union wants to discuss a particular proposal, it will do so on its own, without any reminders from management.

Generally, it is inadvisable to write contract language during negotiating sessions. A much better practice is to draft the agreements after the sessions and submit them, after careful review, at a subsequent meeting. Careful draftsmanship helps to avoid disputes over the meaning and application of the contract. Hasty draftsmanship almost inevitably results in future difficulties. As for language, simplicity and brevity are valuable. A collective bargaining agreement essentially is a statement of limitations on the power and authority of the school board and its officials to administer the school system unilaterally. Every "right" conferred by the agreement upon the employees and their representative means that a corresponding "duty" is imposed upon the employer. The more lengthy and complex the agreement, the greater the limitations and the possibility of disagreement over the meaning and application of its terms.

Concessions to the union should not be made too quickly or impulsively. If concessions are made too quickly, union negotiators will feel they should have asked for more, which only promotes intransigence on other subjects and extravagance in the next negotiations. Unions, particularly teachers unions, are highly political organizations that justify their existence to their members by allegedly achieving increased wages and benefits that the employees would not otherwise have received. If the employer agrees too readily, the union can't take credit and—even worse—may be accused of not asking for enough.

Although management may be willing at the outset of negotiations to agree to a union demand, it should not necessarily express its willingness to do so at the outset; instead, it should make sure the union offers an appropriate concession for it. It is also unwise to make a concession on an item that was left unresolved after the prior session without first ascertaining the union's current position on that item. The union may have changed its position since the previous meeting, so a concession on an item may result in an unnecessary giveaway. One of the few absolute rules of negotiations is never to give away more than is necessary; in future years, management will need all the concessions it can muster for subsequent negotiations.

It is always better to agree to a union demand than to try to get the union to accept management's proposal. This is particularly important in the final stages of negotiations; management should try to structure negotiations so that the final proposal is the union's, and management is accepting it. If this isn't possible, it is sometimes helpful to propose alternatives so that the union can choose which management proposal it accepts. Of course, the union may not want either of them, but in many cases, offering a choice results in some movement. It is most important, however, that in the final stages of negotiations, management should avoid making any significant concessions unless the offer is contingent upon reaching a complete agreement.

Side letters (sometimes referred to as sidebars) can be a useful device to resolve items that would cause the union political problems if they appeared in the collective bargaining agreement. Because a side letter of agreement is not part of the labor contract, it need not be presented to the union's membership.

Throughout the negotiations, the board's chief negotiator should have complete control over who says what and who responds to what question. The chief negotiator should be the only person to make concessions and exercise the authority to make a move. Moreover, the same person should remain in charge. To change chief negotiators from meeting to meeting is sheer folly. To avoid losing credibility, the board's negotiator should not characterize an offer as final unless no future movement will be made and the negotiator is prepared to stand by that position. Otherwise, "final offers" will be regarded as rhetorical ploys.

Management Rights Doctrine

Prior to negotiating any labor agreement, management negotiators should have a firm philosophy to guide them in negotiations. In the private sector, management negotiators have generally relied on the management rights doctrine as their guiding philosophy. A management rights doctrine means that management retains all rights it does not negotiate away. Integral to this doctrine is the concept that it is management's duty to act and the union's duty to issue a challenge if it feels that management's action is contrary to the negotiated agreement. In other words, management acts and the union reacts.

This functional basis for management rights does not allow any room for the union to acquire rights to manage and slide in as a "joint manager" of the district. Nevertheless, public employee unions, particularly teachers unions, are increasingly asserting the right to co-determine matters of public policy. *These attempts should be resisted*; management is not required to negotiate matters of inherent managerial policy. Moreover, proposals requiring that management must first obtain the union's agreement before acting in such areas as discipline, scheduling overtime, or subcontracting should be avoided. These "mutual agreement" or "veto" clauses are contrary to the management rights doctrine.

Because management's rights come from the duty of management to carry out its designated public policies and to operate efficiently, management should be considered the "acting" party and the union the "passive" party in the context of day-to-day relationships under a collective bargaining agreement. It is impossible for any school district to be run properly if there are two "acting parties." Thus, union leaders should never participate in day-to-day decision making under a labor agreement.

If union representatives are not to participate in day-to-day decision making, then what is their function under an agreement? During the negotiation of a collective bargaining agreement, of course, union representatives must be recognized as having bargaining rights equal to management's, except on subjects declared by law to be outside the scope of bargaining. However, once agreement is reached, union representatives should assume an entirely different role: ensuring that actions taken by the school district are consistent with its contractual commitments previously agreed upon by the parties. Thus, the union's function under an agreement can best be described as a "watchdog" function—watching the actions of the employer, the "acting" party—to see whether such actions comply with the agreement.

If being the watchdog is the union's proper function under the agreement, then the union must have the necessary rights to perform this function. In the private sector, these rights are contained in grievance and arbitration procedures. About 95 percent of collective bargaining agreements in private industry include such provisions, and some state laws specifically authorize public school employers and unions to agree to arbitrate disputes over interpretation or application of the contract. A binding grievance and arbitration procedure may be logically consistent with the management rights approach, however; unless carefully drafted, grievance procedures can erode management rights during the term of the agreement.

In addition to providing a basic framework for negotiation, the management rights doctrine provides a test by which to analyze union contract demands. Thus, to preserve the district's right to carry out its designated public functions and to manage its operations efficiently, one fundamental question should be asked as each union demand is presented: Does the proposal prevent the district from taking actions necessary to implement the public goals entrusted to it by law in an efficient manner? If it does, the proposal should be resisted.

In the private sector, this management rights philosophy is incorporated into the labor contract in the form of a management rights clause. Such a clause usually begins with a provision to this effect:

> It is understood and agreed that the board retains the right to operate the district and that all management rights are reserved to it, but that such rights must be exercised consistently with the other provisions of this contract. These rights include but are not limited to the following....

After this kind of preamble, the basic management rights should be listed. Some of the basic management rights include the right to:

- Hire, assign, or transfer employees
- Determine the mission of the school district
- Determine the methods, means, and number of personnel
- Introduce new or improved methods or facilities
- Change existing methods or facilities

- Establish and require observance of reasonable rules and regulations
- Discipline and discharge for just cause
- Contract outside for goods or services.

Management rights are one of the most controversial areas in collective negotiations. To what extent should school management accept limitations upon its discretionary power over such common areas of controversy as compensation, transfers, assignments, schedules, workday, workyear, and promotions? Undoubtedly, the union will oppose any attempt to obtain a strong management rights clause, but such opposition should not deter management from attempting to negotiate as broad a clause as possible.

The effectiveness of a management rights clause can be reinforced in other provisions of the contract. For example, a provision might state, "If the employer changes the hours of the school day, it shall notify the union two days in advance of the effective date of the change." This language constitutes contractual recognition that the employer has the right to change the hours unilaterally, i.e., without prior negotiations with the union or agreement by it. Thus, what appears to be a restriction (the requirement that the employer notify the union in certain circumstances), actually enhances management's rights.

Legislation may constitute a kind of management rights clause by limiting the scope of representation. For example, the California statute limits the scope of representation to "wages, hours of employment, and other terms and conditions of employment." The statute goes on to define "terms and conditions of employment" as meaning:

Health and welfare benefits..., leave and transfer policies, safety conditions of employment, class size, procedures to be used for the evaluation of employees, organizational security..., and procedures for processing grievances....

The statute further provides that "all matters not specifically enumerated are reserved to the public school employer and may not be a subject of meeting and negotiating." This constitutes a kind of management rights provision because it relieves school management of the obligation to negotiate over matters not specifically listed in the statute. Nevertheless, it still is important for public school employers to negotiate a management rights clause in their labor contracts. The reasons are several:

- Although the union has the statutory right to negotiate over the subjects listed in the statute, it has the legal power to waive these rights during the term of the labor contract. It is important that management obtain a waiver in the form of a management rights clause covering these subjects in order to protect itself from having to bargain over the subjects during the term of the agreement. Thus, a public school employer has a duty to bargain over class size when negotiating a new contract, but it may seek a management rights clause that authorizes the employer to change class size.
- A management rights clause constitutes contractual recognition by the union of the school district's basic rights.
- A management rights clause notifies the union and the employees that the public employer expects to exercise its rights.
- It reinforces the argument that union activity interfering with the employer's rights is prohibited.
- It protects the public school employer in the event the present statutory guarantees are modified or eliminated.

It should be noted that specific clauses in the agreement will limit the exercise of management rights, no matter what the management rights clause states. Accordingly, a management rights clause, standing alone, is only a general charter of reserved rights. Management rights often will be limited, in whole or in part, by the general language or specific terms of the remaining clauses of the agreement. To the extent that other clauses restrict the management right in question, the expressed restrictions will control.

Negotiating and drafting labor contracts in public education is a difficult and challenging task. However, the task can be greatly facilitated if management negotiators understand the roles of the public employer and of unions, both during negotiations and during the term of the agreement. Moreover, the recent history of collective bargaining in the private sector should be studied carefully. Management negotiators in the private sector have learned the importance of careful drafting by trial and error. In this regard, arbitration awards are a rich source of information. They reveal the importance of a sound negotiating philosophy and highlight the mistakes to avoid in negotiating, drafting, and administering labor contracts.

The outcome of any negotiations depends upon many factors that vary from district to district. The likelihood of negotiating a sound collective bargaining agreement is substantially increased, however, if the district's negotiators and board understand and vigorously defend the employer's right to carry out its designated functions in an efficient and orderly manner.

Collective bargaining differs from other negotiations in that it is a continuous process. Unlike the negotiation for the sale of a house, it does not end with the signing of the contract. The parties to a labor contract continue to interact during the specified term. When the contract expires, the parties will need to negotiate a new one. The necessity for a continued, close relationship must play a role in all of management's strategic decisions. If it acts through weakness or unnecessarily inflicts wounds today through deception or overkill, it will pay the price in future negotiations. If it deals with the union firmly and honestly in the present, it will reap the benefits for years to come.

Specific Contract Clauses

All union contract demands must be carefully analyzed. Even something as innocuous as the preamble can be important. A typical preamble, when written by the union, might read as follows:

> Whereas the board and the union affirm that providing quality education for the youth of the district is in their mutual purpose, and whereas the achievement of that purpose can be only fully realized through qualified capable and dedicated teaching, and whereas the members of the teaching profession are particularly qualified to assist in formulating policies and programs designed to improve education, and whereas the board has an obligation pursuant to the state laws to negotiate in good faith with the teacher union, as an exclusive representative in respect to hours, salaries, terms and conditions of employment, and whereas the parties have reached certain understandings they desire to confirm in this agreement, in consideration is hereby agreed as follows....

Management is best served by not including a preamble in a contract. A preamble is an attempt at editorializing. Because the language is unnecessary, it should not be included in an agreement, The controlling concept should be for management to include as little as possible in a contract. In the case of a preamble, arbitrators might use it to provide information concerning the intent of the parties and a paragraph that implies that teachers are "uniquely qualified" and "particularly qualified to assist in formulating policies and programs" could result in detrimental future ruling against the board. The subject matter introduced in the preamble should not deviate from the board's legal requirements for what must be bargained.

The agreement clause, on the other hand, offers management an opportunity to place certain restrictions on the union. When presented by the union, such a clause might read as follows:

> This agreement will become effective on the first day of January 199– and shall continue in full force and effect through December 31, 199–. If no new agreement is reached upon the expiration date of the agreement, it shall remain in full effect and force until 60 days after either party is given written notice to terminate the agreement. Negotiation for renewal of the agreement shall commence no earlier than June 1, 199– and shall commence upon written notice by either party. The school district and the union both agree to negotiate during the above period in a manner which will insure a timely settlement.

An agreement clause should be included in the contract but kept as simple as possible. A good management counter would not include any hint of a successor agreement and would be limited to a simple statement of agreement. A model article might include the following:

> This agreement is entered into by and between the Board of Education, hereafter called the Board, and the Teachers Association, hereafter called the Association. (A duration of agreement statement should be separated from the agreement statement and placed at the end of the contract. In that statement, the board should try to include language that sets the contract expiration date well into the school year.)

The basic purpose of any clause is to set forth clearly the intent of the two parties, something they frequently fail to do. They know what they wish to say, but actually write something else. Specialized words should be carefully defined so that the original parties or arbitrators will know their meaning.

In addition to the management right statement previously discussed, two other clauses may be beneficial to the board cause: a no-strike provision and a "zipper" clause.

A zipper clause "zips up" a contract and prohibits it from being opened to allow for discussion or—more important—additional bargaining during the life of the document. The board should never present these items for discussion unless it intends to stand behind them. This includes the threat or invoking of an actual strike by the union. By introducing an item and then withdrawing it under duress, a board could lose it. On the other hand, by including one or more of the provisions noted, the board's position will be strengthened accordingly.

A model zipper clause might look like this:

> The parties acknowledge that during the negotiations that resulted in this agreement, each party had the unlimited right to make demands and proposals with respect to any subject or matter not removed by law from the area of collective negotiation. The parties therefore, voluntarily and without qualifications, waive the right, for the life of this agreement, to negotiate collectively with respect to any subject or matter not specifically referred to or covered by this agreement. This contract represents the entire agreement between the parties and no other agreement or practice is binding to either party hereto with respect to wages, hours, or working conditions. This agreement shall not be modified in whole or in part by the parties. All negotiable subject matter that might have or should have or could have been included was and therefore, things that were not specifically included remain outside the contract.

A model peaceful resolution of differences—or a no-strike clause, as it is sometimes called—might read:

> Both parties recognize the desirability of continuous and uninterrupted operation of the instructional program during the normal school year and the avoidance of disputes that threaten to interfere with such operation. Since the parties are establishing a comprehensive grievance procedure under which unresolved disputes may be settled, the parties have removed the basic clause of work interruption during the period of this agreement. The Union accordingly agrees that during the period of this agreement no strikes of any kind shall be caused or sanctioned by the Union.

The union frequently seeks to eliminate or restrict managerial rights regarding personnel action. Such union proposals raise the danger that management will lose its rights to manage personnel effectively. It could be that some of these rights have already been lost through bargaining, in which case the issue of how to regain them becomes important.

One way to protect management rights is to include contractual language that explicitly spells them out. Although such language is highly desirable, it is a red flag to the union and therefore difficult to incorporate into the contract. A less threatening way is to include language that does not refer explicitly to management rights but which nevertheless weakens union ability to limit them. For instance, let us compare two contractual definitions of "grievance."

1. A grievance is a claim by an employee that there has been a violation of the express terms of the agreement, personally affecting the employee.

2. A grievance is a claim by an employee or the union that there has been a violation of the contract, or that a provision of the contract has been interpreted or applied in an unfair or inequitable way.

Definition 1 provides much better protection for management rights than definition 2. Under 1, the union cannot initiate a grievance; only an employee can do so, and only if the employee has been personally affected by the alleged violation. Under 2, the union can file a grievance regardless of whether any or all the employees support or are affected by it. Furthermore, under 2, the union could file and successfully pursue grievances that do not allege a violation of the express terms of the contract.

Every step of the grievance procedure presents a series of options relating to the union's ability to challenge management rights. Some contracts provide no time limits for initiating grievances; others require that grievances be initiated within 48 hours after the act or condition giving rise to the grievance. Some contracts require the grievant to submit the grievance in writing, state the provision of the contract allegedly violated, provide an account of the circumstances, and spell out the remedy sought; other contracts omit one or more of these requirements. If the terminal point of the grievance procedure is binding arbitration, limitations on the authority of the arbitrator will generally enhance management rights; broad arbitral authority has the opposite effect.

In practice, it is a mistake to rely solely on a strong management rights clause to protect such rights. Of course, union negotiators are well aware of the implications of a tightly worded grievance procedure; they will resist limitations or restrictions on union rights to file and pursue grievances. The resolution of management rights issues often comes down to the priorities of the parties. If management can offer a reasonably good compensation package, it should do so subject to union acceptance of management's position on management rights. The success of this approach depends on whether the union believes that management is determined to prevail on this issue. Ordinarily, teachers will not risk losing part of a wage increase over the mechanics of the grievance procedure.

If binding arbitration is required in a contract, management negotiators will find a good example of a strong grievance procedure that benefits management in a New Orleans teacher agreement.[1] In this agreement, the definition statement of a grievance is

> ...an alleged violation of a specific provision of the AGREEMENT, provided that the term grievance shall not apply to (a) any matter for which a method of review is prescribed by law, or (b) any matter which according to law is either beyond the scope of BOARD authority or limited to unilateral action by the BOARD alone, or (c) a complaint of a nontenured teacher which arises by reason of his/her not being reemployed, or (d) a complaint by any certified personnel occasioned by appointment to or lack of appointment to, retention in or lack of retention in any position for which tenure is either not possible or not required.

After presenting the usual time limitations specified in grievance procedures, the statement continues:

> In consideration of the decision of any questions involving arbitrability, it is the specific agreement of the parties that:
>
> (a) Except for memos of understanding signed and agreed upon by the parties, the AGREEMENT sets out expressly all the restrictions and obligations assumed by the respective parties hereto, and no implied restrictions or obligations are inherent in the AGREEMENT or were assumed by the parties in entering into the AGREEMENT.
>
> (b) In the consideration of whether a matter is subject to arbitration, a fundamental principle shall be that the BOARD retains all its rights to manage the school system, subject only to the express limitations set forth in this AGREEMENT: it is understood that the parties have not agreed to arbitrate demands which challenge action taken by the BOARD in the exercise of any such retained rights, except where such challenge is based upon a violation of any express limitation set forth in this AGREEMENT.

---

[1] Teacher contract between United Teachers of New Orleans and the Orleans Parish Board of Education, 1980-83; p.13, 7:3, 10.

(c) No matter will be considered arbitrable unless it is found that the parties clearly agreed that the subject involved would be arbitrable in light of the principles of arbitrability set forth in this article and constitutes a grievance under the definition of a grievance set forth in the definition of a grievance and no court or arbitrator shall or may proceed under any presumption that a request to arbitrate is arbitrable.

If a final judgment of a court has determined that a request raises arbitrable issues, the court's decision shall specify in reasonable detail the issues as to which arbitration is directed. The arbitration shall thereafter proceed only upon the issues specified in such final court judgment, and the arbitrator shall have no authority or jurisdiction to consider issues other than those specified.

None of the provisions hereof shall deprive a court of competent jurisdiction of its power to determine questions of arbitrability, or the jurisdiction of the arbitrator or validity of any decision or award of the arbitrator in any proceeding seeking to require arbitration or to enforce, modify, or set aside a decision and award of the arbitrator.

The decision of the arbitrator as set forth above shall be restricted to a determination of whether or not there has been a violation of the AGREEMENT as alleged in the written grievance. He shall limit himself to the issue submitted to him and shall have no authority in any case to add to, subtract from or alter in any way any provision of the AGREEMENT.

Reaching Final Agreement on Management Rights

Ideally, agreement on management rights should depend on two considerations. One is whether discretion on the issue is essential to effective management. The other is the importance of the issue to the employees. For example, discretion in assigning classes to individual teachers is important to management in order to make full use of personnel. If seniority prevails, management may not be able to assign teachers in efficient ways. Suppose, for example, that the teachers cannot be assigned more than five classes but the district needs to cover six classes. Should the district be required to hire an additional teacher? Note that teachers could be paid an additional amount for additional classes. In other words, there would be no limit on the number of classes teachers could be required to teach, but the teachers would still have some protection on the issue.

In any event, management rights must be negotiated on both a comprehensive and an issue-by-issue basis. Merely lamenting the erosion of administrative discretion is really irrelevant to bargaining. Furthermore, careful thought must be given to what, if anything, will replace administrative discretion. Sometimes, the most honest posture is not that administrative discretion is good, but that it is better than any proposed alternative, such as seniority or rotation. If a decision is discretionary, mistakes can be corrected. In any case, if management discretion is needed, management should negotiate the restoration of its rights in the next contract. It should not accept the demonstrably false argument that management can never regain rights once lost.

Many difficult problems arise over claims that discretion leads to or is a cover-up for favoritism. Favoritism is unlikely to be perceived as such by administrators who never have to defend their decisions in bargaining sessions. They may believe that certain teachers are better able to teach advanced students every year, but the teachers left to struggle every year with slow learners may have a different view. It is often salutary for administrators to be required to defend their decisions in negotiations, provided that doing so does not lead to negotiating over a specific grievance. Granted, such situations may embarrass individuals, but that is less harmful than never requiring administrators to account for exercising their discretion.

One frequent problem involves the distinction between "qualified" and "most qualified." Suppose the issue is extracurricular assignments for compensation. The union may propose that those appointments be based upon seniority from among those "qualified." The administration will argue that it wants the freedom to choose not just any "qualified" person but the "most qualified." This can be a troublesome issue, especially if teachers with less seniority are appointed before veteran teachers. The union attitude tends to be that if the senior teacher can do the job, the teacher should be promoted regardless of fine distinctions among those qualified.

Here again, solutions must be ad hoc. Suppose there is an opening for head football coach. The district may not want to appoint the assistant coach who has applied for the position, but it will not want to assert that the assistant coach is unqualified. This is the kind of problem that may not arise often, but it illustrates the importance of contractual protection for managerial discretion.

Consider also the teacher who has had an extracurricular assignment for several years. Should the teacher have tenure in an extracurricular assignment for pay? Some stability and assurance of continued employment seem reasonable here, but so does some flexibility for management.

The larger the system, the greater the pressure for automatic rules, such as rotation or seniority, to replace administrative discretion. Union leaders do not see anything wrong in this, especially under pressure from teachers unhappy about the exercise of administrative discretion. In practice, many administrators discover that things function about as well—or even better—when a measure of seniority or rotation is introduced.

On some issues at least, administrators often prefer automatic solutions to discretionary ones. As with merit rating, administrators often feel that they must support "managerial discretion" publicly, even though they are relieved privately not to have it. Without it, they do not have to separate the "qualified" from the "most qualified" or make other difficult decisions that increase their vulnerability.

The Comparison Game

The most important influences on negotiated contracts are the terms of other contracts. The closer other districts are to a district still in negotiations, the more their settlements will influence the settlement in the latter. For example, teacher bargaining in St. Paul is affected more by teacher bargaining in Minneapolis (or vice versa) than by teacher bargaining in New York or San Diego. A cost-of-living increase granted to firefighters in St. Louis will have more influence on teacher bargaining in St. Louis than will a cost-of-living increase won by teachers in Seattle.

A school board that pays more than nearby boards for supplies and equipment would be criticized for waste and extravagance. The same point applies to teacher salaries. Teachers are not as standardized as chalk or desks or projectors, but it is difficult to demonstrate meaningful differences in teacher effectiveness between school districts. Clearly, taxpayers rarely distinguish one district staff from another on this basis. For this reason, a school board that pays teachers substantially higher salaries than neighboring boards is risking political retaliation.

Minor differences usually are ignored or can be safely explained away, but sizable differences cannot be so easily rationalized and are not likely to be ignored.

The political process is also at work on the teacher side. Obviously, union negotiators would like teachers to be paid as much as possible. In most cases, however, the concern of the union is not so much achieving a victory as it is avoiding a defeat, i.e., a settlement that is visibly inferior to others in the immediate area. Comparisons thus are the keys to the politics of bargaining.

To maximize concessions, the union tries to show how disadvantaged its constituents are. When agreement is reached, however, the union must try to portray it as a victory, which means emphasizing how the teachers have fared better than their counterparts in nearby districts. A union negotiator frequently is obliged to disparage the district offer as being very inadequate, then walk into the next room to tell the union negotiating team what a terrific contract they have been offered.

In bargaining, each side emphasizes comparisons that strengthen its case. If the salary schedule in district A has lower maximums than in district B, the union negotiator in A will stress the injustice done to deserving teachers at the top of the schedule. Nothing is said, however, about the fewer steps that may be required to achieve the maximum, or the fact that the teachers at maximum in district A received more on their way up the schedule than did teachers in district B.

Of course, school board negotiators follow the same strategy. District A's board negotiators are likely to propose increasing the number of steps to reach maximum, on the grounds that this aspect of the schedule is too generous (again, in comparison with nearby districts). The same board negotiators, however, can be expected to ignore the lower maximum, the point stressed by the union negotiator.

The search for supportive comparisons extends beyond individual items to entire settlements and patterns of settlements. Suppose a school district has the third lowest salary schedule in a metropolitan area that includes 20 districts. To raise its rank, it would need to offer a higher percentage raise than neighboring districts offered.

Suppose, however, that a district cannot match the percentage raise in neighboring districts. In that case, it will emphasize the fact that it provided the most generous percentage increase last time. This argument normally falls on deaf ears. The union negotiator will stress the district's comparative position. "We rank tenth in salaries paid, but your offer will drop us to the fifteenth lowest district in the area. My teachers will never accept such a lousy settlement." And so it goes, on both sides.

If a school board can maintain a favorable comparative position even with an unfavorable percentage increase, it will stress its after-settlement position; the union will stress the unfavorable percentage increase. Consistency from year to year does not count for very much in the search for comparative advantage.

An understanding of the comparison game is essential to negotiate effectively. In the first place, most school districts and teacher unions are necessarily pattern followers, not pattern makers. What would be acceptable to one side for an early settlement is often unacceptable to the other. Early settlement involves the risk that subsequent settlements elsewhere will make the early settlement look bad. For this reason, the union normally will not settle early, except on terms the district cannot offer. In most districts, much time is wasted in trying to get a settlement before the time is ripe; that is, before a pattern materializes.

In the second place, a district negotiator should note the basis for comparisons, even though union negotiators will try to shift the basis next time to justify a better offer. If the district settles on the basis of comparisons that are not likely to favor the union in the future, it should emphasize this fact in negotiating the successor contract. The situation to be avoided is one in which the district negotiates items on which it lags behind in isolation from items that are favorable to the district.

Some contracts specify that the salary schedule is to have a certain rank in district's geographical area, but such clauses are of dubious legality and practicality. Apart from the fact that such clauses probably constitute an illegal delegation of authority, they ignore the need to compare settlements as a whole. As fringe benefits consume larger and larger shares of contract costs, school management must compare the cost of total packages as well as the costs of individual items. If a district's total compensation package compares favorably with others, the district can be less concerned about comparisons of individual items in the package. The amount devoted to a particular item, such as sabbatical leave, can be left to the preference of the teachers as to how they want welfare funds allocated. From a management point of view, the allocation may not be of great concern if the district's overall costs are less. Districts cannot completely ignore the allocation of total funds among various benefits, but because the funds are being spent for teacher benefits, teachers should play a major role in their allocation.

Negotiating Procedures

The board's chief negotiator should outline the procedures under which he/she feels most comfortable. The procedures for calling a caucus, as well as the arrangements for taking and transcribing notes, should be made in advance, discussed, and approved. Tape-recording negotiating sessions should be rejected; a tape recorder has a tendency to inhibit open discussion and to encourage posturing for propaganda purposes. The importance of body language should be pointed out, and the negotiator may wish to assign someone to monitor this aspect of negotiations. All notes, materials, backup sources, data, and arguments used in the process of negotiation should be preserved. Proposals that may have been advanced and then dropped can play a very important role in mediation and arbitration. The district should take a position on each item presented for negotiation by the union.

Keeping track of all of the proposals and counterproposals that emerge during negotiations is a major problem. Unless this is done efficiently, the board team is likely to make unnecessary concessions. A system for keeping track of negotiations is essential and is one of the hallmarks of an experienced negotiator. Fortunately, computer programs enable a novice negotiator to keep notes like a professional. A notebooklike organization tool marketed under the name of Spiral[2] was designed specifically for taking and organizing notes. It provides tabs, bookmarks, page marks and an option for automatically expanding abbreviations. After the session, the negotiator can retrieve the information immediately. With this tool, and with use of consistent negotiation procedures, the novice bargainer should be able to keep track of the most complicated proceedings.

An agreement on news releases should also be reached at the first negotiating session. Management's position should be that no press releases are to be issued without mutual agreement on them. This is an instance where the word "mutual" is advantageous for management. One normally does not want to negotiate in public through print, television, or radio; it normally suffices to say that negotiations are proceeding and both parties are working to settle outstanding issues. It is always better to start by trying to get agreements, not by trying to write press releases.

---

[2] Available from Technology Works Inc., Austin, Texas.

The site of negotiations is often resolved at the initial meeting. Ordinarily, the board office is the most desirable site. The rationale for this position is that both teams will have ready access to all needed records, data, and materials. Of course, the board negotiator should offer the union team free access to district copiers and telephones if the board office is to be the site of negotiations.

The meeting schedule may also be an issue. The union position will be that teachers on the union team should be released from their classrooms so that negotiations can take place during the workday. The board should normally insist that negotiations be conducted during off-duty time; teachers are paid to teach, not negotiate. Depriving children of their regular teachers is not in the best interests of the school district. Furthermore, teachers who do all their work in a classroom often enjoy their release from this setting and are not inclined to give up their new celebrity status. They are seen on television and are quoted in the newspapers. Members of the teacher team are stopped by other teachers and asked, "What is happening? You are on the inside." The longer the teams remain at the bargaining table the greater the likelihood that the board team will bargain away rights; for this reason, the board should refrain from giving teachers any additional incentive to avoid agreement. In large districts, some released time is unavoidable. Elsewhere, the board should insist that negotiations take place in the evening, on weekends, and on holidays. It should try to conduct negotiations from 4 to 11 p.m. and avoid extending the evening deadline. In general, more damaging language is accepted after midnight than at any other time. It may make sense to extend a session if agreement on a critical issue appears imminent, but board teams tend to be too optimistic about the likelihood.

Although the board negotiating team also will be working extra hours, additional compensation should not be paid during negotiations. To do so would result in headlines reading "Teachers give up their time to negotiate but administrators get paid for it." After the contract has been approved, the board might provide compensatory time or some other recognition of the additional work required of the management team. The number of members on each team could also become a subject of dispute. Guidelines that reflect a reasonable number for each team should be established. If the number is open, 250 teachers claiming to be members of the team may appear at every meeting, wildly cheering teacher suggestions and hissing management's response. This can be an intimidating factor, especially if the negotiations are open to the public. A five- to seven-member teacher team with provision for specialists to be brought in as required by either side will usually meet the needs of both negotiating teams. Members of teams should be introduced, so that both teams know who will be present on a regular basis. Members of the management team should not ordinarily be replaced as team members, but the board should provide substitute help for administrators, particularly principals, who are on the bargaining team. It should avoid paying for substitutes for the teacher members of the union's negotiating team.

The issue of what materials to provide should also be considered. Ideally, only items that are in the public record should be made available to the union team. Notes, staff communications, and confidential materials that have been developed for the management team should not be made available to the union.

At the initial meeting, it is desirable to have the union state its demands first, making sure that the board team receives a complete package containing *all* the demands the union intends to include in the negotiations. Although both sides do have the right to make further demands as counterproposals, this possibility should not be allowed to justify the introduction of new items unrelated to a previous proposal.

The board team should question any union demand that appears to be unrelated to the district's operating procedures. For example, the union may have proposed clauses on the use of paraprofessionals in a district that does not employ them. This can happen when a local teachers union submits a contract proposal based on a contract in another district or a model contract supplied by the state union. Many times, the union negotiator will drop items that are obviously not defensible. At the same time, the board team should not exchange proposals in the initial meeting. Its position should be, "Our proposals will be based in part upon what we receive from you and after our discussions with you."

The chief negotiator speaks for the team; other team members should not respond verbally unless called upon by the chief negotiator to comment or to provide statistics or other pertinent information. Nothing can be more devastating than an ill-prepared or idle comment by a member of the administration team that has the effect of undermining the team's position.

Patience is important, because bargaining moves slowly, often becoming an endurance test. Counterproposals can be withheld for legal opinion, costing out the impact, and/or further clarification. The board team should resist offering salary benefits until bargaining is well under way. In one sense, the union is playing with "Monopoly" money and can ask for any item it wishes, regardless of cost. On the other hand, every dollar offered by the board translates into tax increases or budget restraints. Salary proposals will provide leverage to gain concessions from the union and keep the negotiation process moving.

Time Management

In many districts, a disturbing aspect of teacher bargaining is the enormous amount of time it takes. No other aspect of bargaining seems to catch districts as unprepared as the ongoing need to devote substantial board and staff time to the process.

Several factors affect the time needed for bargaining: size of the district, sophistication of the parties, history of bargaining in the district, timing of the negotiations, the state aid situation, the economic environment, and so on. Some of these variables are subject to control by school boards; for example, whether the board's chief negotiator is a knowledgeable professional usually is within the scope of board control. Other factors, such as the general economic environment, are not subject to board control or influence. Controversy may arise over how to interpret or assess these factors, but school boards cannot change them.

Another set of factors, although not subject to unilateral control by the school board, can have a marked effect on the amount of time devoted to bargaining. For example, ordinarily it would be futile to begin negotiating in November for a contract that won't take effect until the following July. Boards and unions alike should realize that there would be no immediate pressure to settle and no patterns to follow. Furthermore, the fact that so much time is available encourages unreasonable demands that probably would not be made if bargaining were confined to a short period.

The time needed to negotiate an agreement ranges from less than one hour to two years or more. The presence or absence of an existing agreement is an important factor, but the time required for renegotiating existing agreements can also vary widely. Much depends upon the range and language of the current agreement. If the agreement is comprehensive but loosely worded and is being renegotiated long before any deadline, bargaining is likely to drag on indefinitely. If the agreement is tightly drafted and meets the basic needs of both parties, they may not need to renegotiate anything but the economic package. If the parties are reluctant to settle until the question of state aid is resolved, it usually is futile to bargain on either economic or noneconomic items, since their resolution is often linked.

Most teacher negotiators are full-time union representatives. After negotiating several contracts a year for several years, many union negotiators focus their concern mainly on how to reach agreement as quickly as possible, consistent with what the teachers will accept and in keeping with the appearance of having worked hard to get it. In contrast, some teacher negotiators are employed on a per-diem or per-session basis. As a consequence, these part-timers may not be as strongly motivated as full-time union representatives to reach agreement promptly.

The best way to conserve time is to use a combination of incentives. Providing released time for the union bargaining team during the school day, if offered at all, should be contingent on seeing significant evidence that bargaining is progressing. Frequently, the union negotiator welcomes such an agreement since it obviates the need for sessions to be scheduled after school hours in several districts during periods of heavy bargaining. In any event, school boards should not provide released time for the union negotiating team until the union is motivated to bargain seriously.

A great deal of time can be saved if the board negotiator insists that the consultation procedure be used during the year. If the union has consultation rights but was not sufficiently concerned during the year to raise an issue, board negotiators should avoid devoting much time to the issue in bargaining sessions. Of course, the same obligation to use the consultation procedure applies to the board.

Board negotiators should avoid wasting time on union proposals that are not offered seriously or offered without any genuine expectation that the proposals will be taken seriously. When union demands are submitted, board negotiators should request their estimated costs. If union negotiators haven't developed such estimates, board negotiators should question whether the union is serious about the demand. When bargaining gets serious, the union typically has a close estimate of costs involved. In any case, the public relations value of estimating the expense of outrageous demands usually is not worth the effort—at least at the outset of bargaining. But if the union is still making excessive demands as deadlines near, management can and should be prepared to cite the costs to the public.

Once a demand has been rejected and explained, it is important to avoid repetition of the same proposals and arguments. The district negotiator should make it clear that, unless there is a change in the union position, the district will not spend time on proposals and arguments in which content never changes. The item must be covered thoroughly, of course, but sheer repetition is to be avoided.

It is also important to make sure that the union's initial demands constitute its entire package; otherwise, the district should avoid bargaining until the package is complete. Of course, this should not be done in a way that encourages additional demands. Occasionally, it may be advantageous to bargain on a late proposal—as distinguished from a counterproposal—but only if the union understands that an exception is being made. If management has overlooked a demand of its own, this is the time to introduce it. If the union is allowed to introduce additional demands at will, the board is placed in an untenable bargaining position; in fact, the submission of new demands can be an unfair labor practice if the delay in proposing them cannot be justified.

Except in large districts, agreements should be consummated in four to six weeks (one to three sessions per week) of serious bargaining on both sides—even more quickly if released time for bargaining is provided during the school day. Long intervals between negotiating sessions usually are a mistake because much time will be needed to review and agree on the status of proposals. Two consecutive days of negotiations near the expiration of an agreement are more productive than 10 to 20 days six months before the contract expiration date. Preparation is extremely important in conserving time at meetings, but not if a long period has elapsed between preparation and bargaining.

Computers can help considerably in saving time. In particular, a PowerBook can be an indispensable aid to management during collective bargaining. A salary schedule spreadsheet can provide instant analysis of proposed changes in the existing contract. Items such as hospitalization costs, or a new sick leave or sabbatical leave provision, can be determined immediately. A computer might even enable boards to increase their offer as the boards become more precise in determining the costs of a proposed new contract. With a computer, the question of keeping adequate personnel records would become a concern of the past. Questions concerning certification, age of the teacher corps, sick leave patterns, use of fringe benefit provisions, and many other topics could be placed into a database and researched as needed. Questions concerning immediate cost, hidden costs, overhead, and administrative costs could be uncovered and analyzed.

Research on promising new curriculum experiments could be analyzed using any one of several commercially available statistical analysis packages. An analysis of the impact of inservice training on instruction could be measured. Demands for more money for teacher center credits, professional advancement, longevity, and so on, could be analyzed for their impact on instruction. The value of released time, instructional aids, paraprofessionals, and other support personnel could be ascertained more accurately.

During negotiating sessions, using a computer to create and modify proposals accelerates the negotiation process considerably, with information assembled and new printed proposals created in minutes. A direct line into an attorney's facsimile machine might enable the bargaining team to clarify legal issues as they arise. Various position descriptions could be developed and stored in a database prepared and approved by the board in advance. The superintendent could also be informed of progress and specific proposals being offered, thus keeping top management informed while saving valuable administrative time.

To summarize, the major considerations in saving time are assigning it an appropriate value and accurately identifying the factors that affect its expenditure. Negotiators who do not respect and value time have concluded that their time isn't worth much. These persons should not be allowed to waste the time of others who appreciate its value.

Bargaining Under Financial Duress

School districts sometimes face financial crises that preclude increasing teacher salaries and may even require reducing them. Teacher salaries and fringe benefits comprise about 80 percent of school system expenditures. Increasing these benefits may have major implications for the conduct of negotiations. In most genuine crisis situations, districts must consider either a reduction in staff, the same or a lower level of compensation, or some combination of the two.

Theoretically, boards that must reduce expenditures first evaluate programs and then establish priorities. This process is inevitably affected by pressure from interest groups that want to shift the sacrifice to somebody else. For example, senior employees want a raise and are usually willing to accept layoffs—"by seniority," of course. Ordinarily, this approach will prevail if it does not run counter to affirmative action programs. The most recent hires tend to include many minorities and females, and these groups are not reticent about protecting their interests. Their proposals for who should be terminated are to use a lottery or some other procedure that doesn't involve seniority. In addition, personnel in special programs (teachers of the handicapped, gifted, disadvantaged) are appealing to parents to speak up for their children. Translation: Save our jobs; eliminate somebody else's. The throw-the-other-fellow-overboard approach to the problem is not edifying, but it is typical of crisis bargaining. Most board members or school administrators caught in a similar squeeze probably would behave in the same way.

The role of the union is a key factor in any budget reducing plan. In most cases, the union will favor raises even if they require layoffs. Layoffs adversely affect newer and younger employees who don't have much influence in the union. Furthermore, the union's *raison d'etre* is threatened more by a wage freeze than by layoffs. A no-raise situation leaves all members dissatisfied with their union; layoffs accompanied by raises for teachers who are not laid off results in fewer dissatisfied union members.

Next to salaries, the largest cost items are likely to be fringe benefits, especially health and dental insurance. The escalation of health costs in recent years is stimulating districts to look for savings in this area. Self-insurance is one possibility; user charges are another. The concept of public education as a right available to everyone will continue, but its application may be limited in the future. Items such as summer and evening school, extracurricular activities, books, supplies, and field trips may be more subject to fees than they have been in the past.

Whatever the solution, financial exigencies typically strain the bargaining process for these reasons:

- When revenues dry up, multiyear agreements become extremely difficult to negotiate. The unions can rarely afford to lock themselves into multiyear contracts with no economic improvements in sight.

- Generally, it is more difficult to negotiate a distribution of sacrifices than a distribution of benefits. Union leaders are more likely to make an all-out effort to avoid catastrophe than they would to improve a good contract.
- Retrenchment forces unions to broaden the scope of negotiations to cover layoffs, severance pay, "bumping" rights, and other items that become crucial in retrenchment situations. When budgets are increasing, there appears to be no need to negotiate on these items. Actually, that is the optimum time for management to negotiate its rights in retrenchment situations, but most management negotiators do not press the issue in good times. In a retrenchment situation, however, those items are crucial, but also more difficult to negotiate.

Whatever the impact on the overall budget, retrenchment generates increasing pressures to bargain every year over economic issues. Paradoxically, a district with decreased revenues generally devotes more time to bargaining. True, the less money there is, the fewer the options, and the fewer the options, the less there is to negotiate. But this situation points up one of the biggest pitfalls in bargaining: the tendency to make concessions on the work rules to compensate for the district's inability to improve economic benefits. This is a road to disaster. The less money, the more imperative it becomes that a district remain able to operate efficiently.

Significantly, the necessity to reduce benefits does not relieve districts of the duty to bargain over them. Example: An increase in class size required by declining revenues does not relieve the district of the obligation to negotiate over class size. The most crucial problem in retrenchment usually is the ability of school boards to establish priorities. Forced to choose among several competing pressure groups, the board is tempted to cut all programs by a certain percentage. This is the easiest solution and has the political advantage of "treating everyone alike." Unfortunately, perhaps not everyone should be treated alike.

Joint Committees

A "joint study committee" can be a useful way to prevent an insolvable disagreement on a single item from holding up agreement on a contract with a teachers union. Such a stalemate often happens when union and board negotiators cannot agree on an item that is important to both.

Finally, as time is running out, and board negotiators are as eager as the union to wrap things up, the union may suggest that a joint committee study the problem and report back to the negotiating teams. In that way, the union can show that it tried to achieve concessions on the item, while the board isn't committed to anything.

This suggestion can appear very attractive to a board negotiating team in the final stages of negotiations. Sometimes, a proposal for a joint committee does make sense for both sides. On the other hand, joint committees may also open up a Pandora's box.

Ordinarily, boards should not establish a joint committee when nothing can be done about the substantive problem involved. The sense of relief over temporarily resolving an issue eventually will be replaced by teacher feelings of outrage. It won't help to point out that the district negotiator told the union that nothing could be done. The union is not likely to put the matter this way to the teachers. To do so would destroy the value of the joint committee from its point of view. The union is usually forced to the joint committee as a way of achieving concessions on the issue when the committee reports.

Sometimes "no" or "we can't make any concession on that proposal" is as legitimate as "yes" or "maybe" or "something can be done." Refusal to accept a negative reality often leads to a joint committee. Instead of getting closure on negotiations, the parties may find themselves in endless negotiations under the guise of "joint committees." Once a joint committee is appointed, the teacher members will want released time for committee work, which can be a drain in a smaller school system.

Joint committees should not negotiate. During the course of negotiations, it is sometimes helpful to refer particular issues to subcommittees of the negotiating teams. One should not overlook, however, that agreements are made between the board and the union, not any of their constituent subgroups.

Most problems referred to joint committees are the subject of negotiations in the next contract. The union will use the report of a joint committee as a point of departure if there is anything in it favorable to the union position. District negotiators should avoid having joint committees perform work that should have been done prior to negotiations. If the facts were available but the teachers did not collect and present them, the teachers should be required to be better prepared at the next contract talks if they want progress on the item. The point is to avoid encouraging poor preparation by agreeing to study something when the union has had ample opportunity to do so.

Of course, new issues may arise or there may be new proposals or questions that legitimately require data not available during negotiations. However, if honest disagreement over the facts arises during negotiations, it may make sense to have a smaller group ascertain the facts and report back. However, it is a mistake to believe that agreement on the facts necessarily means that the parties will agree on the issues involved. As Richard H. Tawney, the famous English historian, once pointed out, the conflicts that really matter are not those resulting from misunderstanding the other fellow, but those that result from understanding him too well.

Mediation

Eventually, most school boards are involved in mediation. Because mediation is so frequent and can be used effectively in certain circumstances, every board should have some understanding of the process. Let us first define "mediation" and contrast it with other procedures that use impartial third parties:

Mediation, sometimes called *conciliation*, is an attempt by an impartial third party to facilitate bargaining or to settle an employment dispute by means of suggestion, advice, or other ways of stimulating agreement short of dictating a solution.

Fact-finding is the investigation, assemblage, and reporting of facts concerning a labor dispute. Fact-finding can be with or without recommendations for settlement. To the extent that it includes recommendations for settlement, it can be considered a form of advisory arbitration.

Arbitration is a procedure in which an impartial third party actually renders a decision that can be binding or nonbinding in a labor dispute. Arbitration is now the most common procedure for resolving disputes over the meaning or interpretation of collective bargaining agreements. Arbitration is seldom used, however, to resolve disputes over what the *terms* of the agreement should be. Although interest is growing in the use of arbitration as a means of reaching agreement on terms, mediation remains the more common method to achieve this objective. Arbitration is discussed in greater detail in part 2 of this book.

Let us now take a closer look at the mediation process. First, who are the mediators? They usually are either full-time employees of a state labor relations agency or individuals employed by them on a per diem basis. Those who work for state agencies may come from the ranks of management, or they may be former union officers or union staff members (perhaps their side has recently lost a union election). Per diem mediators are often moonlighting college professors. Whatever the case, prior employment is usually irrelevant, at least from the standpoint of ensuring impartiality. Judges start out as legal advocates; mediators start as negotiators for labor management, and although they may be biased, their professional origins are seldom relevant to the issue.

The mediator's lot is not always an easy one, as illustrated by a controversy in New York. There, the state Public Employment Relations Board (PERB) asked 150 per diem neutrals to work one day for nothing because of a fiscal crisis affecting the agency. When the neutrals agreed to do so, the president of the state teachers union charged that the PERB neutrals had compromised their impartiality by working a day at no pay. Admittedly, the notion that one can't be impartial if one has voluntarily worked a day for nothing may be difficult for school boards to accept, but it illustrates the problems of being impartial.

How does a mediator get involved? Usually, state law prescribes or authorizes the conditions under which mediators become involved in bargaining between boards and unions. Some states trigger mediation any time the parties have not reached agreement by a certain time—for example, 30 days before adoption of the final budget for the coming year. Other states prescribe mediation when the parties have reached an impasse, usually defined as a state of affairs in which continued bargaining on *any* item is futile. Some state laws give the state labor agency discretion to send in a mediator, or they stipulate that mediation is invoked automatically under certain conditions.

Whatever the trigger, Mr. or Ms. Impartial appears on the scene in due course. Frequently, his or her first move is to convene the parties to find out what the issues are. Having done this, the mediator then meets separately with the parties to ascertain whether movement is possible on various issues. In doing so, the mediator must gain and keep the respect and confidence of the board and union.

Taking sides too soon or too openly can undermine a mediator's effectiveness. Ultimately, if and when an agreement is in sight, the mediator may exert pressure on one or both parties to modify their positions. Consequently, mediators are likely to phrase their suggestions in terms of their negotiating impact, not their educational merits. Here is a typical exchange:

Mediator (to board negotiator): You know, if you could shorten the teachers' work day a little, I might be able to get the union to soften its stand on the number of work days.

Board negotiator (aghast): What? They already have the shortest work day in the county. Why are you defending this outrageous demand?

Mediator (sympathetically): I'm not defending their position. I'm only telling you how they look at it. They claim the nervous strain of teaching the kinds of kids in this district justifies a much shorter day. I'm not agreeing with their argument, but merely suggesting what might work in this difficult situation.

A few minutes later, the scenario could be:

Mediator (to union negotiator): You know, if you dropped your demand for a shorter school day, I might be able to get the board to move on the calendar.

Teachers union negotiator (aghast): Drop our demands for a shorter school day? Not as long as we have the largest class size in the county—not a chance. How can you ask us to drop such a clearly meritorious demand?

Mediator (sympathetically): I wasn't questioning the merits of your proposal. My purpose was only to let you know what could happen if you modified it.

The above dialogue illustrates that mediators avoid taking sides until they have reason to believe their initiatives will be successful. Frequently, mediators state their suggestions in terms of contingencies: "If I can get the union to agree to X, will the board agree to Y?" If the parties agree on the contingencies, the mediator in effect has achieved agreement. This technique illustrates an advantage of mediation over direct bargaining. A mediator can float ideas without indicating their sources. If a proposed idea is rejected, neither a loss of confidence nor an escalation of conflict is likely to ensue, as might be the case if the proposal were made by one of the parties during bargaining. The fact that a mediator can test proposals without confrontation tends to loosen up the parties and to encourage them to suggest solutions they might not be willing to propose directly.

The contingency approach is a good mediation technique, but it poses serious problems for school boards. To a mediator, the test of success is whether the board and union reach agreement. Whether the agreement reached is good or bad for the school system (or for education) is of secondary concern, if indeed it is relevant at all. A mediator who has achieved 10 agreements in 10 disputes is regarded as more successful than one who has achieved agreements in five out of 10 disputes—even though all of the agreements were undesirable from a public policy perspective. If a mediator concludes that one side can be pressured into agreement, pressure almost certainly will be applied to that side without regard for ultimate consequences. It is not that mediators view the merits of disputes as irrelevant, but frequently they are unable to assess the merits accurately. Under such circumstances, it's easy to understand why reaching agreement dominates their outlook.

Needless to say, boards ought to be cautious in reacting to the mediator's suggestions. The fact that the mediator leans on management doesn't necessarily reflect a prounion bias; the mediator may be leaning even harder on the union in the other caucus. In any case, the question of how much to tell the mediator can be a tricky one. If both parties refuse to make any concessions, the mediator will be helpless. The difficulty is that if one party is willing to make concessions and the other side is not, the confiding party is placing itself at a disadvantage. However, an experienced and effective mediator is not likely to be influenced by unjustified intransigence on either side.

When should a mediator be called upon or made available? Theoretically, this should happen only after the board and union have bargained in good faith to impasse. Have a substantial number of tentative agreements been reached before a mediator enters the scene? If the answer is no, the state agency may prohibit mediation, on grounds that the board and union have not tried hard enough to reach agreement on their own.

What happens if no agreements have been reached because one side has been intransigent and unyielding from the beginning? The position of the state labor relations agency may be that the other party should file unfair labor practice charges in such a case. In effect, the state's rationale would be as follows: "We aren't going to provide mediation services where the parties haven't fulfilled their obligation to bargain. Furthermore, it isn't up to us to decide who is responsible for the lack of progress. Charge the other party with refusing to negotiate in good faith if you really believe that's what underlies your lack of progress."

This rationale makes sense, but to take advantage of it, boards need adequate records of the bargaining history; then, if the union alleges that the board is responsible for the lack of progress, the board has available a record to refute the charges. Policies sometimes dictate the need for a mediator. To illustrate, the union leaders, having made a continuing public display of their alleged militancy, may fear that they will look weak to their membership if they reach agreement without third-party intervention. Similarly, school board members who may be willing to make certain concessions may be fearful of public condemnation should they do so; thus, both parties may welcome a mediator who can take them off the hook by making the recommendations. In both cases, the combatants seemingly are displaying sweet reason by agreeing to a compromise suggested by an impartial third party rather than one reached by making concessions to the other side.

Whatever the method of payment, the major costs of mediation are the time devoted to mediation. Ordinarily, when the mediator is meeting with one side, the other is waiting in a nearby room. Consequently, both sides find themselves devoting large blocks of expensive time to waiting for the mediator to return with news, they hope, of progress toward an agreement. Inasmuch as the mediator can achieve concessions only from the side conferring with the mediator, mediation strategy calls for persuading or stimulating the mediator to spend as much time as possible with the other side.

How effective is mediation? Sometimes it is extremely effective; in other cases, a dismal failure. The outcome often depends on what follows mediation. If mediation is the final stage in efforts to reach agreement, it is far more likely to be successful than if mediation is followed by fact-finding. If fact-finding is in the offing, both sides are likely to withhold "final" offers in mediation to protect their positions in fact-finding.

4. BASIC BOARD ISSUES AND STRATEGIES

Introduction

Education, more than most enterprises, is people-oriented. Individuals who run for election to membership on school boards often see themselves as caring individuals representing the parents or children of the district. Therefore, it is not surprising that many board members find confrontation difficult. The problem with being open and humanistic under conditions of collective bargaining is that openness frequently undercuts one's fellow board members and those administrators who are striving to protect the viability of the district. Providing confidential information to outsiders frequently results in the teachers union's knowing management's position, while management remains blind as to the union's objectives. Conflict among board members will most assuredly be exploited by the union team. Learning how to handle pressure and how to reach a consensus when doing so is in the best interest of the school district is an important attribute of a successful board member. The following chapter describes several of the most troubling issues involving internal board and administrative relationships that frequently occur during pressure bargaining.

Maintaining the Confidentiality of Board Positions

Despite naive theories of "win-win" bargaining, collective bargaining is an adversarial process. For this reason, confidentiality of board positions, including strategy and tactics, must be maintained. A board member who leaks critical information to the union undermines board objectives in negotiations. Distasteful as it usually is, the problem must be faced by the board when it arises. The person leaking information is usually a board member closely allied with the union. Some states prohibit teachers from membership on the school board of their district of employment; other states prohibit board members who are also union members from participating in negotiations with their union. Unfortunately, some problems do not involve board member affiliation with a union but rather a political or personal relationship that leads to breaches in confidentiality.

For instance, a board member may be married to a teacher who is also a union leader. Taking some precautionary measures concerning such situations is not to suggest that the individuals involved are unethical; if action is taken as a matter of policy, the board is protecting the individuals as well as the district. Federal officials are required to sever their business connections and put their investments in a blind trust. They do this not on the assumption that they will be dishonest in office (then why appoint them in the first place?) but because they must not even *appear* to have a conflict of interest. The same principle should be applied to collective bargaining situations and relationships.

Guarding against leaks by board members is a difficult problem. Board member X may be leaking board positions to the union, but it may be practically impossible to prove this during the time when the leak is especially damaging. Proposals that board members refrain from talking to teachers can split the board, because board members who do not leak board positions may still insist upon their right to talk to teachers. Ideally, boards should not discuss matters being negotiated outside of board meetings, but some boards will not accept or comply with this sensible policy.

One alternative is for the chief negotiator to consult key members informally about strategy and bottom lines. This is probably the most convenient solution, and it is common practice even in the absence of leaks. The negotiator needs to know the board and must be confident that those consulted can deliver a board majority when final decisions are made.

Another way to protect against leaks is for the board to appoint a bargaining subcommittee that excludes the guilty party. The subcommittee could have a less controversial rationale, namely, the need to avoid tying up the entire board. The operative word here is *appoint*: If a request is made by volunteers to serve on the subcommittee and the board member responsible for leaks volunteers, establishing the subcommittee solves nothing.

As long as school board members talk to teachers about matters subject to negotiation, there will be a double standard that works to the union's advantage. Meanwhile, alert board members must cope with the problem as best they can.

Intraboard Conflict During Bargaining

Bargaining sometimes places heavy strains on relationships between board members. Disagreements within school boards and/or bargaining teams can be one of the greatest difficulties of collective bargaining. Every experienced negotiator, whether for management or the union, can cite cases in which disagreements on the negotiator's side were more difficult to resolve than disagreements between the negotiating teams.

Disagreements among union team members usually become obvious during the course of negotiations. Teachers earning maximum salaries want the salary package to stress higher maximums; those in the middle or beginning years want a reduction in the number of steps. Single teachers may prefer individual employee health coverage to more funds for sabbaticals; married teachers with families may want the priorities reversed. Dozens of such conflicts emerge during negotiations. Typically, they are resolved by "negotiations" within the bargaining team.

Generally, it is advisable not to let the other side know about the disagreements within one's own team, because such disagreements can be exploited by a skillful adversary. Suppose, for example, that the board negotiator perceives that a particular group of teachers has achieved its major objective in the negotiations. In that case, these teachers will not be greatly motivated to hold out for benefits that would go to other teachers. In contrast, the teachers who have not achieved their major objectives are more likely to be adamant on the remaining items that pertain especially to themselves.

Problems frequently arise when a benefit granted to some teachers reduces the benefits granted to others. For this reason, it is easier to agree upon items that affect all teachers equally. This is why clauses relating only to subgroups within the negotiating unit are often troublesome to both negotiating teams.

The interests of members of the management team may also affect their reactions to a proposal. Suppose the teachers propose that teachers be paid for unused sick leave upon resignation or retirement. In most systems, administrators receive the same sick leave benefits granted to teachers. For this reason, administrators may react very differently, depending upon their own situation. An administrator on the verge of retirement may be much more receptive to the union proposal than a first-year administrator. The latter might prefer to see board funds spent for immediate instead of long-range benefits that may be lost on transfer to another district. In the example just cited, the administrator about to retire is not going to say, "I favor the teacher proposal, because I'll get a year's salary in unused sick leave if the teacher proposal is accepted." Needless to say, the administrator will give other reasons for favoring the union proposal.

From time to time, positions recommended by management negotiators are camouflaged for this reason. It is difficult to resolve disagreements over them when the real reasons, interests, and motivations are not discussed frankly; because the justifications are rationalizations, not reasons, controversy over them is futile. Furthermore, negotiators may exacerbate matters by referring to the underlying motivation; nobody likes to be characterized as profiting personally from a position allegedly espoused as a matter of principle.

These comments do not imply that management positions should be resolved by votes within the administration team. The chief negotiator should solicit views from team members and try to get a unified management position, but should not be bound to any ratio of support. Ordinarily, a chief negotiator would be ill-advised to negotiate a clause strongly opposed by most of the management team, but this is necessary in some situations. Of course, disagreement at the board level is another matter; even individual opposition cannot be easily ignored at this level.

Even at the board level, however, conflicts of interest disguised as differences of principle arise occasionally. A board member may believe that approval of a proposed agreement would be fatal to his or her reelection. As a result, the member may oppose the agreement while privately hoping that the board adopts it. Then the board member can avoid the responsibility for sabotaging an agreement while simultaneously taking credit for opposing it.

On occasion, board members or union negotiators may try to renege on an agreement. Such action may be an unfair labor practice, but even if it is not, the practice should be avoided if possible. If such situations occur, the reasons one gives for disavowing an agreement are critical. It is one thing to try to rectify an honest mistake—for example, when board members have approved a proposal because of an honest misunderstanding. But deliberate efforts to repudiate an agreement because of adverse political repercussions are much less defensible. Boards have the right to try to change something they have agreed to, but they should be prepared to offer something in return for such a change. Offering someone an inducement to change a bona fide agreement is different from offering spurious reasons for not living up to the agreement or simply refusing to abide by it.

Resolving Internal Disagreement

Usually, some palatable way can be found to resolve internal disagreements. For example, consider a board disagreement where the board was able to pay the highest salary schedule in the state. The board's reluctance to do so was strictly political; some board members up for reelection were afraid that opposing candidates would benefit politically by criticizing the incumbents for adopting such a generous salary schedule. Substantively, none of the board members had any real objection to it. This was made evident by their efforts to reduce the salary schedule by very small amounts that would prevent it from being the highest in the state. This might not have been a problem except that the teachers had the same problem in reverse. Their leadership was under pressure to achieve the highest salary schedule in the state. For the teacher leadership also, the dollar amounts involved were not very important substantively, but their political impact was crucial.

This problem was resolved by an increase in the board contribution to a tax-deferred annuity. The board contribution was virtually as good as a salary increase, since the teachers could withdraw the contributions at the end of the year if they so chose. This enabled the teacher negotiators to claim that they had negotiated the best package in the state; the salary schedule plus the board's contribution to the tax deferred annuity (unique at that time in the state) was more than any other schedule. At the same time, the board members believed that their political flanks would not be exposed; the salary schedule was among the highest, as the community expected, but it could not be clearly identified as "the highest."

Although obligated to seek an agreement that is consistent with the instructions from the board and superintendent, when his principals are adhering to an undesirable or unrealistic position, the chief negotiator must be prepared to tell them the nature of the problem. Otherwise, the negotiator will be in an untenable negotiating position, having to defend positions that are clearly indefensible. Unrealistic objectives at the beginning of negotiations are not necessarily a major obstacle to an agreement; if the board's bargaining position is an unreasonable one, that fact will become evident during negotiations.

What can be done, however, when a board or board members insist upon a final offer that the teachers reasonably cannot accept? At this point, the negotiator must be ready to take drastic action. One alternative is to declare an impasse, then have some third party come in and educate the board about the facts of life. Chief negotiators on both sides frequently adopt this course of action if they are unable to persuade their principals to adopt a realistic position.

Unrealistic boards sometimes can be persuaded to change their positions by a two-stage process. In the first stage, the board is persuaded to improve its offer, to weaken teacher determination to use impasse procedures. The negotiator should emphasize the long-run danger that the union will achieve significant improvements by third-party intervention; if this happens, teachers will be more reluctant in the future to settle before such intervention. If appropriate, it should also be emphasized that the board's position is building militancy among teachers.

Negotiators who can get the board to accept these possibilities can usually persuade it to make an offer that will bring about an agreement. Suppose the parities are officially $750 per teacher apart, but the board negotiator believes the union will accept $250 per teacher. Suppose, also, that the negotiator believes that the board should be but is not willing to make such an offer. In that case, the strategy would be to move the board closer to the settlement figure, so that the $250 figure comes as an offer from the union. With the board, emphasis is placed on the foolishness of going to impasse for so little more money and for such a blow to morale of the "defeated" teachers. The negotiator docs not and cannot make a "final offer" of $250 more per teacher; instead, he tries to find out if—assuming that by some miracle he could persuade the board to improve its offer—the union negotiator could persuade his or her constituents to accept it. At this point, the parties should reach an agreement.

The Policy/Administration Dichotomy

Conventional wisdom has it that school boards formulate educational policy and administration implements it. Unfortunately, conventional wisdom is out of touch with political realities. Indeed, collective bargaining illustrates why this tidy division of labor does not and cannot be made to work in many districts.

Generally, the larger the school system, the greater the likelihood that it will be controlled by administration. Board members in large school systems may not agree, but the point is hardly debatable. After all, even full-time elected officials often are unable to control the bureaucracies they supposedly supervise. Not surprisingly, school board members who are part-time, unpaid public officials exercise even less control over school district bureaucracies.

Staff control of information is a crucial factor. In a large district, the staff tends to control the flow of information to the board. If the staff is opposed to a policy, its communications will emphasize the negative aspects of it. If the staff favors a policy, its communications to the board can support the policy directly or by omitting its negative aspects. By the time issues and policies come to its attention, the board may have little room to maneuver. In small school districts, however, board members are more familiar with issues. Also, they have fewer problems to resolve, thus are less subject to bureaucratic control. Because smaller districts operate fewer schools, they have fewer problems of maintenance and renovation. Because they tend to enroll a more homogeneous student body, they are less likely to face social, racial, and religious conflicts over educational issues.

Bargaining illustrates the wide disparities in board control between large and small districts. For example, the grievance procedure in a large district may require that appeals of grievance decisions by principals be directed to an area superintendent. Impartial arbitration may be the next and terminal point of the procedure; appeals to the board of education may not even be one of the steps in the grievance procedure.

In contrast, grievances in districts with a few hundred teachers or fewer may go from the superintendent and terminate with the local board. In short, school boards in small districts can and do play a role in implementing policy that would be impractical in larger districts.

In large districts, the school board must coordinate its program with other public services and officials. Police, fire, sanitation, transportation, and recreation agencies tend to develop a measure of control—or strong influence—over school board policies, and rightly so. School systems outside large cities often constitute the largest public agency in their communities; integrating school programs with other services presents fewer problems.

Clearly, therefore, the division of the labor between school boards and administrators depends partly upon district size. The distinction between policymaking and administration is relatively unimportant in small districts where a teacher transfer would normally constitute an item of business for the board. The actual transfer, not the policy covering transfers, could be the item for consideration. Meanwhile, in large districts, the board doesn't have time to consider individual transfers, even if it wished to do so. In other words, school boards in big districts can't ordinarily consider individual situations, whereas boards in small districts routinely do so; they implement as well as formulate policy. In medium-sized districts, the distinction between policy and administration is or can be a rough working guide. In large districts, boards lack the time to develop policy in many areas; their problem is determining which policies will be resolved by the board and which will be delegated to the school administration. Even in large districts, however, boards will be deeply involved in individual cases that receive a great deal of publicity for one reason or another.

Collective bargaining illustrates another reason that the policy and administration dichotomy breaks down in practice. In the prebargaining era, school boards could consider personnel policies on their own schedule. A specific policy, such as sick leave, could be placed on the board agenda and considered in due course in isolation from other personnel policies. If events forced a delay, the item could be rescheduled at a time convenient to the board. Collective bargaining, however, forced school boards to abandon this leisurely approach. With the arrival of bargaining, personnel policies had to be resolved as a package by a specified time. To do this, school boards were forced to delegate a great deal of their authority over district policy to their administrators, especially their chief negotiator. The latter cannot ask the super-intendent to convene the school board to consider every policy proposed by the union during bargaining. Consequently, teacher bargaining resulted in the loss of school board authority over district policy for school administrators as well as for unions.

Strike Plans and Public Relations

A strike is one of several means by which labor creates pressure on management for the purpose of inducing concessions. A strike is not always an effective weapon. When a strike is ineffective in producing an immediate compromise, pressure builds and vandalism and violence may occur. In order to combat these events, it is highly desirable that the board have a comprehensive strike plan in readiness before under-taking negotiations with the union. Without such a document, the union is likely win the battle for community support and achieve aims that may be detrimental to effective operation of the schools.

Union influence is often a major consideration that must be considered when developing a strike plan. The union may orchestrate several different scenarios in a strike situation. (*Note*: if the authors were to attempt to cover all of the ramifications of trying to operate schools during a strike, a separate book would be required. For this reason, we are not including a comprehensive discussion on the topic of strike plans. However, the policy aspects of teacher strikes are covered in part 2 of this book.)

Although they are greatly oversimplified, here are some of the strategies a school district might use when faced with a strike:

• Keep schools open if possible. When schools are closed, the pressures on board members from the community, the press, and politicians to open them are frequently overwhelming. Trying to negotiate under conditions of heavy duress frequently forces board members to "cave in" to unreasonable demands.

• Prepare a strike plan with as many contingencies as possible. Be aware that the union will have a comprehensive plan that will have the advantage of having been tested under real conditions in other districts. Prepare required letters of notification to teachers, the community, and the press in advance. Install private telephone lines immune to union jamming. Provide for emergency food service. Service unions, such as the cafeteria workers, may join in the strike, or even more likely, refuse to cross union-generated picket lines. Setting up meetings with the heads of the service unions may result in some agreements that will lessen the likelihood of these unions joining in the strike.

• Include the school building principals—managers responsible for keeping the buildings open—in the plan. Let them know what will be expected of them in the event of a sizable walkout of their building staff. Give principals support and immediate access to district officials and district public information personnel. With the assistance of the principals at each site, prepare a substitute procurement plan well in advance of actual negotiations.

• Help board members understand the heavy pressure they will face. The administration should meet frequently with the board and keep it informed on all aspects of the strike and the nature of the discussions with the union or mediators should mediators become involved. Make board members realize they need to stand firm on any "retroactive pay" issue, which is the only way to prevent a rash of strikes in the future. Pressure may cause individual board members to try to negotiate privately with the union or selected politicians. When board members crumble under pressure, the advantage always accrues to the union side. Prestrike board member training, which covers the actions likely to be taken by the union during a strike, should be provided.

• Build a legal foundation for possible action in the courts. Although laws vary from state to state, there are usually several legal recourses that should be considered.

• Finally, keep the plan as secure as possible. Strike plans have a way of being discussed in public, or worse, getting lost. Assign a secretary who is management confidential to type the document, then guard the actual plan and share it only with trusted employees.

Here are some additional observations (based on actual experience) that may be valuable in anticipating union activity. Security will quickly become a problem. The union will take steps to force the principals to shut down the school buildings. Union members will make attending school a hazardous experience for both students and working teachers. Off-duty police can be very helpful in augmenting the district security force. Principals may have to escort teachers and other school personnel through picket lines. Protection of employees who report for work is imperative. These employees must be aware of the security of their future, their immediate safety, and the protection of their possessions, such as automobiles.

Finally, most strikes are won or lost based on the perceptions of the community. Community groups need to be involved, properly advised, and consulted at regular intervals by the administration and by individual board members. Members of the working press are also likely to be union members and may, perhaps unconsciously, exhibit bias in reports on the strike. In an effort to counter such a possibility, the board or superintendent should arrange meetings with media editorial boards, where the management viewpoint is more likely to be understood and, it is to be hoped, conveyed to the general public.

An effective strike plan should also take into account the actions and needs of the students. Student attendance in a particular school tends to reflect teacher absence in that school. In other words, when a high percentage of teachers in any one school walk out, student attendance in that building will be low. The opposite is also true. This predictable linkage allows the board to pinpoint the assignment of reserve personnel. Student attitudes, especially the attitudes of secondary students, may also affect the outcome of the strike. In schools where large numbers of students are absent, the union may attempt to organize a student walkout. This action provides a circus atmosphere, which attracts television coverage detrimental to the desired image of an orderly and safe school atmosphere. Student leaders should be included in the development of contingency planning.

A strike is damaging to everyone it touches. Nevertheless, the board should not give in to unreasonable demands just to avoid the consequences of a strike. If the board and management plan carefully and stay united, the advantage lies with the board and may discourage the union from using the strike threat as a weapon of intimidation.

Joint Bargaining

In the private sector, several companies often bargain jointly with unions representing employees in all of the companies. The situation arises most frequently where many companies must bargain with a large, powerful union. The hotel, restaurant, and trucking industries in various communities are an illustration of this situation, in which, the companies jointly hire a negotiator (usually a law firm specializing in labor law) who negotiates an agreement that applies to all of the companies. This set of circumstances must be distinguished from one in which the same negotiator bargains separately for different companies. The latter situation is common in education; in many areas, several school districts employ the same negotiator. The issue to be discussed here is the feasibility of joint bargaining; that is, the negotiation of a single agreement that applies to teachers in several school districts.

It is not difficult to see the advantages of joint bargaining. One is the potential to reduce the substantial costs of district-by-district bargaining. Another advantage is that in most districts, settlements are based upon settlements in neighboring districts. This reason is not so applicable to pattern-setting districts, but few districts set rather than follow the pattern of settlements. Furthermore, under present arrangements, most school boards operate at a disadvantage. Board members find it difficult to track bargaining settlements or developments in their area. Sometimes they lack information about the factors underlying a specific agreement in a nearby district. The result is that they are unable to evaluate the relevance of concessions made elsewhere to their own situation. When union negotiators in district Y argue, "If district X can make this concession, why can't you?" the administration in Y may have no answer. Nevertheless, there may be good reasons for the concession being made in district X but not in Y. It may be that union negotiators in district X dropped many demands to get the item in dispute, demands that are still on the table in district Y. Lack of information can thus be a severe tactical handicap for district negotiators.

In contrast, having a single negotiator for two or more districts eliminates or minimizes problems of interdistrict communication during negotiations. This is especially helpful where the teachers are represented by the same union, the same negotiator, or both. Such arrangements give the union a significant tactical advantage in negotiations, in that the union can coordinate its strategy and secure the most advantageous agreement first. Then the early agreements can be used as leverage against other school districts that are resisting union demands. Finally, despite large expenditures of time and resources, many districts end up with an agreement that is substantially similar to agreements reached in nearby districts. To many administrators and board members, it seems pointless to expend so much time and energy to achieve so little that is different from agreements negotiated in neighboring districts.

As a practical matter, many districts have relatively little discretion in negotiations. The teachers will not allow districts to pay too little, and the public will not permit school boards to pay much more than other districts. As a result, discretion is more apparent than real, applying mainly to peripheral issues. At least that is the case if the board and the administration wish to avoid a major battle with the taxpayers or the union in their district.

One additional advantage of joint negotiations should be cited. Typically, the participating employers share the cost of the joint negotiator. As a result, the cost to each board would be less than the cost of a separate negotiator for each board; a group of school boards thus can employ highly skilled negotiators at minimal cost to individual boards.

Despite these advantages, joint bargaining also exhibits formidable disadvantages in public education. Suppose a board agrees to initiate joint bargaining with neighboring school districts. Wealthier districts might be opposed to the idea, feeling that they would lose their competitive advantages if their terms and conditions of employment were the same as those of poorer districts. Poorer districts may also be reluctant to participate in joint bargaining because they cannot afford to pay salaries and benefits paid by affluent districts.

Suppose that districts are able to overcome these obstacles. Perhaps they do so by persuading districts with very similar resources, problems, and conditions of employment to join together for bargaining. Suppose further that the districts manage to come to agreement on a negotiator and the fee involved. The negotiator must now receive negotiating guidelines from the employer districts. It is virtually impossible to do this while meeting with only one board at a time; issues arise with board C that will affect the guidelines of boards A and B. Thus, joint bargaining introduces an additional layer of decisionmaking that can be more complex and time-consuming than the relations between a negotiator and single board.

Achieving Common Agreement

The negotiator who represents several districts must achieve common agreement on concessions. Unfortunately, positions that make sense in one district may not in another, so negotiations between the participating school districts will be required merely to achieve agreement on guidelines. In joint bargaining, there is the constant danger of concessions that are acceptable in most districts but unworkable in some because of special elements overlooked by the joint bargaining team. When the administration negotiating team bargains for only one district, that team is more likely to be thoroughly knowledgeable about the district. Under joint bargaining, however, the negotiating team would become too large if it included knowledgeable members from every participating district.

Troublesome as they are, these problems are probably not as difficult as the problems of delegation and ratification. In the first place, the participating boards must agree to be bound by the agreement negotiated; however, such an agreement can be interpreted as an illegal delegation of authority to a third party not responsible or accountable to the public. Furthermore, each board will need to ratify the agreement separately. Imagine the union reactions if one or more school boards refused to ratify an agreement negotiated jointly. The teachers would be outraged and probably refuse to engage in joint bargaining again, at least with the nonratifying school board.

Ratification highlights one of the most important ways in which public sector bargaining differs from that in the private sector. In the latter, employers are free to delegate authority to negotiators representing all of the employers. Because private companies need not worry about illegal delegation of authority, joint bargaining can proceed on a much firmer basis in the private sector.

Interdistrict Differentials

Another obstacle to joint bargaining relates to interdistrict differentials in conditions of employment. Some districts have more liberal policies than others relating to sick leave, transfers, sabbaticals, and so on. Teachers who enjoy the most generous benefits will object to giving them up. School boards, however, cannot simply accept the most generous benefit provisions from each contract and apply these provisions equally throughout all the districts. Union negotiators will try to achieve this, but boards normally would find it impossible to accept such an outcome. To do so would be as unrealistic as expecting the teachers to accept the least generous provision in all the districts. In short, providing adequate and universal salary and benefit differentials would be a very troublesome point in making the transition to joint bargaining.

One possible solution to this problem is "two-tier" bargaining. At the regional level, bargaining could proceed on items that are or could be relatively uniform throughout the region; bargaining at the local level would still be used to resolve other issues. Although this approach has merits, its long-range viability is doubtful. It would not materially reduce the cost or the time to individual districts and might inhibit needed flexibility on items negotiated locally. Bargaining issues do not stay categorized very neatly; the implications of a policy that seems amenable to uniform treatment may vary widely from district to district.

The foregoing discussion has been devoted largely to the merits of joint bargaining from the employer viewpoint. For unions, joint bargaining is much easier to achieve legally, but it is likely to lead to severe organizational problems, especially in the transition period. Teachers unions tend to be favorably disposed toward joint bargaining because it leads to more efficient use of union resources. Nonetheless, local union leaders may be just as reluctant as local boards to give up the prestige and autonomy associated with the individual district approach.

Once initial contract demands concerning union recognition, union security, some improvement of working conditions, and adequate salaries are reached, successor contracts become centered on working conditions and monetary advancements. There is also the question of erasing inappropriate language in successor contracts by demanding union givebacks.

Ratifying The Contract

Relationships between the board and its negotiating team become extremely important when the board negotiator recommends board ratification of a negotiated agreement. A split board can cause serious problems. The contract vote should focus on the *total package*. If the issues are separated, it becomes difficult, if not impossible, to get a positive ratification vote. As long as the board negotiator has stayed within the guidelines established by the board, ratification should be forthcoming.

The alternative to the proposed agreement is likely to be a bruising battle that ends in the same—or virtually the same—agreement. Consequently, the basis for refusal to ratify must be serious enough to justify the battle that may follow. A serious question of ratification usually signals a breakdown of communications between the board's negotiator and the school board. Board negotiators should avoid unpleasant surprises, particularly to the school board during the critical stages of negotiations. A negotiator who is aware that an item may lead to refusal to ratify should not ordinarily include the item in the proposed agreement without consultation with the board. If the item is included, the negotiator should explain very clearly that the proposed agreement may be rejected as a result. If the negotiator believes that the board should accept the item, the negotiator should try to persuade the board informally to accept it; including the item in a proposed agreement submitted to the board for ratification is rarely defensible.

During negotiations, the negotiators sometimes reject proposals because their principals allegedly would never accept them. Alleging that the board or the teachers would never accept a proposal becomes a convenient way to avoid dealing with its merits. To be sure, negotiators must take ratification problems into account; there is no point to insisting on items that will lead to rejection of the proposed agreement. At the same time, negotiators cannot allow the other party to avoid unpopular concessions merely by declaring that they are unacceptable. Even highly unpopular concessions will not necessarily lead to rejection of the contract if there is a legitimate basis for them. In some situations, the fact that the contract has been recommended by an impartial third party helps the negotiators avoid criticism for unpopular agreements that should be ratified.

The timing of ratification is extremely important. Normally, the board should ratify *after* the teachers do so. Prior board ratification leads to all kinds of problems if the teachers reject the contract. Suppose, for example, that a board ratifies a contract in July, even though the union constitution calls for ratification when the teachers return in the fall, and begins implementing benefits under the new contract. In the fall, the teachers vote against ratification. When the union tries to reopen negotiations, the board refuses. Both sides file unfair labor practice charges that are later dismissed, but the entire controversy could have been avoided if the board had waited.

Ratification can be too late as well as too early. This is especially true if the teachers are divided over ratification. Some union members may want time to block or overturn the union's ratification. If the board ratifies promptly, however, the contract is a *fait accompli*, and further opposition is futile.

School boards sometimes want to ratify, but only if one clause can be changed. If only one clause is unacceptable, it may be possible to modify or eliminate it. If the board wants to change an item, however, the union will propose to change a different item to compensate for the change sought by the board. The danger is that the entire agreement will unravel when one of the parties proposes to modify one item in an agreed-upon package.

To avoid this outcome, negotiators should be prepared to offer appropriate concessions for changes in an agreed-upon package. If such concessions are not available, it may be advisable to accept the package rather than risk reopening the entire agreement. The best procedure is for the school board and its negotiator to work closely together so that refusals to ratify simply do not happen.

5. SHARED DECISION MAKING

The conventional wisdom is that unions protect teachers from the capricious and arbitrary actions of management. Today, however, it may be management that needs to be protected from the unions. Supported by powerful allies, the teachers unions have gone beyond seeking concessions on working conditions and wages to demands that teachers run schools without "interference" from administrators and boards of education. The vehicle for this takeover is "shared decision making," a new variation on traditional collective bargaining. Most modern reforms call for teachers to be involved in decision making on professional issues. Several good mechanisms can be devised for this, but collective negotiation is not one of them.

The educational process is better served if the scope of bargaining between school boards and teachers unions is limited. If management's rights are bargained away, it is extremely difficult—if not impossible—to operate an effective education program. Unfortunately, some teacher empowerment advocates propose placing responsibility for school management and instructional programs in the teachers' hands.

Paradoxically, most teachers do not want to make management decisions or serve on more committees. Instead, most teachers want responsible leadership, support (both moral and material), some influence over decisions that affect them, and time to teach.[1]

From the very beginning of public sector bargaining, the experts predicted problems over the rights of the parties. The more "professional"

---

[1] Robert Brasco, *Organizational health as a predictor of a desire for teacher empowerment* (Doctoral dissertation, St. John's University, 1991).

the employees, the more managerial decision making they are likely to demand. In a tax-conscious society, the public employer, when offered an opportunity to trade off monetary demands for shared decision making, is faced with a dilemma. As a public sector employer, the school board holds a public trust and spends tax dollars to uphold that trust. Board members must worry about both cost-effectiveness and managerial control, but what if they are told that they can gain effectiveness by trading away control to an increasingly "professionalized" labor force? Can they take that risk?

The dangers of doing so are illustrated by events in the Rochester, N.Y., public schools. In 1987, the schools announced an increase in teacher salaries of more than 52 percent, up to a maximum of $70,000, together with "real teacher control." One newspaper report saluted the Rochester superintendent and the union president for their achievement and implied that what they had done was in the national interest.

Exactly what the parties had accomplished was made clear in the "Career in Teaching Plan," an agreement between the school board and the Rochester Teachers Association (RTA) that had the force of a legal contract.[2] In its initial form, the plan, which structured career options and incentives for teachers, was governed by a seven-member panel composed of four members appointed by the RTA and three members appointed by the superintendent. Decisions required a five-to-two vote, effectively giving the union veto power over the decision-making process and prohibiting management from taking unilateral action.

In 1988, the agreement was revised, expanding the joint governing panel to 10 members, five appointed by the union and five by the superintendent. In this new agreement, decisions by the panel required an affirmative vote of at least six panel members. The union no longer controlled the majority of panel seats, but the effect remained the same: Management no longer retained the right to manage and to make decisions.

The Rochester contract also called for school-based planning teams, which, according to the 1988-89 guidelines, consist of the principal, who serves as chairperson; the principal's designee(s); three parents; two students for high school level teams; others chosen by a consensus of team members; and a number of teachers "determined by adding one to the total number of all other members selected for the team." These

---

[2] *Career in teaching plan*, an agreement between the Rochester Board of Education and the Rochester Teachers Association, 1987.

teams, which are described in the guidelines as "deliberative, decision-making bodies," are "empowered to act on behalf of the school when their decisions and actions are arrived at by consensus" and when those decisions "are supported by each constituency represented on the team."[2] Teachers constitute not only the majority of the team members but the largest constituency on the team.

One naive notion in the empowerment debate is that school boards can trade away their governance prerogatives in return for a "less adversarial relationship" between administrators and union members. Unfortunately, it is less adversarial because one of the adversaries, the administrator, has been effectively eliminated from the relationship.

Establishing the Scope of Bargaining

The question of what should be the scope of bargaining should be answered by an analysis of the effect of the negotiations upon the educational process. It is essential to provide a system that will permit the managerial function to be performed as efficiently as possible. This does not mean that teachers should be excluded from other areas of decision making. Almost every textbook on education administration written in the past 25 years implores administrators to use some form of consultative participation. Administrators are taught to exercise the concept of teacher involvement in decision making. The concept of democratic supervision of schools permeates graduate departments of education administration, and graduates of these programs tend to practice what they have been taught. As a result, decisions that have an impact on classroom activities are frequently the result of recommendations from teacher committees. Textbooks often are selected by committees predominantly composed of teachers of the subject under study. The placement of children by grade level and subject is normally made as a result of joint teacher and principal discussions. Materials and supplies are frequently ordered as a result of teacher requests.

Under collective bargaining, teachers unions frequently attempt to gain more control over educational issues by proposing union designation of teacher representatives on decision-making committees. As far back as 1968, the New Jersey Education Association's proposed master contract stated:

"The Association shall select a Liaison Committee for each school building which shall meet with the principal at least once a month during the
school day for the duration of the school year to review and discuss local
school problems and practices, and to play an active role in the revision
or development of building policies. Areas for consideration shall
include, but not be limited to, such matters as curriculum, textbooks, distribution of materials and supplies, discipline and parent visitation."[3]

More recently, the Missouri Education Association demanded (but
failed to secure) language that provided for a paid "professional development" teacher committee selected by the association that would:
"...develop the procedures and policies in regard to: In-Service Programs,
Educational Reimbursement, Professional Conferences, School
Visitation, Sabbatical Policy, Mentor Committees, Curriculum Revision,
Professional Assistance Programs, and Peer Counseling/Assistance."[4]

Elsewhere, when such provisions were included in contracts, teachers
appointed to the committees by the union president promptly espoused
union positions. This injected a new dimension into a collegial relationship; what had been a professional relationship quickly became an
adversarial one. Under the guise of mutual decision making, administrators were confronted with union efforts to control various educational programs. Quite understandably, school districts were urged to protect
these extremely important decision-making rights. Even on the issues
that accompany collective bargaining, effective administrators typically
subscribed to the philosophy that classroom teachers should be involved
in decisions that have an impact on the classroom. Teachers frequently
have better information that may bear on the classroom problems to be
solved. For this reason, school-based administrators frequently discuss a
proposed policy with teachers prior to making a decision on that policy.
In leadership courses, administrators are encouraged to involve teachers
in decision making. Note, however, that in a consultative model, management does not abdicate its responsibility for making decisions. If
there is no consensus on the best way to proceed, the *administrator*
makes the decision, after ensuring that the group members have disclosed all of the relevant facts. Accountability remains in the hands of
those appointed by the board of education to exercise responsibility.

---

[3] New Jersey Education Association proposed master contract disseminated to local affiliates,
1968.

[4] Missouri Educational Association proposal to the Fort Zumwald Board of Education, 1990.

Industrial models of employee involvement in organizational decisions are often cited as one reason that management should encourage, not resist, teacher involvement in educational decision making. However, before incorporating industrial incentives into school settings, decision makers should proceed with considerable caution. Industrial models are not necessarily applicable to schools. For example, teachers, unlike industrial workers, receive pensions from the state, not the "company." Another significant difference between education systems and private industry is the absence of the profit motive. Increased production frequently brings with it increased income. No comparable incentive is available to most teachers engaged in consultative activities.

How Much Involvement of Teachers?

Administrators need to determine when to involve teachers in decision making. Too much or too little involvement in school decisions is detrimental, detracting from teacher satisfaction with the school. Although some studies indicate a desire by teachers to increase their involvement in school decisions, it is typically assumed that the increased involvement would take place on "school time," not otherwise.

In a study of the potential costs and benefits of teacher involvement in school decision making, Duke, Showers, and Imber indicated that teachers may not want to devote much time to it.[5] In addition, administrative roles assumed by teachers that are not rooted in the technical expertise of the teacher may result in less—not more—effective teaching and learning. These studies are samples from a strong body of research that emphasizes the need for a selective use of teacher involvement in decision making by school administrators.

Teachers unions state that one of the their goals is to increase teacher autonomy by having teachers share control of the management and instructional programs of schools. The unions propose to organize schools so that teachers have more authority to make important instructional and policy decisions. In such a setting, teacher committees, led by lead teachers, would supposedly replace the principal in running the school. The unions assert that these changes would increase teacher

---

[5] D.L. Duke, B.K. Showers, M. Imber, Teachers and shared decision making: The costs and benefits of involvement. *Educational Administration Quarterly*, 16, pp. 93-106, 1980.

autonomy, reduce bureaucratic regulation of schools, and encourage collegial decision making. Decisions under teacher control would include instructional methods and materials to be used, the staffing structure to be employed, the organization of the school day, the assignment of students, the hiring and use of support staff and consultants, and the allocation of resources available to the school.

In effect, the unions propose to diminish the authority of building principals at a time when extensive research demonstrates that successful schools require strong instructional leadership from the principal. The unions not only ignore the role of the principal, superintendent, and school board in implementing reform, but also undermine school board authority by replacing building level administrators (who are subordinate to the superintendent and school board) with influential members of teacher unions.

School boards and school administrators are already overregulated by state government and the contractual restrictions imposed by collective bargaining. These restrictions are largely the result of teachers union efforts to decrease flexibility in decision making. Union propaganda would lead one to believe that the teachers are stifled by regulation, despite the fact that most state legislation affecting teachers is intended to enhance teacher welfare and teacher protections. The teachers unions support management by teachers on the grounds that decentralization would decrease bureaucratic regulation in schools. In our opinion, however, increasing the number of decision makers in the schools would greatly complicate school level management. Even more important, persons involved in this new bureaucracy would not bear individual accountability, which would result in a system in which no one would be in charge.

School board officials are expected—and specifically empowered—to make policy and operate schools and are held accountable for their actions. The participation of teachers or any other employees in this process is a means to an end. Like any other means, it has limits and conditions that must be subject to managerial discretion.

Concerns of the Teachers

Teachers themselves often have concerns about shared decision making. Are teachers performing so poorly that they need externally

imposed restructuring of the system? Teachers may be upset with recommendations for paying some teachers more than others and for relating teacher pay to pupil performance. Teachers may also be concerned
with the problem of accountability. Under the present system of governance, the building principal is the individual responsible for teacher
evaluation. In many union proposals, committees of teachers would be
given the responsibility for evaluating the performance of peer teachers. In such cases, who makes the decisions and what happens to individual accountability? How could there be any continuity of leadership
if designated standards were not met and committee members were
subsequently removed and/or demoted? The maneuvering to gain
power at the expense of others in this new bureaucracy could have only
a negative effect on education in the classroom. The accountability proposed by the union is "collective accountability" for student perfor
mance, with the suggestion that the entire school staff work collabora-
tively and take collective responsibility for student progress. How
could anyone ever prove that a decline in student performance was
because of collective teacher incompetence rather than external, uncon-
trollable factors? The truth is that school boards would never be able to
show that individual teacher incompetence was a contributing factor in
lower student achievement.

If a teacher were to be accused of incompetence by a union-con-
trolled committee, to whom would the accused teacher grieve? The
union representative for that school might very well be the lead teacher
who recommended dismissal. Because union strength depends on
avoiding controversy within its ranks, problems with inadequate
teacher performance in a school building would never be adequately
resolved when the situation results from conflict between union members. The union simply would not be able to serve as prosecutor and
jury as well as protector of teachers.

Teachers under fire from fellow teachers would not be the only individuals at risk. To seek relief for a building-level problem involving
their child, parents might be forced to appeal to union officials, inasmuch as school board members and district administrators would lack
decision-making authority in school buildings. A teachers union proposal requiring parents to grieve a teacher's action, as proposed in
model contracts disseminated by state unions, might become a reality.
For example, a California Teachers Association proposed master contract reads as follows: "Any complaints regarding a teacher made to the

administration by any parent, student or other person will be promptly called to the teacher's attention. No teacher will be disciplined, reprimanded, reduced in rank or compensation or deprived of any professional advantage without just cause. Whether just cause exists in any case, shall be subject to the grievance procedure."[6] Middle management would be thoroughly undermined if such a proposal were adopted. In reality, the principal is in the best position to explain why a particular contract demand might restrict his/her ability to manage the school effectively. The implementation of a collective bargaining contract calls for principals to be consistent, to act fairly, and to enforce contractual provisions. School boards and superintendents need school-level administrators who will act to ensure the instructional integrity of educational programs in the district and the rights of parents and children. In a school system operating under shared decision making, district and community proposals and concerns would be subject to veto by unionized teachers.

Undoubtedly, the United States educational system would benefit if teaching became a profession held in higher esteem. However, creating school organizational structures and leadership roles as envisaged by advocates of shared decision making is not the way to achieve this objective. Proposals that replace principals with lead teachers and teacher committees not only run counter to a strong body of effective schools research, but are likely to result in unmanageable schools.

School boards and school administrators need to be fair, but at the same time they must protect themselves and the district against those who would take advantage of their fairness. Sharing decisions with teachers unions will not provide that protection. Reforms that propose to "empower unionized teachers" or "replace hierarchical structures with peer group control" or accord "professional autonomy" to teachers are ludicrous intellectually and devastating in their political and policy consequences. Such proposals are tantamount to prescribing the germs to cure the disease. The only question is how long the patient can survive these misguided prescriptions.

---

[6] California School Employees Association proposed contract, 1977, p. 24.

6. STATUTORY BENEFITS AND TEACHER CONTRACTS

Every state has enacted legislation dealing with teacher welfare. State retirement systems are probably the most important example, but minimum salaries, tenure, sick leave and duty-free lunch periods are also common subjects of state legislation. A few states have even enacted statutory grievance procedures.

Board negotiators should carefully consider the relationships between statutory benefits and the negotiating process. For example, suppose state law mandates that teachers receive at least one 30-minute, duty-free lunch period per day, but in bargaining the teachers ask for a 60-minute, duty-free lunch period. If the district cannot provide more than the 30-minute statutory benefit, it will be asked to include it in the contract. The union will urge that the statutory benefits be included in the contract to make it more attractive to teachers, without any substantive concession by management.

How should management react to such apparently harmless requests? First, the board negotiator should recognize that incorporating a statutory benefit into a collective bargaining agreement is not just a symbolic gesture. Such incorporation may constitute an extremely important concession to the union, for the reason that the union finds it much easier to enforce contractual rights than statutory ones.

Presumably, the district will provide teachers a duty-free lunch period whether they are entitled to it by statute or by contract. Suppose a controversy arises as to whether a teacher's right to the duty-free lunch period was violated. If the right is statutory, the teacher is not likely to pursue an alleged violation by filing a lawsuit against the school district. Very few teachers would be willing to initiate such a lawsuit.

Furthermore, the statutes seldom prescribe any remedy for violations; in many situations, the remedy would not compensate for the time and expense of a lawsuit.

By contrast, consider the situation in which teachers have the duty-free lunch period pursuant to a collective agreement. In most cases, the teachers will have recourse to a grievance procedure, terminating in binding arbitration by an impartial third party, to remedy any alleged violation of their contractual rights. Contractual grievance procedures are far less costly and less time-consuming than lawsuits. Furthermore, the union can be the moving party in the grievance procedure, whereas an individual teacher or group of teachers must file the lawsuit to sustain the statutory right. True, the union could provide the funds in either case. However, the union, like individual teachers, is much less likely to initiate a lawsuit than a grievance to remedy an alleged violation of teacher rights.

Inclusion of Statutory Benefits: a Significant Concession

In short, the inclusion of statutory benefits in a collective agreement can be a very significant concession to teachers. This does not mean such a concession should never be made, but the board should reject the argument that inclusion doesn't give the teachers anything they don't already have. It will have given teachers a contractual remedy that may be crucial in specific situations. Teachers initiate many grievances that would be ignored if the teachers' only recourse was a lawsuit. Suppose the union negotiator does not pretend that no concession is involved but tries to negotiate for the concession on its merits. His argument might be as follows: "It's true we would be getting additional procedural rights if you include these statutory benefits in the contract. However, what's wrong with that? The reason we have a grievance procedure in the first place is to facilitate speedy resolution of grievances. If one really believes in the principle of speedy resolution, then why not apply the principle and force a teacher to file a lawsuit if the teacher sincerely believes he or she is not getting a duty-free lunch period or some other statutory benefit?"

This argument has some merit, but it also overlooks some cogent considerations. In the first place, there is always the possibility of abuse of a grievance procedure. The more costly the grievance procedure is to teachers, the less the likelihood that it will be used for harassment of the administration or for organizational propaganda. If the board reduces the cost of initiating grievances, it increases the likelihood that teachers will initiate invalid as well as valid grievances. A board negotiator should think carefully before making a concession that has this effect. A statutory right seems more secure, but contractual rights are much easier to enforce.

It is not suggested that board negotiators should never incorporate statutory benefits in a contract. Much depends on the quid pro quo for doing so. Often, the board itself will want certain statutory provisions in the contract; for example, the statutes may prescribe certain penalties for teachers who violate their contracts of employment. It can be to the board's advantage to have such statutory obligations of teachers included in the contract. Therefore, if the board wants inclusion of statutory teacher obligations in the contract, it can sometimes reach agreement on the basis that either both parties get inclusion of the statutory provisions desired by each, or neither does. This approach can be used very effectively to get a strong management rights clause into the contract. Under no circumstances, however, should the board agree to the language that incorporates all of the statutory benefits in the contract. Such language converts every statutory benefit, present and future, into a contractual obligation of the board.

Board negotiators also should be very careful about deciding what is an item of teacher welfare. A state law requiring that schools be in session 180 days per year does not constitute the legal work year for teachers. One could keep schools open for 180 days per year without having any one teacher work more than 90 days. The number of days required by state law for state aid, accreditation, or whatever is often the crucial factor in how many days teachers are asked to work, but the items should not be confused. Another example relates to the length of the school day. A state law might require that schools be in session at least five hours to count toward the state aid requirement. Such a requirement would not mean that state law requires teachers to work at least five hours a day; schools could be kept open five hours a day by employing a large number of teachers who worked fewer than five hours a day. Unless board negotiators are very careful in this area, they may end up relying upon nonexistent statutory conditions of employment.

The view that the collective agreement should govern the relationships between the parties has merit, but if the teachers advance this argument, they should be required to accept its consequences. Among other things, this requires that teachers give up their statutory remedies for contractual rights. Statutory remedies for statutory rights and contractual remedies for contractual rights—this should be the board's general position on incorporating statutory benefits in the collective agreement.

Teacher Tenure Decisions

In the prenegotiations era, the question of whether tenure decisions should be subject to grievance arbitration was not even considered. During the 1960s, the issue was seldom raised in negotiations. Subsequently, however, teachers unions have sought to make tenure decisions subject to the grievance procedure. These efforts raise some practical issues that are frequently overlooked.

Let us first compare the statutory dismissal procedure with the contractual one. Typically, states provide that boards have an unlimited right to discharge a teacher during the probationary period (usually three years). After that period, boards can fire teachers only by following a statutory procedure. The problem is that the statutory procedure makes it all but impossible to terminate tenured teachers. In some cases, the administrators may not have done their job adequately, but many tenure statutes undoubtedly impose an excessive burden of proof on districts seeking to terminate teachers. Even so, there is usually no legal barrier to negotiating a contractual procedure in which binding arbitration is the terminal point of grievances over dismissal. The contractual procedure might be more favorable to teachers in some ways—for example, by reducing the probationary period from three to two years. The district might also negotiate a contractual procedure that is less favorable to teachers than the statutory procedure, but obviously the union is not going to propose it.

What a district can do legally and what it should do from a practical standpoint are two different things. Usually, even though there is no valid reason to negotiate two remedies for the same grievance, the district should consider replacing the statutory procedure with a contractual one. The union will argue that it cannot legally negotiate away any of the statutory rights of teachers. This may or may not be true, depending on the language of the statute governing negotiations by unions representing school district employees. If it is not true, both the union and the district might be better off with a contractual procedure. In making its argument for a contractual procedure, the union will argue that this approach is more expeditious, less expensive, and less likely to embarrass the district and the teacher. The problem is that these benefits turn out to be illusory if the employees retain the option of using the statutory procedure. As dismissals arise, the union and the employee will try to decide which forum offers the best chance to overturn them.

In private employment, unions often bargain for more protection for regular employees in exchange for management's unlimited right to terminate probationary employees within a specified period, such as 90 days. This is a perfectly routine trade-off in the industrial setting: more protection for regular employees in exchange for less protection for probationers. School board negotiators may see no reason to accept any such proposal, because state laws usually give boards the right to terminate, usually within three years, without having to hold a hearing.

Much depends on the language of the tenure statute: If it renders dismissal virtually impossible or highly doubtful after the probationary period, and if the union can legally waive the statutory procedure for all teachers, the district should consider a contractual procedure. Indeed, under these circumstances, the district should consider taking the initiative to replace the statutory procedure with a contractual one.

Another possibility is to specify that use of the contractual procedure constitutes a waiver by the grievant of any statutory rights on the issue. This is not desirable because the objection is to the option, but if the option exists, either choice should rule out resorting to the alternative. In short, what the district should not do is add a contractual remedy to a statutory one, on the fallacious assumption that doing so does not give the teachers anything they do not already have.

The practical issue may come down to whether the district is willing to reduce the probationary period and use arbitrators instead of judges in exchange for a more expeditious way of resolving tenure cases.

Teacher Evaluation

Teacher evaluation is one of the most troublesome issues in collective bargaining. On one hand, teacher unions are constantly seeking to expand contractual protections for teachers. On the other hand, school administrators are becoming more concerned about their eroding authority to discipline or discharge teachers, and such authority is often related to teacher evaluation. If teacher evaluations do not meet all of the administration's contractual obligations, its authority to discipline or discharge teachers may be successfully challenged.

Case Example Involving Arbitration

An actual arbitration case dramatically illustrates these points. The case involved a probationary teacher who was not hired after three negative evaluations. The collective agreement in effect at the time included the following clauses:

> Prior to March 15 of each year, the principal shall submit a recommendation to the superintendent regarding the employment of all teachers. Should this recommendation include dismissal or additional probationary status, it shall state fully and completely the reasons therefor, and a copy shall be sent to the teacher. The teacher may submit a counterreport in writing to the superintendent within five days if he chooses to do so.

> No teacher shall be disciplined, reprimanded, reduced in basic salary schedule, or deprived of any professional advantage without just cause. Any such discipline, reprimand, or adverse evaluation of teacher performance asserted by the board or any representative there of resulting in reduction in rank and/or compensation, shall be subjected to the grievance procedure hereinafter set forth.... All information forming the basis for the disciplinary action will be made available to the teacher.

The teacher, "Miss B," was first evaluated in November and then in January by her principal. The evaluations, although negative, were specific and included recommendations for improvement. The third evaluation was conducted on March 10 and was followed by a conference on March 12 between Miss B and the principal. During the conference, Miss B learned that the principal would not recommend her reemployment. She did not receive a written copy of the evaluation until the afternoon of that day and did not sign it.

On the same day, March 12, the principal sent the superintendent a long, detailed memorandum explaining his recommendation that Miss B not be hired. On March 25, 10 days after the date required by the contract, Miss B received a letter from the board informing her that it had voted unanimously not to offer her a contract for the upcoming school year. The letter quoted the principal's memorandum verbatim to explain the reasons for this decision. In other words, Miss B saw the principal's evaluation and his adverse recommendation prior to March 15 but did not see the board's detailed memorandum justifying her nonrenewal until March 25. This memorandum included some points covered by the three evaluations prior to March 15 and others not discussed or implicit in the principal's evaluations.

It should also be noted that Miss B prepared a report on March 17 that attempted to rebut each of the three evaluation reports prior to March 15. Miss B also stated at this time, "I must receive a list of specified reasons for the recommendation that I no longer be employed....When this list is forthcoming, I shall submit a rebuttal of those specific reasons."

To summarize, Miss B did not receive a copy of the board's reasons until after the board had acted upon the principal's recommendations. The teacher did have an opportunity to respond to the principal's evaluations, but the principal's recommendations to the board included some items and references that were not on the evaluation forms. Because these recommendations were relied upon by the board, and the board acted upon them prior to deciding against renewing the contract, the teacher filed a grievance.

In its argument, the board contended that a refusal to reemploy a probationary teacher should not be construed as a disciplinary action or deprivation of professional advantage. The arbitrator cited a number of cases to show that this issue had divided courts and arbitrators, but as a matter of law and policy, he supported the view that refusal to rehire constituted a deprivation of "professional advantage." In other words, a district can't refuse to rehire a probationary teacher and then claim that the teacher hasn't lost any professional advantage. Because the contract specified that the board could not deprive a teacher of any "professional advantage without just cause," the board had to show just cause.

The basic issue in the case, therefore, was whether the board had complied with the contractual requirements concerning notice to the teacher. The arbitrator ruled that this had not been done. True, the teacher knew about the negative evaluations by the principal, but these did not meet the contractual requirements. The teacher was entitled to know the board's reasons prior to the time the board took action on them. Otherwise, the teacher would be denied her contractual rights to rebut the reasons while the matter was still open. The arbitrator gave little weight to the possibility that the teacher would have a fair opportunity to rebut the reasons after the board had refused to rehire: At this stage, because the board would have developed a vested interest in upholding its prior negative judgment, its objectivity was suspect. For this reason, the arbitrator ordered reemployment of Miss B with back pay as a result of the board's refusal to reemploy her.

This case is significant in several ways. One is that the arbitrator did not challenge the competence of the principal's evaluations. The problem was due to the fact that the board's reasons, which must be distinguished from the principal's, were not communicated to the teacher by the contractual deadline. Although based upon the principal's memorandum to the superintendent, the board's reasons differed in some important respects from the reasons communicated to the teacher by the principal before March 15.

What if the principal's recommendation to the superintendent about Miss B had relied upon precisely the same points he had made to Miss B before March 15? In other words, suppose the board had given as its reasons the evaluation report made available to Miss B before March 15 instead of a separate memorandum that the teacher did not see until after March 15. The arbitrator probably would have upheld the grievance, although it would have been a closer case. Unless and until the board adopts a set of reasons recommended by a subordinate, the reasons remain those of the subordinate, not the board. Realistically, a teacher might adopt a very different approach with the board than with the subordinate of the board, even though both are citing the same reasons. For example, an effort to discredit a reason cited by the board might involve data concerning the principal that would be omitted from efforts to discredit the same evaluation at the principal's level.

The practical implications of the case under discussion seem to be clear: (1) Administrators must make sure that the substance of their observations and evaluations will support the recommendation they make; (2) they must scrupulously observe the procedural requirements spelled out in the collective agreement before taking action adverse to a teacher; and (3) boards must recognize that the reasons for a personnel action recommended by a subordinate are not those of the board unless and until the board officially adopts them. Such adoption, however, cannot be used to deprive teachers of their rights to know the board's reasons by a specified date. (Of course, the board might have avoided the problem altogether by different contract language, but any language on the issue is likely to be interpreted as very rigorous by arbitrators.)

In this case, the failure to fulfill the procedural requirement was the fatal weakness in the administration's position. To avoid such situations, administrators should systematically review teacher evaluations with the principals and supervisors. Such review should aim at ensuring that evaluations are comprehensive and are completed in time to fulfill all contractual deadlines. An essential ingredient of effective contract administration requires fulfilling both the substantive and procedural requirements pertaining to teacher evaluation.

Because the negotiated evaluation procedures must be followed strictly, the procedures must be negotiated very carefully. Every aspect of teacher evaluation can be a battleground: the number and duration of observations, time limits for presenting the teacher with the evaluations, the teacher's rights to respond to evaluations and to follow up observations if requested, the union's role in the procedures, deadlines of management action based on the evaluations, and so on. Board negotiators must resist the temptation to "stop haggling over the details"; the "details" are all-important in the context of teacher evaluation. If each teacher must be observed three times a year for at least 45 uninterrupted minutes each observation, consideration must be given to whether staff will be available, in the light of emergencies and interruptions. Quite frequently, the union will insist upon as few observations as possible, and subsequently will cite insufficient observation as the reason adverse action against the teacher must be overturned. Like any other employees, most teachers do not welcome frequent observation of their performance on the job. This attitude is not always articulated openly, but union proposals on the number and duration of observations confirm it. The union typically emphasizes the importance of a "cooperative" instead of a "punitive" approach and management's obligation to assist teachers who are not performing adequately. In considering such proposals, management should bear in mind that even the most successful coaches drop team members for inadequate performance or failure to follow team regulations. That is one of the reasons these coaches are successful.

Should Teachers Evaluate Other Teachers?

Management negotiators frequently are confronted by teacher proposals for "peer evaluation." Union negotiators typically assert that principals and supervisors are too busy or lack the expertise to evaluate teachers. "Let's have experienced classroom teachers help probationary teachers," the union negotiator may assert. Teachers are allegedly more receptive to suggestions from other teachers than from management, and because the purpose of evaluation is to improve teaching, it would be better for everyone to have experienced teachers conduct the evaluation. Thus the argument goes.

Such proposals usually include the procedures for selecting the teacher evaluators. Peer evaluation, when included as a contract provision, is undesirable in theory and practice whether or not the union designates or approves the evaluators. If teachers unions propose peer evaluation, management should reject it. The reasons are contained in the following illustration: An experienced teacher evaluates a probationary one, but the probationary teacher believes that the evaluation is unfair or incompetent. In such case, whom does the union represent— the teacher evaluated or the evaluator? Because both teachers are in the bargaining unit, the union must either neglect the probationary teacher or adopt an adversarial stance toward the experienced teacher, who is likely to have more union influence than the probationary teacher. The latter, who is more likely to need effective representation, turns out to be the one least likely to get it.

Teachers, along with administrators, sometimes forget that a basic purpose of the union is to protect teachers from unfair or incompetent evaluation. If bargaining unit members conduct the evaluations, the union is likely to support the teacher with the most organizational influence. The union is not likely to provide effective representation for new teachers pitted against experienced teachers.

Teacher negotiators tend to dismiss this possibility. They often assert that if peer evaluation results in a difference of opinion, the union (or its grievance committee) can decide who is right. This view is naive at best. A lawyer is not as likely to defend a client vigorously if the lawyer is also serving as the judge in the case. If the teachers union tries to serve as judge as well as advocate, it will inevitably weaken its role as teacher advocate.

At first glance, peer evaluation looks attractive to administrators. It seems especially attractive if the union has been challenging evaluations and personnel actions based thereon. The prospect of having the teachers union and/or teachers assist management in the unpleasant task of evaluation often appeals to beleaguered management. In practice, however, the teacher evaluators come under severe pressure to avoid rigorous evaluation. Many yield to such pressure, reasoning that teachers were not employed to evaluate their peers. Teachers may not relish the prospect of evaluating others, feeling that it is not one of their major functions and that they may not be well prepared for the task technically or psychologically.

Furthermore, suppose teacher and management evaluations differ significantly. If the peer evaluation is favorable, management is more likely to hesitate to make negative evaluations; the difference will be cited as evidence that management is biased or incompetent. If the teacher evaluation is unfavorable and the management evaluation is favorable, management will be accused of recommending incompetent teachers for tenure. Either way, the peer evaluation is likely to have undesirable effects. If peer and management evaluations coincide, there is no need for both. Is an evaluation right because of who makes it, or is it right because whoever made it followed appropriate criteria and procedures?

Collective agreements should spell out the criteria for evaluation. It then becomes management's job to interpret and apply these criteria. If management fails to do so properly, the aggrieved teacher has a remedy through the grievance procedure. In other words, teacher protection should flow from managerial adherence to specified criteria in the evaluation process.

Emphasis on who evaluates, instead of the criteria and procedures, will lead both teachers and administrators into a hopeless morass. Peer evaluation might be acceptable where it is not used in personnel administration. If teacher A observes teacher B, and offers only suggestions and criticisms, peer evaluation might be acceptable. The question is whether the benefits are worth the costs. Is it worthwhile to pay for the released time of teachers to conduct evaluations or observations that will not count in personnel administration? Ordinarily, it would not be. In any case, peer evaluation should not be accepted where the evaluations are included in the files of the teachers being evaluated. Evaluation should be management's responsibility. When management abdicates this function, the outcomes are likely to be confusion and mismanagement.

Fringe Benefits

Fringe benefits have outgrown their label. In public education, they average 20 percent or more of salary. This development is similar to private sector experience. In the early years of private sector bargaining, fringe benefits were just that. They seldom amounted to as much as five percent of wages. Over the years, however, the costs of fringe benefits rose faster than salaries. This was especially true when contracts stated employer obligations in terms of benefits instead of dollars. As the costs of the benefits escalated, employers were forced to absorb them even in the absence of negotiations on the issue. If employer obligations had been stated in terms of dollar amounts, employers would not have been so vulnerable to the rising costs of fringe benefits.

When the federal government opposed inflationary wage increases, it did not oppose increased fringe benefits. Also, as income tax rates increase, so does the attractiveness of fringe benefits, which are usually tax-free. If the costs of medical insurance were paid directly to employees, it would be taxable income; also, employees would lose the benefit of group purchasing power if obliged to purchase health insurance individually. Although fringe benefits will probably be subject to more taxation in the future, they undoubtedly will continue to show tax advantages over equivalent wage payments.

The leading cause of the increased costs of fringe benefits is health insurance, which has gone up much more rapidly than salaries and the cost of living generally. Once districts began providing health insurance, their costs escalated rapidly even if they did not provide increases in benefits to employees.

Theoretically, the costs of fringe benefits could constitute an alternative way of spending similar dollar amounts. A district and teachers union might agree to devote more money to insurance benefits and less to the salary schedule. The result could be a lower salary schedule but greater insurance benefits in comparison to districts in which the parties allocated more to the salary schedule and less to fringe benefits. In such cases, there is no overall inequity between the districts—only a difference in how each district allocates the same dollar amounts.

When it come to bargaining, however, the parties don't always see it this way. The salary schedule is the most visible part of the package, so it tends to dominate perceptions about teacher compensation. When pay schedules are compared, districts may not get full credit for liberal fringe benefits. This is especially true of fringe benefits to which it is difficult to attach a dollar value. Example: A school district may have a generous leave policy for which it pays heavily in terms of higher substitute teacher costs and increased allocations of management time to recruit and orient the substitutes. The budget, however, may lump together all substitute costs, making it impossible to ascertain the costs of specific leave policies.

Because the costs of fringe benefits are not always visible, they can be used to conceal increases in compensation when neither board nor union wants to publicize them. Unfortunately, a fringe benefit that is inexpensive when first established can become a financial burden. A one-week increase in vacation allowance for employees with 10 years of service may seem an inexpensive way of getting support from a few key senior employees. Five or 10 years later, however, with an older work force the same concession will be much more costly.

Districts should minimize or avoid altogether providing substantial benefits to a few employees. Sabbatical leave is one such benefit. It can be a sizable benefit, but because of teacher turnover, only a few teachers may enjoy it. This would not be objectionable if sabbaticals were a form of merit pay, but they are usually based only on length of service.

Although it can be difficult to cut back on fringe benefits such as salaries that include retirement contributions, it is impossible to make cutbacks. Once a fringe benefit is established, it tends to remain in existence, and its cost, like all others, tends to increase. Technically, as far as the bargaining position of the district is concerned, it should not matter whether salaries or fringe benefits are increased; practically, as a result of the greater public awareness of salary schedules, the district may be better off allocating funds to salaries instead of to fringe benefits.

In addition to financial considerations, fringe benefits have important policy implications. In the private sector, fringe benefits are viewed primarily as cost items, i.e., a method of allocating resources. In education, the issues are more complex. For example, whether teachers must be paid for evening meetings is not simply a compensation issue; it is also a school/community relations issue because of the importance of having teachers available to parents who cannot meet with them during the day. District payment of family health insurance may lead to an excessive number of visits to doctors and stays in hospitals and make higher salaries for all teachers prohibitively expensive. All such factors should be considered in negotiating fringe benefits.

Due Process: Rhetoric and Reality

Why do teachers unions make it difficult for school boards to terminate incompetent teachers? Unions argue that they are only trying to make sure that no adverse actions are taken against teachers without affording them due process. On the surface, this is a plausible argument, but union emphasis on due process is suspect. Consider the following proposal submitted by hundreds of local affiliates of the California Teachers Association (CTA). "A teacher who is supervising an instructional aide or voluntary aide shall be empowered to terminate the services of such aide if such teacher alleges that the aide is interfering with the teacher's performance or is not performing his own services satisfactorily."

This proposal would give teachers the unrestricted right to fire aides. Teachers need not file charges against the aide, alert the aide to deficiencies, nor give the aide time to correct such deficiencies. Teachers need not afford the aide a hearing, give the aide the right to cross-examine the teacher, nor supply the aide with a written statement of charges. Significantly, the teachers aren't asking for the right to exclude unwanted aides from their classrooms. They are proposing that a teacher has the right to fire an aide at any time for any reason. This is hardly consistent with the principle of due process.

The union proposal also ignores the possibility that aides have union representation and bargaining rights. A school board that accepted such a clause would be guilty of an unfair labor practice directed at the union representing the aides. The aides could rightly argue that the board had adopted a term of condition of employment without bargaining with the union representing the aides.

Actually, some California school boards countered the union proposal with the following: "A principal who is supervising a teacher shall be empowered to terminate the services of such teacher if such principal alleges that the teacher is interfering with the principal's performance or is not performing his own services satisfactorily."

In short, healthy skepticism is essential in assessing union rhetoric about due process. The sincerity of that rhetoric is called into question by the following proposal, also made to hundreds of California school boards by teachers unions.

1. The Board shall, upon recommendation of the student's teacher, exclude from a class any student who, in the teacher's opinion, has filthy or vicious habits; or suffers from a contagious or infectious disease; or suffers from a physical or mental disability which would cause his attendance to be inimical to the welfare of other students; or acts in such a way that the teacher believes good cause exists for such student's exclusion.

A. The Board shall act upon the teacher's recommendation within five days.

B. Should the board fail to follow the teacher's recommendation, it shall provide the teacher with its reasons in writing.

2. A student excluded under paragraph 1 above shall not be entitled to return to any classroom until such time as the board determines that the condition that prompted the exclusion no longer exists and the teacher into whose class the student is to be assigned concurs in such assessment.[1]

Clearly, any school board that accepted the union proposal would swiftly be in deep trouble with civil rights agencies. Under the union proposal, a teacher could exclude a pupil from class forever, regardless of the basis for the exclusion. Although teachers probably should have more authority over pupils than they do, the union proposal would be an outrageous violation of the due process right of students. Fortunately, most school boards are sensitive to the due process needs of pupils, even if the unions are not.

In bargaining with unions, board negotiators frequently encounter proposals implying that teachers can do no wrong. For example, the unions often propose that teachers be given leave benefits with no obligation to provide reasons or evidence to demonstrate that the leave was used for its designated purposes. In negotiating hours of employment, unions frequently demand that school boards simply trust the teachers to appear on time and stay until they have completed their duties. When a board insists upon safeguards on this issue, its position often is characterized as an attack upon the integrity or professionalism of the teachers.

When proposals such as those just discussed are challenged, the union response may be that the proposals merely represent a bargaining

---

[1] California Teachers Association, model contract disseminated to its local affiliates in the 1980s.

position, that because the union doesn't expect to achieve everything it proposes, the extreme nature of some of the proposals should not be serious cause for concern. Unfortunately, this rationalization simply isn't good enough. It is one thing to ask for more than is expected and prepare to settle for less, but it is quite another to submit proposals that have no justification regardless of whether the other party is sure to reject them. In other words, there is a crucial difference between a proposal that is unacceptable in principle and one that is unacceptable from a practical standpoint. As an extreme example, suppose the union proposed that black teachers be paid less than white teachers. The fact that the union did not expect the board to agree to the proposal would not constitute justification for it. The elimination of due process rights for aides or pupils cannot be justified as merely a position from which to begin bargaining.

Union rhetoric frequently implies or directly asserts that school boards and administrators are tyrants who ignore the rights of teachers. For the sake of argument, even if every such allegation was assumed to be true, remedies proposed by teacher unions suggest that their proposed cure would be as harmful as the disease. Managerial tyranny would simply be replaced by teacher tyranny.

7.   NEGOTIATING WITH MIDDLE MANAGEMENT

Middle management refers to school-level personnel who exercise administrative/supervisory roles: principals, assistant principals, and supervisors; department chairmen with significant responsibilities for hiring, tenure, promotion, and discipline; and some central office personnel (depending upon the nature of their work, size of system, appropriate legislation, and other factors). Management is "middle" between top management and teachers, not between upper and lower echelons of management.

As a general rule, a school board should make every effort to provide an alternative to bargaining with its own management. Bargaining with middle management presents a number of special problems. In many states, questions related to bargaining with middle management have been resolved at least temporarily by statute or state regulation. Should middle management be included in the same negotiating unit as classroom teachers? Should middle management have the right to be represented by the same organization that represents teachers? What impasse procedures should be used in case of an impasse between middle management and board negotiators? Who belongs in the middle management bargaining unit (often referred to as an administrative/supervisory unit)? These are some of the special issues related to negotiations with middle management.

In states where such issues have not been resolved statutorily or judicially, administrators should be aware of experience in states that have mandated negotiations with middle management. On the whole, this experience confirms the conclusion that it is not desirable to legalize collective bargaining by middle management. Significantly, management in the private sector is not required to bargain with middle management. When the National Labor Relations Act (NLRA) was enacted in 1936, management was required to bargain with unions representing supervisors, but the requirement was so destructive of efficient management that it was deleted in the 1948 amendments to the NLRA. Thus, many school boards and superintendents who lament "the introduction of industrial practices into education" regret the failure to follow "the industrial model," at least on this crucial issue.

Where there is no statutory obligation to negotiate with middle management, the decision on whether to do so will rest upon several factors. Ordinarily, a board is unlikely to be faced with such a request unless it is already negotiating with teachers. Other than that, size of the system is probably the crucial factor. A large urban district cannot determine individual conditions of employment for several hundred principals, assistant principals, supervisors, and coordinators. Some type of collective representation or administrative team structure may be desirable. Nevertheless, collective bargaining with middle management involves some difficult problems.

First, administration is likely to be shorthanded in negotiating with middle management. This is especially likely if management is simultaneously negotiating with a teachers union and one or more unions of noncertified personnel. It is preferable to negotiate with middle management after negotiations with other groups have been concluded. As a practical matter, boards should avoid concessions to middle management that undermine their bargaining position with other unions. For example, it is usually undesirable to negotiate a higher percentage raise for middle management than for teachers if the middle management contract is negotiated first. The teachers are not likely to expect a smaller percentage raise, and they will be adamantly opposed to any final board offer that proposes a lower percentage increase than that offered to middle management. If the order of negotiations is reversed, however, the board has more flexibility. It can correct administrative inequities without raising teacher expectations to unrealistic levels.

In all cases, the board should be careful about making any concession to middle management that it does not intend to make to teachers in their next contract. Suppose middle management has asked for sabbatical leave at full pay and administration has just negotiated an agreement with the teachers union providing sabbatical leave at half pay. In this situation, the board could hardly agree to full pay for middle management sabbaticals unless it was prepared to do so in the future for teachers. In fact, it probably would be a serious mistake to make any such concession unless the board had first made it to teachers. It would be much better to have the teachers feel they had obtained this benefit for middle managers than to have them feel they received it only because it had been first given to their supervisors.

Some agreements with organizations representing middle management expressly base benefits for middle managers on the teacher contract. For example, the administrator/supervisor salary schedule may be based on certain steps in the teacher salary schedule. Despite the frequency of such clauses, they can be extremely undesirable and should be avoided. To illustrate, consider a district in which both the school board and the supervisors want to avoid yearly contract negotiations. Assume that both sides are willing to negotiate a two-year or three-year agreement but have deep uncertainty over the appropriate salary terms for the second or third year. Middle managers will seek a salary that minimizes the risk of a two-year or three-year contract. This will often require a higher commitment than the board should make. Under these circumstances, gearing the salaries for middle management to changes in the teacher schedule appears to be an attractive solution. However, this should be avoided because it gives supervisory employees a stake in raising teacher salaries, an unacceptable conflict of interest.

Grievance procedures for middle managers are also problematical. In general, school boards and superintendents should have wide latitude in selecting and directing middle managers. Nevertheless, unjust treatment of middle managers is a possibility. Again, the size of the system is crucial. Suppose the middle management unit includes only 15 persons. If the grievance procedure provides for impartial arbitration as the terminal point in the grievance procedure, it might cost each member of the unit $50 to $100 per grievance going to arbitration. The cost would be prohibitive unless a basic employee interest was involved. Nevertheless, middle management groups with only a few members sometimes propose that grievance arbitration replace a board hearing, even though the middle management organization could not ordinarily pay its share for grievance arbitration.

Many middle managers allegedly support bargaining because they believe that they have been "bypassed" in teacher/board negotiations. Even if this is true, collective bargaining for middle management is not the answer to the problem. Rather, needs of middle management should be incorporated into the positions adopted by the school board's negotiating team. Usually, but not necessarily, this requires that capable middle managers be included on the board's negotiating team. (An effective administration negotiating team may understand how various proposals and counterproposals affect middle management, regardless of whether middle managers are on the team.)

If a board does not provide fair terms and conditions of employment for middle management, middle managers are encouraged to take a hard line with the board. Budgetary commitments should leave adequate resources and flexibility for dealing with middle management. School boards and superintendents who recognize this ordinarily will not find negotiating with middle management to be a traumatic experience.

8. EFFICIENCY ISSUES IN CONTRACTING FOR EDUCATION SERVICES

In addition to controversies over school choice, contracting for education services is becoming a major issue in public education. Although school districts frequently contract for pupil transportation or custodial or food services, they seldom privatize instruction. This reluctance, however, appears to be changing.

For example, many small school districts that do not have a high school send the high school–level students to other districts with high schools. Vermont does not restrict the funding to public schools in this situation. Because the pupils have a choice of public or private schools, the Vermont practice is more akin to a voucher system than to outside contracting. Regardless of how it is characterized, however, the practice is limited to school districts that do not offer high school instruction.

Similar considerations apply to the education of pupils who are handicapped in various ways. If a school district enrolls only one mentally retarded student, providing educational services needed for such a pupil would be prohibitively expensive. In such cases, school districts typically pay to have the pupil educated by another school district or by an educational contractor who serves a large number of such pupils.

These examples illustrate the point that contracting for instruction is a last resort, used mainly by small districts without any feasible alternative. Nevertheless, school districts are likely to contract for instruction much more frequently in the future than they have in the past. One reason is that conventional approaches to school reform are ineffective. As a result, state and local policymakers are under growing pressure to develop alternative delivery systems for instructional services. Another reason is the growing interest in privatization, especially in contracting outside for municipal services. Because school districts tend to be separated from municipal governance, the privatization movement has not affected education as much as other municipal services. Nevertheless, because education budgets require one-third to one-half of state and local government expenditures, instructional services are likely to be affected by privatization in the future.

We can conceptualize decisions on whether to contract for a service as decisions to "make" or "buy" a service; in the case of instruction, the school board decision is whether to "make" education, i.e., produce it by means of school district employees, or "buy" it by purchasing instructional services from independent contractors. To make such decisions rationally, school boards need to know the costs and outcomes under both delivery systems. Typically, boards have been providing the services directly; consideration of the "buy" option will require them to decide what costs will be shifted to contractors. The "buy" option will also require boards to specify the outcomes—or at least the services—being purchased. In other words, school boards and contractors alike have to know what is being purchased. Otherwise, there is no way to decide whether the "buy" or the "make" option is preferable. If one knows the costs but cannot specify the services to be delivered, one has no basis for choosing one option over the other.

Several problems arise in comparing costs and outcomes under the "make" or "buy" options. Let us first consider some problems in comparing the costs of contracting to the costs of service delivery by public school teachers. Subsequently, we shall consider some problems on the outcome side, but first it is essential to clarify some ideological issues that often play a major role in privatization controversies.

Rationale for Outside Contracting

The literature on privatization falls into two general categories, the first of which emphasizes the ideological dimensions of privatization. Some individuals in this category view privatization as much more than a management option; it is a way of diminishing the role of government, enhancing the role of the private sector, and of avoiding inefficient government activities that would be difficult, if not impossible, to eliminate. Privatizers in this category regard efficiency as important, but they view it as intimately related to the functions of government, the role of the economic system, and the relationships between political and economic freedoms.

By the same token, privatization has its ideological detractors as well as supporters; that is, some critics of privatization also do not separate the broader philosophical issues from the immediate, practical ones. These critics are the counterparts of the ideological supporters of privatization. Whereas supporters view privatization within a favorable philosophical framework, the ideological opponents view it within an unfavorable one. Although both groups agree that privatization proposals should be evaluated on a case-by-case basis, they seldom agree on the merits of specific proposals.

The second major category of privatization literature discusses the concept primarily as a management tool. In this context, efficiency issues are resolved without much regard to their philosophical implications. This group can be labeled "the practical decision makers." For this group, outside contracting does not raise any broad philosophical issues; if it is a more efficient way to get the job done, so be it. A decision on whether to contract for instruction is like a decision on whether to drive or take the bus to a football game. All important practical considerations taken into account, what is the best way to get there? There is no need to relate the decision to the role of public transportation. Similarly, practical decision makers might see no need to relate "make" or "buy" decisions in education to ideological issues. In this analysis, contracting for instruction is considered primarily from the standpoint of practical decision makers. Such consideration does not imply that the ideological issues are unimportant, or that the discussion can always avoid them. Nevertheless, school managers are practical decision makers who may or may not be ideological supporters or opponents of privatization as such. Furthermore, although efficiency issues are not the whole story, they are a large part of it, and if interested parties could reach a consensus on the efficiency issues, the ideological ones would be much easier to resolve.

Efficiency Issues and State Regulation

Arguably, the efficiency argument for contracting for services is much stronger in education than it is in most state and local public services. The reason is that state regulation of education is usually more detailed, more restrictive, and more conducive to inefficiency than it is in other public services. Persons not professionally involved in public education find it difficult to grasp the sheer volume of regulations and how they result in inefficiencies. Let us first review the broad categories of statutory regulation before citing some specifics:

1. *Regulation of governance and financial procedures.* State statutes normally govern eligibility to be a candidate for a school board: how board meetings are to be conducted; district financial and business procedures; budget categories and schedules; board authority to contract; school district bond and insurance requirements; bidding procedures for district supplies and services; legal authority to appoint administrators, teachers, and support staff; and health and safety standards and procedures.

2. *Regulation of the educational program and of students.* State statutes prescribe the minimum and maximum age for compulsory education; the subjects to be taught; pupil workday and work year; instructional materials, graduation requirements, and maximum class size; vaccination and medical examinations; how to deal with handicapped, migrant, and delinquent children; and other categories deemed worthy of special attention.

3. *Regulation of teachers and administrators.* State statutes control eligibility to teach or administer schools (often by grade level or subject), discipline and dismissal procedures, layoffs and recall procedures, mandatory leave benefits, eligibility for retirement, pension procedures and benefits, duty-free lunch periods, seniority, and teacher evaluation.

4. *Regulation of support staff.* State regulation of support staff (secretaries, bus drivers, custodians, cafeteria workers, groundskeepers, data processing technicians, and others) differs in degree but not in kind from state regulation of teachers and administrators.

It is hardly possible to overemphasize one basic point about state regulation. Insofar as teachers are concerned, there is very little regulation of their classroom conduct or decisions. Most state statutes affecting teachers provide teacher benefits; they were enacted at the behest of state teachers unions. They are restrictive, but the restrictions overwhelmingly apply to school management, not to teachers. When teachers are restricted, it is usually an indirect result of a direct restriction on management. For example, if a state law restricts a district's choice of textbooks to those approved by a state textbook commission, the restriction upon teacher choice is derivative from the restriction on management choice.

Although the amount and nature of regulation varies enormously from state to state, some regulations force districts to be inefficient throughout the state. A few examples from California illustrate the tremendous scope of these inefficiencies.

According to the California Education Code, "It is the intent and purpose of the Legislature to encourage, by every means possible, the reduction of class sizes and the ratio of pupils to teachers in all grade levels in the public schools and to urge every effort to this end be undertaken by the local school administrative authorities."[1] This statement of policy is absurd on its face, because it does not take account of the fact that class size is often extremely low. Nevertheless, the next section of the code penalizes school districts if their class size exceeds 30 in grades 1 through 8, or 31 or 33 in kindergarten.

There is no credible evidence that these limits have any relationship to educational achievement or educational productivity. Let us suppose, however, that adding another first grade pupil to a class of 30 has a discernible negative effect upon the educational achievement of class members. In order to decide whether to split the class or to add another pupil to the existing class, we should compare the costs as well as the educational outcomes. The costs of splitting the class would perhaps be $50,000 (average salary plus benefits for an additional teacher). The underlying issue, however, is not the impact of the additional student upon the class as a whole. Rather, it is whether spending $50,000 for an additional teacher is the optimum educational use of the $50,000. It is preposterous for a legislature, or anyone else, to make this judgment without an understanding of the other needs and resources of a school district. In nearly all cases, adding a pupil to a class of 30 would not result in any perceptible educational gain; it would, however, cost the district $50,000 that could be used more productively on other needs. Nevertheless, a California school district is penalized by the state statutes for making the most cost-effective use of its resources.

In California, school districts cannot assign teachers to extra duty, even with the extra pay agreed to by their union, against the wishes of

---

[1] *West's annotated California code, reorganized,* sections 41375, 41376.

the teacher. As a result, teachers who had been employed partly because of their ability to supervise certain extracurricular activities sometimes declined to perform such duties after receiving tenure. When the districts were unable to recruit individuals not on the regular staff to take the assignment, the districts were forced to overpay existing staff or drop the extracurricular activity.

Again in California, any benefits provided full-time support personnel must be prorated for part-time employees. Thus, if a school district increases vacation benefits for full-time cafeteria workers or for bus drivers who work a full year, it must increase vacation benefits for employees who work only two hours a day for only 180 days a year. Not surprisingly, the legislation was enacted at the behest of the California State Employees Association (CSEA), the union representing most classified employees in the state. CSEA sought the legislation primarily to avoid internal conflicts between part-time employees seeking health benefits (a significant proportion of its membership) and regular full-time employees. The legislation was also intended to discourage part-time employment.

A specified minimum percentage of the operating budgets for school districts must be spent for teacher salaries. The minimum is 50 percent for elementary districts, 55 percent for districts including both elementary and secondary schools, and 60 percent for high school districts.[2] The effect is to discourage school districts from introducing any changes that would reduce the proportion of their budgets devoted to teacher salaries. Districts that are able to operate satisfactorily while paying teachers less than their state-mandated share of the district budget nevertheless are forced to increase teacher salaries. In some cases, the increases result in higher salaries than the teachers unions have already accepted. By contrast, a private company would rarely if ever try to become more efficient by requiring itself to be labor-intensive.

If a district wants to suspend an employee for as little as one day, it must follow the same procedure as for firing a tenured teacher. The district and the employee each appoint someone to a three-member commission to conduct a hearing on the suspension. The third member is a hearing examiner appointed by the state. If the school district loses, it must not only pay any compensation lost by the employee but the

---

[2] *West's annotated California code, reorganized,* section 41373(c).

employee's hearing expenses as well.[3] Not surprisingly, teacher suspensions have virtually ceased in California.

California is regarded as a leader in the school reform movement, but the California Education Code still includes scores of such indefensible statutes, virtually all of which are ignored by reform leaders in the state. If California regulated garbage removal as it does education, its laws would prescribe what days and during what hours garbage would be picked up, qualifications for supervisors of garbage disposal, standards and procedures for disciplining or firing sanitation workers, insurance policies governing equipment and personnel, policies governing layoff and recall of sanitation workers, size and safety requirements for sanitation department trucks, and so on. All these regulations would be imposed on a statewide basis, without regard to the economy of the community or the wishes of its citizens. Under such circumstances, it would be astonishing if garage removal by public employees were even close to efficient.

To illustrate how pervasive state-mandated inefficiencies are, let us cite a development in New York. In 1987, the state enacted legislation requiring that school districts provide training for 20 percent of the time required by teachers who did not meet regular certification requirements.[4] Under this statute, New York City could continue to employ teachers on emergency certificates, but such teachers could be required to carry only 80 percent of a normal teaching load. During the remaining time, the school districts had to provide the teachers with additional training to assist them in achieving regular certification. The school districts, therefore, lost 20 percent of the teachers' instructional time and had to pay for their additional training. New York City school officials estimated the district's additional costs in 1987-88 would be about $25 million.[5] The actual costs, which are impossible to measure precisely, undoubtedly have increased substantially since the program was initiated.

---

[3] State of California, Senate Bill 813, section 35432 (b), approved by Gov. George Deukmejian July 28, 1983.

[4] See Amendment to the Regulations of the Commissioner of Education, pursuant to sections 207, 3004, and 3006 of the Education Law of the State of New York, repealing section 80.18 of the Regulations of the Commissioner of Education and adding a new section 80.18 effective Sept. 1, 1987, approved March 20, 1987.

[5] The estimates were given to the writer (M.L.) informally in April 1987 when he was serving as a negotiations consultant for the New York City Board of Education.

Whatever the costs of such an arrangement, it will not contribute to better teaching in the city's schools. The reasons some teachers are not certified have nothing to do with their teaching effectiveness. Where additional training might be helpful, there is no assurance that qualified persons are available to provide it. The district vigorously recruited retired teachers to provide the training, but their qualifications do not necessarily meet the needs of the teachers they supervise. Once teachers acquire a regular certificate, they may seek teaching positions outside the state.

These examples from California and New York illustrate the point that public education operates under a crushing burden of mandated inefficiency, that those who preach "education reform" are often the ones most responsible for its absence, and that there is no diminution of legislation mandating inefficiencies.[6] As numerous as they are, the inefficiencies mandated by statute are undoubtedly outnumbered by those mandated by collective bargaining contracts. About 80 percent of the nation's public school teachers work pursuant to such contracts. In varying degree, these contracts impose a wide range of inefficiencies on school districts. They restrict district flexibility in employment, assignment, transfers, scheduling, workday, work year, class size, and a host of other matters. Although some school board leaders have become more outspoken against these restrictions, it is highly unlikely that a reduction will take place without some form of privatization.

Realistically, there is no movement within public education to change its governance structure.[7] Desperately needed as they are, such changes are not even being discussed in political forums. Even a rollback in teacher collective bargaining, which will happen as a result of judicial decisions if it happens at all, would not overcome most governance and regulatory obstacles to better education. Ideally, school board members should be public-spirited citizens who volunteer for public service in order to help children. In the real world, however,

---

[6] For an earlier survey of state-mandated inefficiencies, see Myron Lieberman, *Identification and evaluation of state constraints on educational productivity, final report, project 3-0231* (National Institute of Education, U.S. Department of Health, Education, and Welfare, June 1975).

[7] "In November 1985, several prominent citizens in New York City, including three members of the New York City Board of Education, urged replacement of the existing board with one appointed *in toto* by the mayor. The purpose would have been to have a board clearly accountable to the mayor, who appointed only a minority of board members under the existing structure. It did not seem to occur to anyone to eliminate the board entirely and have the school system operate as a municipal department under the mayor." (*New York Times,* Nov. 28, 1987, p. 27).

school board candidates have the same need for support as other candidates for public office. At the same time, the unions of teachers and support personnel have a larger stake in who is elected to the board than does any other group. Parents may be interested, but it is practically impossible or too expensive for most parents to try to change school district policies or practices. Furthermore, parental interest in school affairs wanes when their children graduate, whereas employee interests in school board affairs are permanent. In addition, school board elections are often conducted separately from general elections, a situation that greatly enhances the political influence of teachers unions in the elections.

This analysis applies also to school boards that are appointed instead of elected. Usually, the appointments are made by a mayor who must be sensitive to the wishes of the public sector unions. Nor is the under-lying argument weakened by the fact that nationally, almost half of school district revenues come from state governments. Again, the dynamics are the same: Elected officials, primarily governors and members of state legislatures, frequently make legislative concessions in exchange for union political support.

The foregoing considerations underscore the potential importance of outside contracting. Because the employees of independent contractors are not public employees, they are not subject to the statutes and collective bargaining contacts that cripple school management. For this reason, private contractors may be able to avoid both the statutory and collective bargaining sources of inefficiency in school district operations.

Costs and Benefits of Contracting for Education Services

Do the preceding considerations establish a case for contracting for instruction? Objectively, the answer is "not thus far." The analysis has shown that conceptually, contracting for instruction might achieve increased efficiency and/or higher quality education.

In order to decide whether to make or buy education, school boards must be able to compare the costs and outcomes of both options. These may not be the only relevant considerations, but they are obviously important. If school boards knew the costs but not the outcomes, they would not be able to make an informed decision. Similarly, if they

121

knew the outcomes but not the costs, they would lack an adequate basis for their decisions. Knowledge of both costs and outcomes is essential because school districts should not necessarily choose the option that results in greater learning. If an option results in a very small increase in learning but requires huge additional resources, it will usually be the less desirable one. At some point, educational improvement is not worth the cost of achieving it.

Unfortunately, it is extremely difficult—often impossible—to ascertain either the costs or the outcomes of public education. For one thing, the costs are virtually always understated, often by substantial amounts. These understatements vary from district to district and state to state. In this analysis, we can only illustrate some patterns of cost understatement; the actual amounts involved ordinarily would need to be ascertained from state and local data.

Local Costs Not Shown on School District or State Budgets

Some of the local costs of public education do not appear on school district budgets. Most school districts are contiguous with local municipal or county governments. In some areas, especially when the school district receives some funds from local government, the latter provides negotiation services for the school district. Such services may include the time of a chief negotiator and members of the negotiating team, use of data processing facilities and personnel, and reproduction and communications costs incidental to bargaining. In large city school districts, mayors and mayoral staffs may be required to devote a considerable amount of their time to school district bargaining. Such time is not shown as a cost of public education.

Similarly, several municipal overhead costs often are not shown on school district budgets. These costs may be for legal, accounting, financial, or personnel services, to cite just a few. In some cases, such as the costs of school board elections, the understatements of the costs of public education are not relevant to cost comparisons of contracting for and direct provision of service. In other situations, such as school board utilization of the city's legal staff, the understatements are or may be relevant.

In some states, contributions for teacher pensions are paid by the state government. As a result, these contributions do not show up in the budget of either the school district or of any local unit of government.[8] Similarly, states sometimes provide textbooks to local school districts at no charge or at a reduced charge. These costs, especially the former, can involve substantial amounts that are relevant to cost comparisons.

Some costs to the state of regulation of education are not included in estimates of the costs of education. Unlike pension and textbook costs, the costs of state regulation would not normally affect comparisons between public and private school costs. This is certainly true when states regulate educational activities regardless of whether they take place in public or private schools. On the other hand, if one's purpose is to determine the total cost of public education to the taxpayer, the costs of state educational agencies and even of noneducational agencies that devote some of their resources to education should be included.

Costs Not Shown on Any Budget

The market value of school district land and property ordinarily is not included in education cost estimates. Economically, this makes no sense; nobody operates a business without factoring in the costs of land and buildings. It is important to recognize that "cost" does not necessarily refer to initial cost. A school district may have acquired a school site 50 years ago for $1,000; today, fair market value of the site may be $1 million. Under conventional school accounting methods, the cost would be shown as zero, since the land is already paid for. Realistically, the cost to the community is the "opportunity cost"; that is, the $1 million the district could get by selling the site. We should not assume there are no costs merely because there are no cash outlays.

The largest opportunity cost systematically ignored in school finance is student time. This omission does not affect comparisons of public to private provision of educational services because the opportunity costs would be the same, regardless of whether a pupil was being educated in a public school, a private school, or by a for-profit contractor. Opportunity costs are, however, relevant to several important educational

---

[8] All the data on teacher pensions are taken from Robert P. Inman, Appraising the funding status of teacher pensions, *National Tax Journal*, 39: 21-33; and Robert P. Inman and David J. Albright, Central policies for local debt: The case of teachers pensions (Paper made available to the author at the University of Pennsylvania).

policy issues, such as the maximum age for compulsory education or the desirability of subsidies to students in higher education. Opportunity costs are closely associated with student age; a college student ordinarily could be earning more than a first grade student if neither was in school.

Depreciation of buildings or capital equipment or both is routinely omitted from district budgets. The omission not only distorts the cost picture but is conducive to inefficiency. Failure to take depreciation into account often distorts comparisons of private to public school costs, even when the item is omitted from the financial statements in both sectors.

In economic terms, depreciation is the cost of using capital facilities or equipment. The depreciation costs of public education include the decline in the value of buildings and capital equipment. If the district builds a school, the cost should be prorated over the life of the school. Likewise, if it buys trucks or typewriters or computers, the costs should be spread out over the useful life of the equipment. When this is not done, the costs are overstated when purchases are made and understated in other years. Quite often, the outcome is excessive costs for repairs, with only lip service paid to preventive maintenance. If budgets allow for repairs but not for replacement, repairs may be made when the building or equipment is actually beyond repair.

Recent history in New York illustrates how and why the neglect of depreciation results in significant underestimates of the costs of public education. In 1987, the *New York Times* published an article describing the deplorable physical condition of the New York City schools. The article portrayed an appalling picture of deterioration and neglect of the city's school buildings. The articles asserted or quoted school officials to the effect that:

- Many school buildings had not been painted in 20 years.

- Holes in some classroom floors were large enough for students to fall through.

- A school visited by the city's mayor had broken window shades, peeling paint and plaster, and no soap or bathroom tissue for teachers and students.

- It took almost 10 years to build a school; only one new school had been built from 1975 to 1987.

- The schedule for painting schools was once every 33 years.

- Most requests for repairs (e.g., broken windows) went unheeded for years unless the repairs were deemed an emergency.

- The only way to have maintenance work done was to have a powerful political leader visit the school.[9]

Seven years later the situation remained essentially unchanged.

How could such an undesirable state of affairs come to be? One reason is the time perspective of political leaders. Inevitably, their major concerns are focused upon the next election, or upon their political careers generally. They tend to sacrifice long-range public interests for immediate political advantage. Furthermore, because few political leaders in large urban centers have children in public schools, they have less awareness or personal commitment to the public school system.

In practical terms, there is a political tendency to overspend on employee benefits and skimp on maintenance of public facilities. The benefits have an active, politically potent constituency; maintenance has only a diffuse public constituency that is unlikely to be effective in the budgetary process.

Although the physical deterioration of New York City schools may be exceptional, underfunding of maintenance needs is not. The cost of meeting these needs is one of the major problems facing state legislatures in the 1990s. Whatever the outcome, it is not likely to include realistic treatment of the costs of educational facilities.

Unfunded Pension Costs

Another major cost that may not be shown on any budget is unfunded pension obligations. Typically, teachers pay a specified percentage of their salaries to a state retirement system for teachers. The local school district and/or the state also contribute to the retirement system according to formulas set by the legislatures. The contributions from teachers and public agencies are invested and total revenues made available for payments to retirees.

Essentially, there are two different approaches to funding; "full funding" and "pay-as-you-go." Under the first approach, funds contributed every year plus the anticipated earnings from investing prior contribu-

---

[9]*New York Times*, May 13, 1987, p. 1, B6

tions cover the costs of the anticipated obligations of the retirement system. With the second approach, the assets of the retirement system meet current obligations (if they can) and the states make up any shortfall. Some states have also added cost-of-living supplements from time to time. These supplements are paid from state (not local) funds.

Most teacher retirement plans are pay-as-you-go. Such plans often have substantial unfunded pension liabilities. This is true regardless of whether the nonteacher contributions come from the local school district, the state government, or some combination of the two. Over the years, the age of retirement and required number of years of service have been reduced. Benefits have been extended to spouses and children; disability and service-related handicaps have been liberalized. Meanwhile, the longevity of beneficiaries has increased, so benefits must be paid out longer than was initially anticipated.

The extent of unfunded teacher retirement obligations varies widely. In some states, it is not a serious problem, but in many others, it clearly is or will be. Furthermore, taxpayer obligations are increasing; in the near future, we can expect several state financial crises from the underfunding. Nevertheless, the state teachers retirement systems are government agencies, and any shortfalls must be made up by state governments. This means that pension costs for teachers currently in service cannot be ascertained by analyzing either the state or the local school district budget, or both of them together. The costs of public education are understated, insofar as such budgets do not show either future cost-of-living supplements or underfunded pension obligations.

To appreciate the importance of pension issues to outside contracting, the difficulties of solving the problems of excessive public employee pensions must be considered. Over the years, most state courts have held that pension benefits of public employees are contractual obligations of government. Most state supreme courts have rejected the view that pension benefits are matters of legislative policy that can be changed by legislatures. In most states, it is legally impossible to reduce benefits for retirees and current employees, regardless of how much greater than anticipated the required payments turn out to be. At the same time, efforts to reduce benefit levels for new employees meet enormous resistance from public sector unions, including teachers unions. Apart from their general opposition to reducing benefits, unions fear that reducing benefit levels for new hires will weaken the union. Eventually, the union would be divided between new hires seeking to equalize pension benefits (thereby reducing the benefits that could be made available to the senior employees) and senior employees seeking to add to existing benefits.

Regardless of whether a state makes up a shortfall in contributions or adds a cost-of-living supplement, its additional contributions are not payments for current services, but rather additional payments for services rendered in the past. In pay-as-you-go systems, the cost figures for pensions are a mix of costs for present and past services. To fully assess the costs of present services, one should deduct the costs for past services and add the unfunded pension obligations that will be owed to current employees. In effect, public school employees are being paid partly in cash and partly in promissory notes, but the cost figures show only the current cash payments to them or on their behalf.

Large, unfunded liabilities must be paid by future taxpayers, the big losers when politicians increase retirement benefits without immediate contribution or tax increases. Future teachers and pupils are also big losers. When the costs come due, it becomes more difficult to increase or even maintain existing levels of public services.

Clearly, outside contracting would tend to avoid most of these problems. Private employers have less incentive to conceal unfunded pension costs, and even when they do, shareholders and the investment industry are likely to monitor the situation. The citizen who monitors public employee pension costs receives an insignificant benefit from detecting excessive pension costs, since the savings would have to be shared with many other taxpayers. In contrast, shareholders may benefit immediately and substantially from information about unfunded costs because they could affect future dividends. For this reason, pension costs are monitored more carefully in the private sector, especially by large institutional investors.

Neglected Costs of Outside Contracting

Cost comparisons often overlook significant expenditures associated with buying services. For example, the costs of the process of outside contracting—or "transaction costs," to use the economists' term—are often omitted. Minimally, such costs include the process of preparing and advertising bids, evaluating offers to provide services, and the costs of negotiating and drawing up contracts. Obviously, the nature of the service involved is an important cost factor. If the service requires substantial investment by the contractor, in the absence of idle district facilities or equipment or personnel, transaction costs can be substantial. Resolving the rights of the parties to terminate and the allocation of payments and costs upon termination may also require substantial transaction costs.

Although transaction costs should not be ignored, they are not likely to affect the desirability of contracting for services. Organizations of public officials have accumulated thousands of service contracts, many of which have been drafted by lawyers knowledgeable about the issues. For this reason, school districts contracting for a service have access to excellent contracts that can serve as a guide. Furthermore, whatever the transaction costs of the initial contract, they are likely to be much lower in future ones.

The costs of implementing as well as negotiating an agreement are sometimes overlooked. Such costs may stem from litigation, labor problems, contractor delay or failure, and many other unanticipated problems.

Once negotiated and implemented, service contracts must be adequately monitored. This can involve significant costs. The basic issue is how the monitoring costs affect realistic comparisons of total costs. Outside of education, monitoring for contracted services typically ranges from 5 to 10 percent of direct costs. Obviously, omission of costs of this magnitude could lead to invalid comparisons. In fact, public agencies sometimes require private contractors to specify monitoring costs, at the same time ignoring costs of monitoring the performance of public employees. Quite clearly, valid comparisons would need to include the monitoring costs of both public and private service delivery.[10]

Overall, it is very likely that inclusion of neglected costs in cost comparisons would strengthen the case for outside contracting. First, the most substantial costs that are frequently ignored, such as pension costs, are nearly always higher in the public sector. Second, political pressures to underfund long-range needs, such as maintenance, are not as strong in the private sector. For example, it is unlikely that private companies in New York City have underfunded their maintenance needs to the same extent that the city's public schools have done. In other words, there appears to be less advantage in the private sector in concealing or minimizing costs; if anything, the reverse is true.

---

[10] See John Tepper Marlin, *Contracting for municipal services* (New York: Ronald Press, 1984).

Although problems of comparing costs are important, they are large-ly technical problems amenable to technical solutions. This is not the case with outcomes. Even full knowledge of the outcomes may not resolve disputes over them. Public schools typically strive to achieve several outcomes, but parents and taxpayers may differ widely on their importance or even their desirability. Contracting for instruction is not feasible in the absence of consensus on the contractor's mission. Citizens may object to contracting for water purification, but their objections will not be based upon support for contaminated water. It will be based on the cost or some other side effect of achieving clean water or on the belief that outside contracting will not result in clean water.

Studies of contracting for services indicate that this policy is applied most effectively when the service involved can be readily identified, measured, and evaluated. Refuse collection illustrates this. Is the refuse picked up by a certain time each day? How many complaints are there? Does the contractor respond within a specified time to complaints? Questions such as these can be answered in a relatively straightforward way. With human services, however, it becomes more difficult to know what the outcomes are and how much weight to give each of them. The contractors naturally try to show beneficial outcomes; their critics try to identify the negative outcomes that are being ignored. Thus, the process facilitates clarity and specificity with respect to both cost and outcomes. This outcome is independent of whether the contractors can provide equal or better service at a lower cost. Outside contracting will tend to reveal the true costs of public education. Public awareness of these costs is likely to help keep them at reasonable levels.

In addition to the general arguments against contracting for services, several others relate specifically to contracting for instruction.[11]

Stated briefly, these objections are as follows:

- Some of the objectives of instruction are not subject to measurement; consequently, it would be impossible to determine whether the contractor is performing adequately.

---

[11] Both the National Education Association and the American Federation of Teachers actively opposed the experiments in educational performance contracting conducted by the Office of Economic Opportunity in the early 1970s. These experiments and union opposition to them are discussed in Myron Lieberman, *Privatization and educational choice* (New York: St. Martin's Press, 1989). Significantly, both NEA and AFT affiliates seek to represent nonteaching employ-ees, a policy that explains teacher union opposition to contracting for even support services. Teacher union opposition to outside contracting has escalated dramatically since the 1970s.

- Instruction has multiple objectives, such as academic skills, respect for others, intellectual curiosity, patriotic sentiments, and good citizenship. It is extremely difficult to measure progress toward achieving some of these objectives. Even if we could do that, we would not know which objectives should receive the highest priority.

- Some instructional objectives are measurable, but if these objectives are specified in a contract, the contractor will focus its efforts upon them and neglect other objectives not so readily measured. This would be undesirable.

It is debatable whether these objections constitute a valid argument against contracting for instruction. As a matter of fact, some of them appear to strengthen the case for it, although that is certainly not the intent of those raising the objection. At any rate, these objections are not persuasive.

First of all, testing can measure educational achievement, regardless of whether the instruction is provided by public schools, not-for-profit schools, for-profit schools, or educational contractors. For all the rhetoric about nonacademic objectives, schools and teachers rely almost entirely upon tests of academic achievement to measure student progress. It hardly makes sense to object to contracts with private contractors that rely upon the same criteria.

Objections to contract services based upon a multiplicity of ineffable objectives is suspect for another reason. Granted, education should have several objectives in addition to educational achievement. However, if public school officials cannot furnish criteria used to evaluate progress on these other objectives, how do they know—how *can* they know—whether the public schools are fulfilling them? When school officials themselves do not know the criteria for measuring an objective, it is difficult to believe these officials regard the objectives very seriously.

Indeed, the assertion of behavioral and attitudinal objectives in the simultaneous absence of criteria to evaluate school performance on them is not accidental. A criterion is a two-edged sword. It can be used to show both progress or the lack of it. Public schools, like public agencies generally, show little interest in developing criteria for evaluating their performance. In the absence of such criteria, school personnel are invulnerable. No matter how poorly pupils perform on any given criterion, it can be asserted that other objectives that cannot be measured must be taken into account. Meanwhile, the deficiencies are useful if pupils aren't learning and the schools need more money for remedial programs, better teachers, and improved instructional materials.

Granted, it may be easier to compare public and private garbage removal or mail delivery than the outcomes of education. The difficulty is probably exaggerated, but whether it is or not is of secondary importance. Why do parents and taxpayers lack usable criteria for evaluating school performance? The answers suggest that the alleged absence of criteria for assessing educational outcomes is an argument for contracting, not a reason to reject it.

Schools do have attitudinal and behavioral objectives, however poorly articulated these objectives may be. The reason that schools do not ordinarily evaluate progress on these objectives is not the inherent technical difficulty of doing so. It is that no one has any stake in establishing the criteria necessary to do so.

Contracting for instruction would provide the incentives for establishing such criteria. The contractor needs to know the criteria for evaluating its services, and the school district needs to know whether the contractor fulfilled district objectives. Consequently, the contracting process forces districts to define their objectives and specify the criteria for evaluating contractor success in achieving them.

Suppose we assume that public schools try to teach respect for others, patriotism, and good work habits. Although these attitudes and habits are distinct objectives, they are not "subjects" like mathematics or reading. Whether pupils learn these things depends on whether the teachers as a group and the school administration foster them. Although all teachers are responsible for helping to achieve these objectives, no individual teacher is held accountable for them. There is nothing necessarily wrong with this, since it may be practically impossible to disentangle the contributions of individual teachers to the objectives. Granting this, it is still feasible to evaluate how effectively schools inculcate these habits and attitudes. The technical difficulty of formulating the criteria to be used is not the problem.

In any event, there is no reason contractors would be less likely to foster the desirable habits and attitudes in question. These objectives are not so much a matter of expertise as they are of being clear about goals and being determined to achieve them. On both counts, there is no reason to assume that public schools would do a better job than private contractors. If anything, the latter should be expected to perform better, because their livelihood will depend upon performance in a way that does not apply to public school personnel. Recent trends in school finance underscore this point. As noted earlier, in recent years, almost 50 percent of school revenues has come from state governments. All that counts in the allocation of state aid is the number of pupils in various grade levels or categories, such as the handicapped or non-English-speaking. Inasmuch as state funds are distributed to school districts regardless of their performance, school districts have no incentive to develop criteria for assessing their performance.

In considering the difficulties of specifying instructional criteria, a double standard of judgment must be avoided. It is improper for public school personnel who lack criteria for accountability to demand that a contractor be held to standards that do not exist in conventional school operations. Initially, the same criteria used to evaluate conventional instruction can be used to evaluate contracted instruction. Those who teach, or allow teaching to go on in the absence of any criteria, should not be allowed to block contracting for this reason. Like public school personnel, contractors might prefer not to be evaluated according to specified criteria, but they could hardly adopt this position in dealing with school boards.

No doubt contractors will propose criteria likely to be favorable to their efforts, but school boards need not accept them without change. Over time, especially if contracting for instruction becomes more common, the criteria can be refined and expanded. Furthermore, national and state organizations of school boards, school administrators and teachers will provide feedback on outside contracting in various school districts. In short, it is essential to visualize the development of outside contracting over time, not to view it simply as a static and repetitive process.

Overcoming Union Opposition to Outside Contracting

As we have seen, the major opposition to contracting for instruction comes from employees and/or the unions that represent them. Can this opposition be overcome or neutralized?

Three basic principles should guide school management on this issue:

1. No special interest group should be permitted to block an action that is in the district's interest. On occasion, it may be impossible to adhere to the principle, but it is better to recognize a violation of it than to rationalize it away.

2. Employees who are adversely affected by contracting should be dealt with fairly. What this requires in any specific situation may be controversial, but it should not be interpreted to give employees or their unions a veto power over proposed changes.

3. Union and employee interests are not identical. This principle is not always recognized, but it is critical from a strategic point of view. Differences sometimes can be used to neutralize union opposition to contracting. On this issue, there is much to be learned from the way the Thatcher government in Great Britain facilitated privatization.[12] From the outset, it sought not merely to neutralize employee opposition but to gain employee support for privatization. To achieve this objective, it offered employees a variety of benefits subject to privatization. For example, in denationalizing several industries, the government offered employees opportunities to buy stock at a deep discount in the companies taking over the government enterprise. Similarly, to overcome management opposition to privatization, it often arranged for incumbent management to remain when the enterprise was privatized. In many instances, even the unions that opposed privatization ended up purchasing shares in the new companies.

Although the specifics of the British approach generally are not applicable to public education in the United States, the underlying philosophy of the plan is clearly relevant in that it underscores the fact that the unions' underlying interests are not necessarily identical to those of the employees. This is especially evident when the contract for instruction is with a nonunion employer. Even when the contractor's employees are or can be unionized, they may come under the jurisdiction of a different union. For this reason, the union representing school district employees may oppose outside contracting regardless of the union status of the contractor's employees.

When employees would be adversely affected by contracting, there is no conflict between union and employee interests. In many situa-

---

[12] See Madsen Pirie, *Dismantling the state: The theory and practice of privatization* (Dallas: National Center for Policy Analysis, 1985); John Goodman, ed., *Privatization* (Dallas: National Center for Policy Analysis, 1985); Stuart M. Butler, *Privatizing federal spending: a strategy to eliminate the deficit* (New York: Universe Books, 1985).

tions, however, employers can satisfy employee interests in ways that do not accommodate the union's. For example, in order to overcome employee opposition to contracting, the employer may offer early retirement, severance pay, and/or transfers under conditions highly favorable to its employees. In some situations, the employer can rely upon attrition or voluntary departures to avoid layoffs that might otherwise arise from contracting. In contrast, union staff who rely on dues income for their livelihood will accord preservation of the union a higher priority than protection of employees from loss of income.

In some cases, union opposition to outside contracting may be contrary to employee interests. Suppose that school boards in a given area propose to contract for instruction in fields in which they are unable to recruit competent teachers. Some teachers in such fields may feel that with extensive use of paraprofessionals and technology, teachers can meet the needs of these districts just as well as the contractors can. The teachers unions, however, will be concerned about the precedent and the loss of dues-paying members. Even if the local unions are not concerned about these possibilities, their state and national affiliates are likely to be.

Obviously, in any such situation, the unions would be denying some members an opportunity to promote their own welfare. For this reason, the union position would be difficult to defend. It is impossible, however, to predict how often such situations would arise: Their frequency would depend partly on whether contracting was only a cottage industry or whether it grew to a scale in which contractors operated entire schools or even school districts.

Normally, the union will be adversely affected by outside contracting, at least in the short run. Although union approval of contracting would always be desirable if it can be achieved without excessive concessions, such approval usually will be withheld, except under heavy pressure. Pressure may include benefits that are contingent on acceptance of contracting. The benefits may apply to employees not affected by contracting as well as those directly affected by it. Efforts to overcome union and/or employee opposition could include one or more of the following provisions:

- Employees remain on the district payroll but work pursuant to arrangements between the contractor and the district. This is a common procedure in certain types of support services.

• As part of the contract, the contractor may be required to employ district employees on a preferential basis. The preference may be limited to a certain time (e.g., up to five years). The district may supplement the contractor's payments. Some type of joint payment often is worked out when employees would lose pension or health insurance benefits if forced off the district payroll.

• Severance pay and/or maintenance of health insurance benefits might be considered to ease the transition.

• Liberalized early retirement might be made available in certain situations.

• Transfers or reassignments might ensure continuous employment without loss of pay or benefits for employees who otherwise would suffer from outside contracting.

Of course, the savings achieved over time by contracting for services must take into account transition costs and costs of monitoring the contracts. The important point is to analyze the circumstances to see what can and might be done to mitigate employee and union opposition.

Undoubtedly, salary and pension problems can be a major obstacle to contracting for instruction. Teacher salary schedules reward years of service. Although significant savings might be generated without loss of quality by using part-time and/or younger teachers, teachers with many years of service will be strongly opposed to a new system that does not pay as much for longevity. Pension issues often exacerbate the salary problem. Teachers are members of state retirement systems for teachers that usually base pension payments on the number of years taught and the average salary of the final one to three years. As a result, teachers within a few years of retirement may oppose contracting because it jeopardizes their anticipated level of pension benefits. One question is whether such teachers can be retained as district employees until retirement or can be bought out without sacrificing the economic advantages of contracting. Obviously, the answer will vary with such factors as the age of the teaching staff, but the issue has to be considered carefully.

Perhaps the most difficult aspect of the problem of balancing fairness to incumbent employees with maximizing efficiency is the absence of any guidelines to resolve it. Obviously, it is undesirable to maintain an inefficient delivery system because some employees will be disadvantaged by change to a more efficient system. Unfortunately, these employees are often able to block the transition. On the other hand, there is no clear-cut standard for government to apply in resolving situations of inefficiency or redundancy. How much protection or compensation should be accorded public employees when more efficient ways to deliver services eliminate or reduce the need for their services? In practice, and in the absence of any economic guidelines, the question is answered on a short-term political or bureaucratic basis: How would a proposed cut affect reelection prospects or bureaucratic objectives? The result is a substantial tilt toward inefficiency in public employment. Essentially, government must find ways to use the savings from more efficient procedures to gain the support, or at least neutralize the opposition, of public employees adversely affected by such procedures.

Role of School Management in Outside Contracting

Unlike teachers unions, school management has no reason to oppose contracting for instruction as an option to be exercised when circumstances warrant. In fact, in addition to the reasons normally cited for the practice, school management has strong reason to resolve any close calls in favor of contracting. Let us see why this is so.

In conventional operations, school management hires staff: teachers, principals, custodians, bus drivers, cooks, and so on. On the other hand, management also is responsible for evaluating these employees. No one likes to admit having employed incompetent employees, especially if there is a political cost in making such a concession; therefore, management tends to be biased toward favorable evaluation. When the legal and practical difficulties of dismissing incompetent employees are added to the inherent management bias in their favor, the outcome tends to favor the employees over the service consumers. Teacher rhetoric notwithstanding, public schools suffer much more from perfunctory evaluation, or none at all, than from unjustified negative evaluations.

Suppose, however, that management did not have the responsibility for hiring certain levels of employees. Would management not be in a better position to evaluate the performance of these employees objectively? Not having any stake in their employment, management would probably be more candid in expressing its conclusions about service quality. Also, because management would need less time for its producer activities, such as hiring teachers, it also would have more time for its consumer responsibilities, such as evaluating services and educational outcomes.

To some extent, therefore, contracting would help management minimize the conflict inherent in being both the producer and consumer of educational services. Management can focus on evaluating the services rendered under less political pressure to justify the results. Nor would the bias resulting from the employment of individual employees be simply replaced by bias resulting from selection of a contractor. This could happen if there was sole-source bidding, and school management was clearly responsible for selecting the sole source. When bidding is truly open and competitive, management is less likely to have a political stake in favorable evaluation of services received.

Furthermore, there is an important difference in the two situations. Ordinarily, management must evaluate employees individually. With contracting, however, management can focus on service outcomes; evaluation of employees is likely to be the contractor's responsibility. Granted, in some cases, it may be difficult—even impossible—to evaluate a service without some attention to the performance of individuals. Education is excessively oriented to evaluation of inputs and simultaneous neglect of outcomes. Outside contracting could help correct this imbalance.

Whether contracting saves management time, and how much, depends on several factors, but contracting clearly has the *potential* to save a great deal of management time. Because they are public agencies, school boards are required to take action on many items of little or no practical significance. Contracting could help to minimize some of these problems. If the competitive process provides assurance that the overall cost is reasonable, management has no reason to be involved in the details of providing the service.

In a 1982 survey, board members indicated that they spent about 45 hours per month on board business. Asked what they would like to devote more time to, 19 percent said curriculum-related matters, 12 percent said policy matters, and 9 percent said visiting schools. When asked how they could save time, 13 percent of the board members—the highest of any time-saving option suggested—preferred reducing the number of board meetings.[13] None of the other time-saving options mentioned even raised the question of whether boards could make better

---

[13] *American School Board Journal,* Oct. 1982, p. 26.

use of their time by contracting in the private sector for some of the services they manage.

It must be emphasized that outside contracting is not an abdication of management responsibilities; instead, it is another way of fulfilling them. Furthermore, the public agency contracting for a service cannot safely ignore what happens after a contract is signed. Contract management, including an adequate reporting system, should be considered an integral part of the process.

Concluding Observations

During the past few years, privatization has become less of an ideological and more of a "good government" issue cutting across party lines. Governments at all levels are facing unprecedented pressures to increase their efficiency. As this happens, privatization becomes a more practical issue to be resolved on efficiency grounds. The preceding analysis has not discussed all the efficiency issues, but the more exhaustive the comparisons, the more they tend to support the outside contracting option. Furthermore, even a small shift to contracting may stimulate greater efficiency in school operations; the threat or the possibility of contracting for instruction may achieve even greater savings than actually doing it. Partly for this reason, school boards should not agree to contractual language that restricts their right to contract for any activity or service for which they are responsible.

PART II
PUBLIC POLICY ISSUES IN
TEACHER BARGAINING

9. PUBLIC SECTOR COLLECTIVE BARGAINING SUBSTANTIALLY DIMINISHES DEMOCRACY

Robert S. Summers

Introduction

My thesis is that public sector collective bargaining, even without the right of union members to strike, substantially diminishes democracy. My aim is to demonstrate the validity of this thesis. I will also show that empirical studies of the actual social effects of public sector bargaining are not required to establish the validity of my thesis.

The conflict between political democracy and public sector collective bargaining manifests itself in a variety of important dimensions. Public sector bargaining:

- Divides public authority and redistributes a share of it to private entities—mainly unions—who are not elected by or accountable to the public.

- Restructures processes for the exercise of that authority to enable these unions to participate in its exercise according to the traditional mode of union functioning, namely collective bargaining—itself an adversarial process.

- Alters in varying degrees the outcomes of these processes for the exercise of governmental authority and thereby modifies the benefits conferred (and their costs) and brings some discontinuation of benefits (strikes).

This chapter was originally published as an article under the same title in *Government Union Review* 1:1, 5-22, (Winter 1980). It is republished here with minor editorial changes.

- Eliminates or reduces public accountability of participants for their share in these processes and outcomes and undermines the general conditions for healthy democratic governance within society at large.

Democracy is a high-priority value in our society primarily because it secures the realization of important "process values."[1] Such values are realized in the course of the workings of democracy and are prized even where the outcomes of democratic processes are bad. These values include (1) determination by the public through elected representatives and their appointees of the nature and manner of conferral of public benefits; (2) direct public participation in ongoing governmental processes of lawmaking and law administration; (3) fairness of those processes, especially to the losing side; and (4) accountability to the public of participants in those processes. The various conflicts between political democracy and public sector collective bargaining entails significant sacrifices of all the foregoing process values.

To develop my thesis in concrete and meaningful terms, it will be necessary to focus on a specific context. Thus, my illustrations will be drawn from the conflict between democracy and collective bargaining at the local level in the field of public school education. My thesis, however, also applies (mutatis mutandis) to public benefit conferral at the state and federal levels as well, and to benefits other than education.

Authority To Make Public Law (and Policy), To Create Public Budgets, and To Interpret and Administer Law and Budgets

Statutes establishing public sector collective bargaining redistribute governmental authority from elected officials and their appointees to private, nonelected and nonaccountable entities called unions (and to various arbitrators and other third parties). This redistribution of political authority inherently diminishes democracy. Of course, such statutes do not in so many words recite that they are redistributing formal governmental authority. If a "truth in legislating" law had required such candor, the public sector bargaining statutes would probably never

---

[1] On the nature of process values, see R. Summers, Evaluating and improving legal processes— a plea for process values, *Cornell Law Review* 60 (1974):1.

have been enacted. These statutes disguise the redistribution of public authority in the language of collective bargaining.[2]

Few would deny that the authority to make public law and policy, to create public budgets, and to interpret and administer the resultant law and budgets is *governmental* authority. Moreover, few would deny that in a political democracy, this kind of authority is characteristically conferred upon publicly elected officials and their appointees, not upon private parties or entities who are neither representatives of nor accountable to the public. Yet, public sector collective bargaining statutes carve out a vast portion of this authority and require that elected officials and their appointees share its exercise with private, non-elected entities—unions (and various third parties).

In the absence of bargaining statutes, public officials and their appointees are not required to share governmental authority with private entities in order to make and administer public laws and budgets. Rather, their authority is sole and exclusive. Under bargaining laws, however, elected officials and their appointees are required to share governmental authority with unions and other private entities who do not, in any way, represent the will of the public. This, in itself, substantially diminishes democracy. The basic democratic process value that is thereby sacrificed is simply that of public self-determination of the nature and costs of governmental goods and services. It will be recalled that a "process value" is prizeable regardless of the nature of the outcomes of governmental processes for the exercise of authority. Even when these outcomes are not good, it remains a virtue of these processes that their outcomes are arrived at by the public rather than by a dictator or private syndicate.

Public sector bargaining statutes sacrifice the democratic process value of self-determination with respect to the making of public law and policy, the creation of public budgets, and the interpretation and administration of these laws and budgets. The budgetary facet of the sacrifice is especially noteworthy. Would our founding fathers, who vigorously opposed "taxation without representation," today endorse the creation of public budgets partly by parties not themselves elected by the people (or appointed by elected personnel)? It is most unlikely.

---

[2] See, for example, the following general state public sector bargaining statutes. Cal Govt. Code §§ 3500 et seq. (West); Mich. Comp. Laws Ann §§ 423.201 et seq.; N.Y. Civ. Serv. Law (McKinney) §§ 200 et seq. See also note 10, infra.

Would unions themselves be quick to oppose the conferral of public lawmaking authority on private interest groups such as agricultural organizations in matters of agricultural policy or, at the local level, churches in matters touching the church-state relation, or textbook companies in regard to facets of the public school curriculum? It is almost certain that unions themselves would oppose such actions, and precisely on the ground that they would dramatically diminish democracy.

The redistribution of governmental authority pursuant to statutes establishing collective bargaining inherently diminishes democracy; that is, empirical studies are not required to confirm this. Of course, the diminution is not something that occurs merely upon formal enactment of such statutes. It occurs only when unions are formed and they step into the role of joint makers and administrators of public laws and budgets. No one denies, either, that the relevant unions have been formed or that they have occupied the role spelled out for them in the statutes.

Observe also that the validity of this conclusion that public sector bargaining diminishes democracy does not depend on any showing that after the introduction of bargaining, public participation diminished from some previously high level.[3]

It is now important to anticipate and respond to several objections. To lend concreteness to the objections, I shall illustrate them with examples from the public school context.

First, proponents of public sector bargaining may respond that when, for example, a school board engages in collective bargaining with a teachers union, the two are not making public law and budgets when negotiating with respect to the application of school policy to an individual teacher or when engaged in "grievance" arbitration. Rather, so the argument goes, they are merely bargaining over "terms and conditions of employment" to be embodied in a "collective bargaining agreement," or merely interpreting and applying the existing agreement, just as do employees in the private sector. Hence, the authority being exercised is not, in this view, essentially governmental authority anyway, and thus poses no threat of any kind to democracy.

The foregoing argument trades in labels and ignores reality. A public employee collective bargaining statute typically carves out a large portion of formerly exclusive legislative and budgetary jurisdiction and

---

[3] Others appear to have failed to see how this is so. See, for example, S. Cohen, Does public employee unionism diminish democracy? *Industrial and Labor Relations Review* 32 (1979): 189.

requires that the agency share that jurisdiction with unions in the guise of "bargaining over terms and conditions of employment." In the educational field, such matters as the length of the school day, class size, teacher recruitment and retention policies, wages and fringe benefits, and much else is taken to fall within the phrase "bargaining over terms and conditions of employment." Yet decisions on such matters are decisions of public law and policy. Indeed, collectively they go far to determine the very nature and quality of the benefit the government unit exists to provide. The fact that they are not embodied in school board bylaws or regulations but in a stack of stapled paper called a collective bargaining agreement does not alter this fundamental fact. In public employment it simply is not possible to divide authority up in the way probargainers advocate without substantially diminishing democracy. What are, to bargainers, merely "terms and conditions of employment" to be bargained over in truth comprise the very subject matter of public law and policy. Public employment is fundamentally different from private sector employment. The "employer" is a public democratic agency, representing the will of the public. The job of that agency is to confer a public benefit. It cannot do this without employees. Yet, that agency cannot be required to forfeit to employees acting through their union basic authority over the nature and quality of the benefit to be conferred without substantially diminishing democracy.

The foregoing analysis is equally applicable to the budgetary side of democratic public benefit conferral. No teachers union would be happy to learn that a process akin to collective bargaining had been instituted to determine the price of books supplied to the district, with the district obligated to bargain in good faith and engage in impasse resolution with a previously screened panel of, say, three book companies. At this point, those teachers who are *taxpayer citizens living in the district* would be almost certain to rise up and say, "The book companies have no right to codetermine in this way how public money is to be spent. There can be no taxation without representation, and the book companies do not represent the public."

By the same token, teachers unions do not represent and are not accountable to the public; yet, when they bargain over wages or other economic items pursuant to a public employee collective bargaining statute, they codetermine important items in the school district budget. This is not to say that what they thus codetermine will always be final. Some school districts put the entire budget up to a vote for approval or rejection. When this occurs, the public *may* have the last word (and even then it cannot discriminate within that last word between particular aspects of the budget). In many districts, public votes on the budget are not taken, or when they are, salaries and other like items in collective bargaining agreements are not reviewed because they are not yet agreed upon by voting time.

Similarly, the interpretation and administration of public law and public budgets are characteristically a governmental function in a democracy. Yet, union negotiation and outside arbitration have usurped this function to a considerable degree, not only in the public school field but in other fields of local governmental activity, too. Many interpretations and administrative issues of significance are now resolved not by public school administrators or school boards but through negotiation or arbitration pursuant to collective bargaining agreements calling for maintenance of standards and for "grievance" arbitration. Note that when an outside arbitrator decides school policies in the course of arbitrating a dispute, the relevant public officials—the school board and its appointees—do not even exercise authority to codetermine the outcome (except insofar as they present their case).

Second, proponents of bargaining may also claim that the public employee union—a teachers association, for example—merely *shares* public authority under a bargaining statute and that the public officials involved—school board members, for example—are not forced by a collective bargaining statute to agree to any particular "term or condition of employment" or to any particular public law or policy. Hence, in this view, the essentials of democratic functioning are preserved. In truth, the essentials are *not* preserved. It is little consolation to a school board that it need not agree to a proposal when failure to do so leaves it with no significant freedom of action anyway. Yet, commonly, a board will not be entitled to alter the status quo at all without securing union concurrence, for the existing contract will bind the board to the status quo. To move away from that position, bargaining norms require that the board give up something in return; hence the board may be induced to do something that it would not otherwise do. The board thus has to "buy" freedom of action. The democratic voice must pay a price to hold sway.

Furthermore, that the union merely *shares* authority must not be allowed to obscure the fact that the union nonetheless remains a private entity not elected by the public or appointed by public officials and not

146

accountable to the public. The union, even when public-spirited, sees its primary role to be that of an arm's length negotiator on behalf of its own employee-members' interest. On many issues—especially economic ones—there will be a genuine conflict of interest between the employees and the government unit. Indeed, the concept of "sharing" authority obscures the highly adversarial nature of much public sector bargaining. It is not too much to say that bargaining statutes set up countervailing power in the form of unions with various legal rights. Unlike in the private sector, where this power exists to countervail private corporations seeking profit, public sector bargaining laws set up private power centers to countervail public *democratic functionaries* such as school boards and city councils.

Third, it may be said that the union is not really a private nonelective and nonappointive body. Rather, the individuals who make up a teachers union, for example, are all public employees appointed by the board. In this view, when teachers engage in bargaining on public policies, one public arm merely deals with another public arm. This analysis is faulty. The individual teacher is not appointed as a prospective codeterminer of school policy and budgets who is accountable to the public. The individual teacher is appointed as a *teacher*. As such, the teacher cannot be viewed as even indirectly representing the public when exercising through bargaining various *legislative*, *budgetary*, and *administrative* jurisdiction. Moreover, it is not the individual teacher who engages in bargaining. Under the statutes, the employee bargaining representatives are union designates, and may even include persons who are not teachers employed by the district. Further, it is the task of union officials to represent the teachers in a genuine adversarial fashion under public sector bargaining statutes. Union officials are not elected, even indirectly, by the public, yet under such statutes they have joint authority to codetermine the law and the budget in relevant respects.

Fourth, it may be contended that unions in public employment should be viewed merely as pressure groups of the kind that traditionally figure in the American political process. Collective bargaining statutes merely recognize and regularize the pressure group status of unions. Democracy is thus facilitated, not frustrated. This line of argument also ignores the truth that a collective bargaining statute catapults the union into a unique position within the political process. In the education field, the union ends up well ahead of the P.T.A., taxpayer groups, textbook companies, and all other "pressure groups" vying for influence upon educational decision making. Unlike these other groups, the union is, by law, entitled to have the governmental agency—the board— negotiate in good faith solely with the union on all issues falling within the scope of bargaining. Moreover, the union has close proximity to the board and thus is strategically situated to exploit the special advantage it has under the statute. Further, the union has a unique cluster of sanctions, including the threat (or actuality) of a strike. To a school board, a "strike" by a nonteacher organization is likely to cause little alarm. But a strike by the teachers is altogether different. The same is true of teacher "slowdowns" or even teacher picketing. The union may also come to have significant local political power, and this may be brought into play.

Processes for Exercise of Governmental Authority

It is one thing to distribute political authority within a system of government and another to specify how—by what processes—it is to be exercised. The processes for exercise of authority, like the distribution of that authority, may be more, or less, democratic in character.

Statutes providing for public sector collective bargaining do not merely diminish democracy by redistributing political authority—the public's right of representational self-determination—to private, nonelected entities called unions (and to arbitrators). The statutes additionally diminish democracy by instituting nondemocratic processes for the exercise of governmental authority. The statutes generally modify preexisting democratic processes (1) to enable private, nonelected entities—unions—to participate in the exercise of governmental authority in accordance with the traditional mode of union functioning, namely, collective bargaining and its corollaries; and (2) to *require* elected public officials and their appointees to exercise much of their governmental authority only via these modes of union functioning.

Again, virtually all would agree that the making and administering of public law (and policy) and public budgets constitutes the exercise of governmental authority. It follows that the processes for the exercise of such authority are essentially governmental too. Furthermore, in the absence of collective bargaining statutes, these processes would themselves be (and by law) democratic in character. Thus, in the absence of collective bargaining, governmental units such as school boards would usually be required by law to exercise their public authority to make laws, policy, and budgets in accord with procedures (often legally prescribed) generally having the following features:

- Only duly elected officials could vote.

- Issues to be voted on would be defined (with or without discussion) by administrators, board members, or some member of the public.

- The public would often (though not always) have advance notice of at least the important issues to be voted on.

- There would usually be considerable opportunity for interested members of the public and for board members to gather information and hear opinions prior to voting.

- As to important matters, some form of parliamentary procedure would be followed with its provisions for amendment of and deliberation on proposals.

- At least on important issues, there would usually be opportunity for opponents and proponents to use publicity, media, and other means to rally public support.

- Final votes by board members would be taken, with the principle of majority rule controlling.

- Resulting rules and policy would be embodied in minutes, board rules and regulations, policy statements, or the like.

With respect to budgetary matters, important issues would also at least be subject to procedures of the foregoing kind, and in many places the law would provide as well for a public vote on the budget. With respect to the interpretation and administration of law and budgets thus made, the story is somewhat different. Generally, interpretation and administration would be left entirely in the hands of administrators appointed by the board, subject to some review by the full board in "policy"-related matters. Of course, administrators might consult in advance with board members and with informal teacher groups. There is scope for great variety here, and most generalizations are hazardous.

We may justly focus on *procedures* of the foregoing kinds for creating public law and policy (including budgets, to some extent). The values such procedures are designed to protect are important democratic values—"process" values. One of these values has already been introduced: self-determination of the public through its elected representatives (rather than autocratic determination by a dictator or a private syndicate). Note that the democratic lawmaking procedures outlined above provide for voting only by those who are elected by the public. Thus, any departure from this norm puts the process value of public self-determination in jeopardy.

The departures from the foregoing democratic law- and policymaking procedures (including budgetary ones) wrought by bargaining statutes put other vital democratic process values at risk too. The two most important of these are public participation and fairness to those who lose on an issue of importance to them. The various procedures outlined earlier generally afford the public notice and an opportunity to be heard. This opportunity and its actual exercise are prizeable regardless of outcome. The potential and actual involvement of the public, in the functioning of its governmental processes, is one of the hallmarks of a healthy democracy. Beyond the process value of participation there is also the process value of fairness to the losing side. This value, too, is independent of outcome. If a bad outcome is reached by a process in which the losers are not accorded a fair opportunity to be heard on a matter of genuine significance, then we have a double, not a single, vice: a bad outcome and a process that is, in democratic terms, unfair.

To be sure, when legislators passed public sector bargaining statutes, they were not asked also to abolish democratic procedures applicable to the functioning of governmental units such as school boards. Such procedures (insofar as they were themselves embodied in statutory or local law) were not explicitly modified. Indeed, if advocates of public sector bargaining had openly asked legislators explicitly to modify these procedures in all the ways required fully to accommodate the intrinsic demands of collective bargaining, it is almost certain that far fewer public sector bargaining statutes would have been adopted.

It will be recalled that public sector bargaining statutes merely state that with respect to "terms and conditions of employment" of public employees, the order of the day would now be collective bargaining and its corollaries. Proponents of bargaining thus claimed that unions would not be engaged in making or administering public laws and budgets. They would only be engaging in collective bargaining over terms and conditions of employment, just as do employees in the private sector. Again, this "argument" trades in labels and ignores reality.

We have already seen that the bargaining statutes carve out vast segments of the legislative, budgetary, and administrative jurisdiction of democratic governmental units and subject the issues thus carved out to a *process* of codetermination through bargaining with private unions. We may now look more closely at the process of collective bargaining itself and consider how it and its intrinsic demands inherently conflict with the process values of public participation and fairness—and thus further diminish democracy.

Public sector bargaining statutes require that relevant governmental units bargain with the union involved. Thus, for example, in the school setting, the statutes require that such vital matters as length of school year, length of school day, class size, teacher recruitment policies, and salaries be decided upon through negotiations with private unions. This requirement implicitly excludes third parties, including the general public, yet the democratic process values relevant there—participation and fairness—are ones to be realized by the public. Of course, it might seem possible to have "multilateral" (school board/union/public) rather than merely "bilateral" (school board/union) collective bargaining. This, however, would be inconsistent with the inner logic of union negotiations, in which two-sided trading with respect to proposals is called for and would very likely be unworkable.

Although relatively few statutes (or court decisions so far) state that collective bargaining *must* take place in secret behind closed doors, this is in fact the usual practice. Moreover, leading labor experts insist that this is the only way the process can really work effectively, given its nature.[4] (It remains to be seen how the process will work in the tiny handful of states that have recently required public sector negotiations to take place in public.) The secret making of public laws, policies, and budgets *ipso facto* thwarts the public and thus drastically delimits the opportunity for members of the public to realize such process values as participation and fairness. It is no answer to say that board members are kept informed of the course of negotiations between the board's chief

---

[4]For further discussion of the intrinsic demands of bargaining, see, in particular, the remarks of Harold Newman, chairman of the New York State Public Employment Relations Board, in: R. Doherty. *Public access citizens and collective bargaining in the public schools.* Ithaca, N.Y.: New York State School of Industrial & Labor Relations, Cornell University, 1979; 8-10, 26-7, 52-3.

negotiator and union leaders. The relevant process values are those of the general public, not the board. Without notice and an opportunity to be heard, the public cannot realize these values.

Also, collective bargaining is often prolonged. Whether this is to some extent intrinsic to the process is not wholly clear. Certainly there are numerous features of the process that tend to prolong it, not least of which are (1) the tendency for the negotiators to "test" and "re-test" each other; (2) the tendency of participants to review and reconsider various aspects of what is, of course, an interrelated agreement during each negotiating session; and (3) the common tactic of one side trying to wear the other down. Whatever the degree to which delay is intrinsic, the fact is that the process is ordinarily drawn out, and this wears down those members of the public who try to "follow it." Changes of mind on the part of the negotiators may also cause these members of the public to lose heart. There simply are limits on the extent to which members of the public can be expected to give of their time and attention even when significant process values are at stake. It is hardly an answer to say that the public is without right to complain when members of the public choose not to persevere. Alternative modes of making public law and budgets in the absence of bargaining do not similarly wear the public down.

For an opportunity to appear and be heard to be meaningful, the public participants must feel, too, that what they say will be seriously considered by those before whom they appear. Yet, if what they are saying to a board or at an open bargaining session conflicts with union interests or proposals, it is not likely to be taken seriously at the bargaining table unless there is a showing of support for what the public participants are saying. Although the school board may take what public members say seriously, the board also knows that the union has special legal status in the negotiations, and that even without the right to strike, the union ultimately may resort to that weapon. (Many labor experts also claim that genuine collective bargaining cannot work without the right to strike.) A realization that unions have such leverage is almost certain to leave some members of the public with a diminished sense of the value of an opportunity to participate in a public meeting devoted to negotiations.

Impasse resolution procedures provided in bargaining statutes also reveal deep tension between collective bargaining and the realization of democratic process values. These procedures are designed to come into play when negotiations falter and call for mediators, fact-finders, and even arbitrators to come into action. Some such procedures are intrinsic to collective bargaining, at least if it be assumed that bilateral negotiations alone will not always produce agreements. Yet, not only are these procedures normally conducted behind closed doors and without publicity; the governmental unit is not entitled to act on its own until these procedures have run their course. That the necessity (under the statutes) of following these procedures can seriously interfere with *all* relevant democratic values may be seen from the following simple illustration.

Assume that all voting members of a small school district gather in the gymnasium during a fuel crisis and vote to instruct the school board (which unanimously concurs) to change the hours of the school day to conserve fuel. If the teachers union insists on its rights under the usual impasse resolution statutes, the union would be entitled to delay and thus frustrate this public decision, at least until the impasse resolution procedures have run their course.

In some states, impasse resolution procedures call, with respect to certain groups, for compulsory arbitration.[5] This is the very antithesis of democratic self-determination. Issues formerly resolved entirely by publicly elected bodies or their appointees are resolved instead by functionaries who are neither elected by nor in any way accountable to the public.

Observe that the conflict between the *processes* of collective bargaining and the realization of democratic process values of community self-determination, public participation, and fairness to the losing side, is, in substantial measure, an inherent conflict. No empirical studies are required to confirm this conflict. It can be seen merely by comparing the nature of the procedures required for the realization of these values with the more or less intrinsic demands of collective bargaining as a process. As we have seen, these demands impinge, at a variety of points and in varying degrees, on the procedures required to secure the realization of democratic process values. Further, the conflict is demonstrable without comparing levels of public participation prior to the advent of collective bargaining with levels thereafter.

Again, it is important to anticipate and respond to several likely counterarguments. First, proponents of collective bargaining may reply that the general public will always get an adequate opportunity to be

---

[5] This is true, for example, in New York. See N.Y. Civ. Serv. Law (McKinney) § 209 (4).

heard at the very end of the process when the school board is called upon to review and vote on the entire proposed collective bargaining agreement that the board's chief negotiator has negotiated over the preceding months. In truth, however, if the chief negotiator has been doing his job as he should, he will have secured board approval of significant concessions piecemeal over the course of the negotiations, and the entire agreement will, at this final meeting, be in no sense "up for grabs." Thus, the final meeting will usually not be one in which a majority of the board will be in a posture of open-minded willingness to hear argument directed for or against just any part of the package. Indeed, often the board chairman will be highly concerned that no one from the public say or do anything that will upset the "long fought-out package deal." Of course, there are and will be exceptional cases.

Second, bargainists may argue that since the public's position on a major issue *sometimes* prevails (with the result that even a strike may be "broken"), it follows that democracy remains sufficiently healthy.[6] Admittedly, when such an event occurs, this does, in the circumstances involved, demonstrate that, as to the issue (or issues) involved, the democratic process value of representational self-determination is not only to some extent realized but also vindicated. Yet, it does not follow from this that the other basic democratic process values of public participation and fairness have been similarly realized and vindicated, even as to the issues involved. The public may have all along been effectively excluded from decision making pursuant to collective bargaining norms and corollary impasse resolution norms. Moreover, we should not make too much of the partial realization and vindication of the public's democratic right of representational self-determination in such cases. For every such case, there are numerous others in which this right of the public is greatly watered down by virtue of the necessity of negotiated codetermination of issues or sometimes even superseded by union predominance in the bargaining process.

It is sometimes said that public sector collective bargaining does not and has not significantly altered outcomes compared to what they otherwise would have been or are. Those who take this view may hold that democracy has therefore not been significantly curtailed. We now turn to this topic.

---

[6] For this viewpoint, see, for example, S. Cohen, Does public employee unionism diminish democracy? *Industrial and Labor Relations Review* 32 (1979): 189, 192-95.

Outcomes of Processes for Exercise of Governmental Authority

Does public sector collective bargaining alter the outcomes of exercises of government authority? And what, if any, bearing does the answer to this question have on whether public sector bargaining substantially diminishes democracy?

There is now considerable evidence (some of it necessarily inconclusive) that bargaining changes outcomes from what they would have been in the absence of bargaining.[7] In the school setting, for example, there is evidence of substantial impact on the content of relevant public law and policy. There is evidence of budgetary impact too. The influence of bargaining on the interpretation and administration of relevant law and budgets is undeniable. Maintenance of standards provisions and grievance procedures provided in collective bargaining agreements have been vehicles for substituting collective negotiations and arbitration for much of what was formerly administrative interpretation and application of relevant law and budgets.

That collective bargaining generally alters outcomes, often significantly, should surprise no one. This was the primary objective of its proponents. The introduction of public sector bargaining was designed and intended "to make a difference." Under the statutes, the governmental unit is obligated to bargain in good faith. To do this, the unit must be ready to make some trades. To make trades, the unit must move away from the status quo in some respect. Furthermore, if the governmental unit refuses to agree to union proposals within the scope of bargaining, the statutes provide, as we have seen, for "impasse resolution" procedures in which third-party neutrals intervene. For this intervention to be effective—that is, for it to lead to "settlements"—these third parties must work out accommodations that inevitably effectuate *some* union proposals. Legal or not, the threat or actuality of a strike may influence outcomes too. When statutes mandate compulsory arbitration of unresolved issues (as they increasingly do in some areas), the outcomes commonly differ from what they otherwise would have been.

To the extent that public sector collective bargaining does alter outcomes of processes for the exercise of governmental authority, this

---

[7] One of the most recent studies is Charles R. Perry, Teacher bargaining: The experience in nine systems. *Industrial and Labor Relations Review* 33 (1979): 3.

alteration may be attributed mainly to (1) the influence of the nonde-mocratic redistribution of authority that bargaining entails, and (2) the influence of nondemocratic processes for the exercise of the author-ity that bargaining entails. It follows that the public, with respect to the altered outcomes, does not enjoy a full democratic right of self-determination through its elected representatives and their appointees.

As we have seen, even if outcomes are not altered at all, public sec-tor bargaining substantially diminishes democracy, inherently so. Bargaining requires the sharing of governmental authority with private entities. Bargaining—its intrinsic demands—excludes or restricts pub-lic access to law and budgetary processes and reduces opportunities for public influence on those processes. As a result, bargaining sacrifices vital democratic process values: public self-determination through elected representatives, public participation in the exercise of govern-mental authority, and fairness to those members of the public who turn out to be in a minority. Recall that process values are prizeable regard-less of outcomes. Even if outcomes remain as they would have been in the absence of bargaining, these process values are sacrificed under a bargaining statute.

Accountability for Outcomes and for the Functioning of Process

Public sector collective bargaining eliminates or diminishes the accountability of participants in governmental processes for the share of the responsibility for outcomes and for the way the processes func-tion. Bargaining, therefore, diminishes democracy in a further funda-mental way. Accountability is a vital democratic process value.[8] It helps secure and is a corollary of the process value of public self-determination through elected representatives.

How does public sector collective bargaining eliminate or diminish accountability? First, it redistributes governmental authority to one major participant—the union—which is not publicly accountable at all for its actions. Under a bargaining statute, the voters of a school

---

[8] Almost all students of democracy agree on this. See, e.g., J. Lucas, *Democracy* (London: Penguin Books, 1976); C. Cohen, *Democracy* (New York: Free Press, 1971); R. Dahl, *A pref-ace to democratic theory* (Chicago: University of Chicago Press, 1956).

district, for example, do not elect a union, nor can they vote a union "out of office" after it has successfully negotiated a collective bargaining agreement objectionable to the voters. This particular law-making and budget-creating entity is neither elected by nor accountable to the public. Even if the voters do vote out the school board or part of it, the union remains in place, and so, too, the objectionable collective agreement. Indeed, even if the voters vote in an entirely new board, the board will not have authority under the usual bargaining statute to repeal the objectionable agreement. That can only be done term by term through future collective negotiations with the union. This is not true, however, in the absence of collective bargaining. Where the governmental agency is not thus hamstrung, the public voice can be heard and translated into action. Existing law, policy, and budgetary matters can be amended, altered, even repealed, more or less freely, in accord with democratic will (to the extent feasible).

It may be argued that at least the publicly elected officials can be voted out, and that this is sufficient. As already indicated, this is not sufficient to afford the public full accountability for past actions of the bargainers where "accountability" does not include relief from those actions. Furthermore, a bargaining setup significantly diminishes the extent to which the public can effectively vote out and thus hold to account even those participants in the process who are elected officials. The *bargaining* process itself affords such an official a whole range of excuses for voting as he or she did—excuses that may distinctively blunt or deflect public criticism—and thus influences voting. These excuses include the following: "But if I had voted the other way, there would have been a strike or serious disruption—our alternatives were limited"; "A deal with the union had to be negotiated as a package— there were some things I liked and some I didn't, but I didn't have the choice to vote for *one at a time*—I had only the choice of voting on them in the context of the parts of the package then being negotiated."

Beyond potentially credible excuses of the foregoing nature that are peculiarly attributable to the bargaining process and which may blur the lines of accountability and thus "save" an official from recall at the polls, the bargaining process undermines other conditions required for ready accountability at the polls. The public may find it difficult, given the extended and nonpublic nature of the process, to accumulate reliable evidence of the piecemeal votes of officials over the course of the bargaining process. The public may be left only with the final general votes of approval or disapproval of the entire package embodied in the proposed collective bargaining agreement. Yet, at this stage, the demands of the bargaining process require that the entire package *not* be up for grabs. At least a majority of board members will, at this point, be more or less "committed." Although it may still be possible and justified to vote them out for having come to this position, the process itself could not work efficiently if such a state of affairs (majority board support on at least a number of matters prior to final vote) could not be achieved. It is possible that some voters perceive this predicament of the majority and decline later to vote them out partly because of it.

Lack of information, lack of clear-cut issues, and the availability to officials of bargaining-generated excuses, then, all combine to diminish the accountability of public officials who are forced by statute to make and administer public law and budgets through collective bargaining (and its corollaries). Moreover, the other major partner to the process—the union itself—is not publicly accountable at all.

It may be argued, however, that as to monetary issues, the public can always hold the governmental unit accountable through public votes on the budget. This, however, is not the safeguard it is often presumed to be. First, it is a safeguard only when provided by law, and it is not generally provided for except in the field of public school education. Second, even within education, not all districts vote on the annual budget. Third, of those that do, often important monetary issues (including the salary feature) are still subject to negotiations at the time of voting. Fourth, a great deal of organized effort may be required to vote down a budget, and it is at best a "blunderbuss tool."

Conclusions

In all the foregoing ways, then, public employee collective bargaining diminishes democracy. It is not good for society in still other respects too.[9] We have not yet told the whole story, even with respect to democracy.

---

[9]For discussion of some of the other respects in which public sector unionism is not good for society, see R. Summers, *Collective bargaining and public benefit conferral: A jurisprudential critique.* (Ithaca, N.Y.: New York State School of Industrial and Labor Relations, Cornell University, (1976); chs. 2,3,5.

The most objectionable counterdemocratic feature of bargaining may be that it undermines the conditions required for healthy democratic governance throughout society. Democracy depends on such "citizen" virtues as public spiritedness and willingness to participate in community affairs. Yet, public sector bargaining does not lead to the nurture and cultivation of these virtues. On the contrary, it stifles them, and at the grass roots level. Indeed, bargaining, especially when itself solemnly enshrined in public statutes, authenticates and positively symbolizes a fundamentally nondemocratic mode of decision making—a form of interest group syndicalism (however peaceful).

In this essay, little has been said about the strike, and it is true that most states do not legally permit public employee strikes. Before noting the bearing of strikes and strike threats on democracy, it is important to stress that in the public sector there is a more apt name for this kind of occurrence, namely, public benefit discontinuation (or some form thereof). When strikes do occur—and bargaining laws have made them far more frequent—the very functions of government are eliminated (or put at risk). The public is often denied governmental goods and services. This is the very antithesis of democratic self-determination of peoples. The *discontinuation of public benefits, whether the union ultimately achieves its ends or not, diminishes social morale and leaves citizens with a sense of powerlessness that can only erode public spirit.* The strike—especially the successful one contrary to law—may also teach social lessons, especially for the young. Indeed, it may even teach that democracy is a low-priority value.

The undemocratic character of *public sector* collective bargaining (as well as other objectionable features) is only now being clearly perceived. Many factors account for the delay: a false analogy to private sector labor relations; an egalitarian preoccupation with according equal rights (and power of control) to all types of employees, public as well as private; a belief that just any social process can be engrafted upon almost any other social process without significant sacrifice (or structural change); and, perhaps above all else, the blinding and self-deluding influence of labelistic thinking.

The illegitimate tyranny of labels is so powerful in political life that it may be instructive to set forth by means of contrasting columns the comprehensive set of labels drawn from the world of unionism and collective bargaining that cloaked—and, for many, still cloak—the substitution of public employee unionism for democratic governance:

Democratic Governance	*Public Employee Unionism*
Democracy	"Public sector"
Government agency	"Management"
Government employees	"Union"
Citizens	"Consumers"
Legislative and budgetary jurisdiction	"Terms and conditions"
Public law and policy	"The bargaining agreement"
Public administration	"Grievance arbitration"
Public debate and deliberation on public issues	"With respect to terms"
Political decision making and public compromise	"Impasse resolution"
Benefit discontinuation	"Strike"

Whether the future holds the immediate prospect of widespread repeal of bargaining statutes is difficult to say. The very institutionalization of such a process imports its own self-sustaining norms and entrenches supporting interests—interests that include not merely union members but statewide union lobbies and state public employment relations boards.[10] Nonetheless, we may hope that the recent and continuing efforts to restore democratic authority and procedures in a few states signify the beginnings of a promising trend.

---

[10] Indeed, arguments are now sometimes even made against democracy on the ground that it interferes with collective bargaining. See, for example, R. Doherty, ed., *Public access: Citizens and collective bargaining in the public schools* (Ithaca, N.Y.: New York State School of Industrial and Labor Relations, Cornell University, 1979); 8-10, 25-7, 52-3.

10.   REFLECTIONS ON THE RATIONALES FOR TEACHER BARGAINING

At least since 1959, teachers unions have tried to enact state legislation providing collective bargaining rights for teachers. In the 1960s and '70s, the National Education Association (NEA) and its state affiliates sought to enact legislation that applied only to teachers. This approach was eventually abandoned in favor of legislation that covered all school district employees. Subsequently, the legislative objective was coverage of most state and local public employees.

One reason was that both the NEA and the American Federation of Teachers (AFT) began to organize nonteaching employees, thus making bargaining rights for them a higher priority. Also, the NEA and the AFT sought to organize faculty in higher education, who were not covered by legislation applicable only to K-12 teachers. In addition, the rationale for state legislation usually included the contention that it was inequitable to grant private sector employees bargaining rights but not teachers. Advocacy of bargaining rights only for teachers appeared to be special pleading for them in relation to other public sector employees.

The AFT always supported broad coverage, but it took some time before the NEA and its affiliates adopted this position. Today, however, the two teachers unions are the most influential supporters of state legislation providing bargaining rights for state and local public employees. To be sure, this reflects the fact that teachers are the largest group of employees affected by such legislation.

This chapter is a slightly modified version of an article by Myron Lieberman under the same title in *Government Union Review* 13: 2 (Spring 1992).

The first state bargaining law applicable to teachers to remain on the statute books was enacted in Wisconsin in 1962. Thus, we have had more than 30 years of experience under one or more state teacher bargaining statutes, ample time to test and assess the rationale(s) asserted when the legislation was enacted. These rationales are still being cited to justify bargaining legislation in states that have not enacted it. For this reason, the issues are relevant in states that have not enacted bargaining laws as well as in those that have enacted some type of public sector bargaining legislation.

Perhaps the most cited and most persuasive argument for public sector bargaining has been the appeal to equality. Private sector employees have bargaining rights; if public sector employees do not, there is, or appears to be, an inequity. Thus, the teachers unions lobby for legislation that will end their "second-class citizenship."

In making this argument, the teachers unions, like public sector unions generally, assume that collective bargaining in the private sector is sound policy. We shall not argue the contrary in this discussion but simply note that the assumption is a debatable one. Debatable or not, it is irrelevant to the equality argument, so we shall focus on the latter.

Practically and legally, employment in and between sectors reflects a mix of advantages and disadvantages. For example, no one argues that military personnel should be governed by the same policies that govern civilian employees, who can quit any time for any reason. Similarly, in the private sector, some employees, such as attorneys, are subject to disclosure requirements that do not apply to all private sector employees. Nevertheless, we do not usually isolate these obligations and refer to them as "inequities."

In practice, we compensate for the disadvantages associated with various fields of employment. Soldiers cannot quit at will, but they receive numerous benefits that compensate them for this constraint. Theoretically, compensation for limits placed on their freedoms might be too generous instead of too little; there is no way to decide except by looking at the total compensation package.

Viewed in this way—and we do not see any other sensible way to consider it—the equality rationale is contradicted by a wealth of evidence. In their totality, terms and conditions of public sector employment are consistently superior to the private sector in every state. Even in states in which public school teachers do not have bargaining rights, their conditions of employment are superior to those of private school teachers, even when the latter have bargaining rights. Many studies comparing public to private sector employment involving the same kind of work have reached similar conclusions.

Why Public Sector School Employment Pays More

What explains the consistent superiority of public over private school employment? One reason is that in the private sector, employment is generally "at will"; that is, with no contract to the contrary, either the employer or the employee can terminate the employment relationship at any time, no matter how long that relationship has been in effect. This is not the case, however, in the public sector. As the result of various U.S. Supreme Court decisions, public employees who have an expectancy of continued employment have acquired a property interest in their position. They cannot be deprived of this property interest in the absence of due process of law. In other words, public sector employees, even without bargaining rights, enjoy constitutional protections against dismissal not available to private sector employees.

The reality is that the presence—not the absence—of public sector bargaining constitutes a gross inequality. This inequality, in fact, favors public sector employees. This is evident if we consider equality from a political perspective. Conceptually, every citizen has equal rights to participate in the public policymaking process. Public sector bargaining, however, constitutes a flagrant exception in both theory and practice. When a school board agrees to a contract with a teachers union, the agreement is public policy for its duration. As a matter of fact, teachers unions often propose that such language be included in the contract. The fact that the contracts cover terms and conditions of employment does not negate their status as public policies. A teacher salary schedule is a public policy just as surely as is a school board policy on discipline, graduation requirements, or curriculum.

Rhetoric aside, the salary policy is the result of negotiations between the school board and the one interest group with the largest stake in the negotiations. The inequality is manifest if we envisage a similar process in other public services. Suppose housing policies were to be resolved by negotiations between housing authorities and the contractors—

negotiations from which other interested parties were excluded. Suppose further that once the housing authority agreed to a housing policy, it could not change its position unilaterally without being guilty of "an unfair housing practice," i.e., a legally prohibited practice. In that case, everyone would recognize instantly that the procedure provided contractors with major advantages over other citizens.

Why is this basic inequality not recognized for what it is? The answer was perceptively stated by Robert S. Summers in 1980: Public sector bargaining is described and discussed in bargaining terminology, and because this terminology conceals its inherent political nature, it also conceals the political inequalities it creates.[1]

To illustrate this point, suppose the teachers union announces that it will strike at 7 a.m. Monday unless it has a contract by that time. The union also states that it is willing and even eager to bargain around the clock in order to reach an agreement by its self-imposed deadline. In an effort to avert a strike, union and board representatives bargain on Sunday and through the morning hours on Monday. At 6 a.m. Monday, say, the union and the school board reach an agreement that averts a strike. In most situations, such an outcome would be regarded as evidence that "bargaining works" if the parties make a good-faith effort to reach agreement.

What has happened here? Stripped of collective bargaining rhetoric, the parties have been swapping public policies in the middle of the night without any opportunity for others to participate in the policymaking process. True, this often happens at the end of legislative sessions, but the differences are crucial. No interest group is favored by law or has any inside track as a matter of law or policy in end-of-the-session tradeoffs. In contrast, bargaining statutes explicitly provide the teachers unions with unique access to the policymaking process, even when unavoidable deadlines are not involved.

In effect, the teachers union in the example has announced, "Unless we receive an acceptable offer by 7 a.m. Monday, we are going to shut down a public service." No other group of citizens or private organization has this right or this power over the policymaking process. Ordinary citizens are not entitled to shut down a public service until public officials adopt policies deemed acceptable to the citizens. Again, the

---

[1] Robert S. Summers, Public sector collective bargaining substantially diminishes democracy, *Government Union Review* 1:1, 5-22 (Winter 1980).

inequity is overlooked because the issues are formulated and discussed in bargaining terminology instead of terms applicable to public policymaking.

Under bargaining, employers are prohibited from changing terms and conditions of employment unless they have either obtained the union's agreement to the changes or have bargained on them to the conclusion of the impasse procedure. In the public sector, this means that public sector unions have veto powers over changes in public policy until the impasse procedures are exhausted. Inasmuch as these procedures can take a long time, union veto power may also prevail for a long time. Not surprisingly, public sector unions use the time to develop opposition to changes opposed by the unions.

The Protection of Tenure

Still another aspect of the equality issue should be noted. In the private sector, employees who strike do so at risk of losing their jobs. The AFL-CIO's major legislative priority is legislation that would prohibit or limit employer rights to employ permanent replacements for strikers. Obviously, the risks of striking vary from industry to industry, company to company, and situation to situation. Nevertheless, from a public policy perspective, employers in the private sector can hire permanent replacements if that is necessary to maintain company operations.

This is not the case in public education. Most teachers enjoy the protection of tenure laws. In most states, efforts to fire teachers for striking would have to comply with the procedures and standards spelled out in the tenure laws. This would be virtually impossible in many states and school districts. Teachers could claim illness or take personal leave or otherwise disclaim personal responsibility for not appearing for work. In fact, teachers unions adopted the slogan "no contract, no work" precisely in anticipation of this issue. If teachers refused to work without a contract, their leaders could avoid the penalties associated with leading a strike. Furthermore, it would be difficult to identify any strike leader if teachers simply failed to report for work in the absence of a contract.

In addition, legislation in virtually all states requires that schools be open a certain number of days in order to receive state aid. Thus, in most cases, the school board reschedules the days lost because of a strike; consequently, teachers do not lose any income by going on strike. In contrast, private sector employees often risk loss of income, if not their jobs, by striking.

Furthermore, legal restrictions on teacher strikes are not necessarily a deterrent to them. Whether they are or not depends on several factors, but especially on whether the illegality is based on judicial decision or statutory prohibitions. Even if based on the latter, however, teacher strikes may occur almost as frequently as if they were expressly legitimized by statute.

Most emphatically, we are not asserting that legal prohibitions against teacher strikes are futile. Our point is that their effectiveness depends on their legal basis and the penalties, if any, applicable to striking teachers.

State legislators sometimes sponsor bargaining laws that explicitly provide that strikes by public employees are illegal. The proposed legislation, however, does not include any penalties for public employees who were on strike. In order to end a public employee strike, public officials must obtain a restraining order prohibiting the strike. The proposed legislation (or judicial decision) may provide that only "equitable relief" be awarded. "Equitable relief" is a term of art; supposedly, only parties who come to court with "clean hands" are entitled to it. Needless to say, the striking unions will assert that the school board has not bargained in good faith or that it has committed some foul act that negates its request for "equitable relief."

In teacher strikes, the first few days are usually decisive. Most strikes are settled within a day or two; very few last longer. Typically, parents, inconvenienced by a strike, pressure the school board to settle, not because the board positions are wrong but because school board is the most vulnerable to pressure to end an undesirable situation. Thus, in the normal course of events, a teacher strike would be over by the time the school board obtained an injunction against the strike. In short, even a statutory prohibition of teacher strikes is no assurance that teacher strikes will not occur frequently. Indeed, the "prohibition" is often formulated in ways that ensure its futility.

More important, the harm done by teacher strikes and strike threats is not the number, frequency, or duration of strikes, but rather in the concessions boards make in order to avert strikes. No one has added up these costs, but by any sensible way of estimation, they must be enormous.

The 'Only Procedural' Rationale

Still another rationale that has been asserted since the 1960s is that teacher bargaining is "only procedural." Bargaining statutes usually include specific language to the effect that the parties are not legally required to agree to proposals or to make concessions. Consequently, the argument is that bargaining ensures only that the teachers' point of view will be heard. Another version is that bargaining ensures teacher "participation" in the policymaking process. Presumably, no sensible person opposes "participation."

Here again, a brief look at the facts exposes major deficiencies in this rationale. Unlike any other group of citizens, teachers are physically present in the schools. They attend grade level, subject, building, and district level meetings—surely ample opportunities to express their views. In addition, teachers unions usually send a representative to attend school board meetings; whether they do or not, they are not legally or practically disadvantaged in this forum. Indeed, school boards often give preferential procedural treatment to union representatives at board meetings. Typically, unions also consult on a regular basis "on matters of mutual concern." Actually, union bargaining proposals typically limit the number and duration of teachers meetings and teacher participation in school-sponsored evening or after-school affairs. The real problem is not any legal or practical lack of teacher opportunities to participate in policymaking or to express their views; it is their overwhelming domination of the policymaking process.

The procedural rationale for teacher bargaining also overlooks the dynamics of bargaining. The union typically initiates the process by submitting a long list of demands, perhaps 100 or more. The school board is not legally obligated to accept any particular proposals, but a refusal to accept any is quite a different matter, both legally and from a public relations standpoint. In that case, the board negotiators appear "hard-nosed" or worse; presumably, they are not "bargaining in good faith." Surely, if they are, they could accept some of the many union proposals.

From the union perspective, the failure to reach an agreement or to make progress toward an agreement must be the board's fault. The union obviously cannot agree that its unreasonable proposals and failure to make concessions are the reasons there is no progress toward a contract. Instead, the board's refusal to bargain in good faith must be the reason, and it must be exposed. Furthermore, it is difficult to achieve concessions if the teachers appear indifferent to union demands. Of necessity, therefore, union strategy must generate teacher support for union proposals when such support is not forthcoming spontaneously.

Another important difference between public and private sector bargaining comes into play here. When teacher bargaining legislation was first being considered, it was widely assumed that teachers did not—and should not—have the right to strike. Union lobbyists argued that teacher inability to strike would undermine the effectiveness of bargaining legislation. Supposedly, school boards could simply say no until the impasse procedures were exhausted, and then the teachers and their unions would have to accept whatever crumbs the boards were willing to offer.

In response to this union argument, state legislatures frequently enacted lengthy, complex impasse procedures that include mediation, fact-finding, and/or interest arbitration in one form or another. These procedures often require several months, sometimes a year or more. Meanwhile, the union posture in the schools and school districts has to be that school board obstinacy and refusals to bargain in good faith are the obstacles to an agreement.

In the private sector, bargaining is largely over economic issues dominated by economic considerations. This is not so in the public sector. There, bargaining is a political contest, decided by political and public opinion factors. If bargaining is protracted, the parties must constantly appeal to public opinion to prevail. The upshot is that teacher bargaining institutionalizes conflict and unrest in school districts.

At any given time, a school board might make an unwise concession in order to end the conflict. Unfortunately, the end is only temporary. What counts is not what the school board has done for teachers lately; it is what it is doing for teachers today. When funding is tight, the unions assert they must have some noneconomic benefits to satisfy their members.

These benefits usually turn out to be new restrictions on managerial discretion. Thus, over time, the school administration loses the ability to manage district operations. Few board members are able to stand up against the constant pounding they take in bargaining. This is especially true if, as so often happens, their position on the board is due to union support.

In other ways, the dynamics affect bargaining in ways that tend to convert the "procedure" into substantive concessions to the unions. School superintendents naturally try to avoid conflict. When their tenure in office is weak, conflict with the union is a real threat to their ability to keep their jobs. In many situations, superintendents can easily make concessions whose costs are not immediately visible to the school board or to the public. The concessions can be rationalized in several ways; often, it is not even necessary to explain them because the board and public do not understand their implications.

In short, the notion that bargaining is "only procedural" seems plausible only to those who are not familiar with the process. Its plausibility derives partly from the fact that it is not always possible to identify the substantive concessions that result from the procedural benefits bargaining confers on teachers unions. Nonetheless, the appeal to "procedure" and to "participation" lacks theoretical as well as empirical justification.

Unable to maintain the early gains made against naive boards of education, union leaders looked elsewhere to sustain the progress needed to placate a membership always on the lookout for increased benefits. The most obvious targets for benefit increases were to be found in the political realm. For decades, union lobbyists achieved success at the state level, forging new benefits for their membership through legislation. The next logical step was to attempt to control local politicians. Board of education members who opposed union pressure tactics seemed a likely target. After achieving considerable success at eliminating individual recalcitrant board members, unions sought the election of entire slates of school board members. These efforts are often successful, even though they reflect a conflict of interest. They also erode the idea of equality in bargaining as school administrators are pressured by their own board members to accede to union demands.

Superintendents of schools sometimes have been dismissed because of their strong opposition to unreasonable union demands. As a result, many superintendents are very reluctant to oppose such demands. Others embrace "shared decision making" and see or claim to see union leaders as partners and not adversaries.

Indeed, perhaps the most discouraging aspect of the situation is the way in which teacher bargaining has been institutionalized and rationalized by the parties who are in the best position to recognize its undesirable consequences.

11. TEACHER BARGAINING RECONSIDERED

Since 1962, collective bargaining has sometimes been sold to legislatures and school boards on a "try it, you'll like it" basis. Others simply inherited bargaining as a fixture on the educational scene, just as its absence was taken for granted in an earlier era. Regardless of how bargaining is presented, however, there is one crucial difference between the present situation and the 1960s: We now have a wealth of experience to guide us. What was advocated or opposed in the 1960s on the basis of logic or intuition or speculation or analogy can be tested today against a body of experience. Today, we know how collective bargaining in education differs from collective bargaining in the private sector. The differences are real and important, justifying the conclusion that providing public employees collective bargaining rights similar to those in the provided private is undesirable public policy.

In the 1960s, the appeal to "equity" was the major public policy justification for teacher bargaining. Without bargaining rights, teachers, like other public employees, are allegedly second-class citizens. Privately employed guards can unionize and strike; those publicly employed cannot. Bus drivers for a privately owned company can strike; if the same routes were taken over and operated as a public utility, the drivers could not bargain or strike. Similarly, teachers in private schools can organize and bargain; those in public schools cannot.

Some sections of this chapter, by Myron Lieberman, originally appeared under the title of Eggs I have laid: Teacher bargaining reconsidered, in the *Phi Delta Kappan,* February 1979.

For the sake of argument, let us agree that teachers ought to have "equity" with private sector employees. To assess the equity argument objectively, however, we must consider all the crucial differences between public and private sector employment, not just the absence of bargaining rights in public education. Among these, one of the most important is that teachers often play an important role in determining who is management. For example, teachers organizations are frequently active in school board elections. In some situations, they have a decisive influence on who is elected. In contrast, private sector employees have no legal or practical role in selecting management, and it would ordinarily be futile for them to try to attain one.

At least in some jurisdictions, the political influence of teachers on public management has been extremely advantageous to teachers. This influence affects not only what is proposed, accepted, rejected, and modified, but the timing of concessions, the management posture toward grievances, and the extent of management support services for bargaining. Sometimes, even the choice of management negotiator is subject to an unofficial but effective teacher veto.

In this connection, teacher opportunities to influence the election of state officials must also be considered. Of course, private sector employees have equal opportunities to influence or to elect such officials. The point is, however, that state officials seldom affect the context or substance of private sector bargaining. Typically, the governor of a state has no role in collective bargaining for private sector employees. Such bargaining is regulated by the National Labor Relations Board, a federal agency. On the other hand, governors frequently play a decisive role in whether there is to be public sector bargaining at all, and if there is, in such matters as the scope of bargaining, the nature of unfair labor practices, the relationship of bargaining to budgetary schedules, the impasse procedures, and the balance of bargaining power between the parties. In addition, governors often play a crucial role in substantive matters subject to bargaining. For example, the governor typically is the most important single individual in the annual aid-to-education controversy. Because states provide nearly half of public school revenues, the gubernatorial role is much more important to teachers than it is to most private sector unions. For teachers, as for other local public employees, the implications are obvious. Political activity at the state level pays the teacher a larger dividend than it does the factory worker or the farmer.

To be sure, every group has the right to use the ballot box to advance its interests; the point is that the opportunity to do so is more advantageous to teachers than to private sector employees. Understandably, state teacher associations typically are among the most influential state interest groups.

Political Dimensions of Public Sector Employment

The political dimension of public sector employment works to the advantage of teachers in several different ways. For example, turnover is greater in public than in private sector management. More important, private sector management tends to have a greater direct and personal stake in resisting unreasonable union demands, particularly those having to do with pension and retirement benefits, an area in which public management frequently achieves bargaining agreements by being excessively generous. Because such concessions may not require any immediate tax increase, management officials responsible for the agreement can be heroes to public employees for being generous and to the public for not raising taxes. Unfortunately, the practice saddles taxpayers with enormously expensive long-range commitments. Significantly, the tendency to "end-load" agreements this way has become evident in local, state, and federal agreements. It is difficult to see the equity in requiring private sector employees to provide retirement benefits for public employees that greatly exceed their own, but that is the present situation.

Another crucial point is that public management has fewer incentives than private management to resist union demands. If private sector management makes a concession that impairs the long-range profitability of an enterprise, this fact is reflected immediately in the value of the company. Thus, unlike public sector management, private sector management cannot avoid immediate accountability for agreement to excessive deferred benefits. Although these observations are subject to exceptions and qualifications, they reflect a significant teacher advantage over private sector employees.

The major disadvantage of public employees relates to revenue-raising and ratification procedures. Normally, a private sector employer can negotiate an agreement without public or political opposition. When the employer representative signs the agreement, the employer is bound. Raising revenue and ratification by a public agency can be more difficult, and the difficulties may serve as a brake on what management is willing to do. For example, a school board may be unwilling to face the opposition to higher taxes needed for justified increases in teacher compensation.

Nevertheless, even on this issue, teachers unions have some advantages. The school board's financial situation is known to the union, as is the board's "maneuver room" on financial issues. Indeed, union representatives are sometimes more knowledgeable than school administrators about the district budget. We are not advocating secrecy in government, but merely wish to point out that teachers have an inherent advantage over private sector employees with respect to their information needs concerning the employer's financial situation.

Another tactical advantage of teachers is that they have very little, if any, obligation of loyalty to their employer. In contrast, private sector employees are under some obligation not to damage the employer. In the context of a labor dispute, private sector employees can urge the public not to purchase the employer's product or service, but otherwise their rights to criticize the employer's product or service are limited in ways that do not apply to teachers. Again, we are not advocating restrictions on the right of teachers to criticize school boards and administrators. The fact is, however, that teachers enjoy legal rights to criticize their employers that exceed such rights in the private sector. Needless to say, this is an advantage over private sector employment, especially in view of the political dimensions of teacher bargaining.

The fact that a public enterprise cannot move physically constitutes still another advantage of public sector employees. Again, although the employer's ability to move varies from industry to industry and within industries, the inability of school boards to relocate as a response to employee pressure is obviously advantageous to teachers. In the private sector, multinational corporations have even resisted unionization successfully by moving certain operations from one country to another. Sometimes, the threat of doing so helps to moderate union demands. On the other hand, Chicago schools cannot be moved to Mexico, or even to Chicago suburbs, in order to avoid excessive demands by the Chicago Teachers Union.

Rights to Due Process

Another major advantage of teachers over private sector employees is that teachers are entitled to certain rights to due process even in the absence of a collective agreement or statutory protection. For example, where teachers have acquired an expectancy of reemployment, they may not be fired without due process. It should be noted that this protection is grounded in the U.S. Constitution, not state statutory enactments. Thus, teachers without bargaining rights frequently have more protection against arbitrary and unjust employer action than do private sector employees with bargaining rights. Teachers sometimes have the benefit of an extensive system of statutory benefits that exceed benefits negotiated in the private sector. In California, for example, teachers and teachers unions have the following benefits, among others, under state law:

- Strong protection against dismissal or suspension
- Ten days of sick leave annually, cumulative without limit
- Right to due process, even as probationary employees
- Substantial notice before termination
- Layoff rights
- Military, bereavement, personal necessity, legislative, industrial accident, and illness leave
- Sweeping protection in evaluation
- Limits on district authority to reduce benefits
- Protection against noncertified employees doing teacher work
- Duty-free lunch periods
- Right to dues deduction
- Right to prompt payment of salary
- Right to notice of school closing
- Protection from legal actions for action in the course of employment
- Protection from being upbraided, insulted, or abused in the presence of pupils
- Limits on the workday and work year.

In the private sector, collective bargaining is the means of self-help to these benefits; bargaining rights were not superimposed on them. Providing bargaining rights in addition to this vast complex of statutory benefits is not equity for teachers; it is more than equity by a wide margin. In the private sector, employees would presumably have had to make various concessions to get these benefits, if they got them at all. In California, as in many other states, the benefits existed prior to bargaining, and no employee concession was or is required to achieve them. This is an enormous advantage to the teachers.

Theoretically, California could repeal all the statutory benefits just mentioned and the teachers could bargain from ground zero. For this reason, it may be argued that the existence of statutory benefits for teachers does not constitute an inherent advantage of public sector over private sector employees. In fact, however, even the legal possibilities are not so clear. In some states, such as New York, public employee pension benefits may not constitutionally be reduced by the state. Unfortunately, this fact did not seem to lessen the generosity of the legislatures, which must now grapple with the problem of funding public employee pension and retirement benefits that require alarming proportions of state revenues.

According to teachers unions, the most glaring inequity between public and private employment is the fact that most states prohibit teacher strikes. If we limit our analysis to the legal right to strike, there appears to be an inequity. Nevertheless, this inequity is more technical than practical, and the typical legislative remedy for it has added to the advantages teachers have over private sector employees.

First, we must recognize that teacher strikes are not an economic weapon for teachers. If they are an economic weapon at all, they favor management. The "loss of production" resulting from a teacher strike is hardly noticeable. Who can say, years or even months after the fact, what difference was made by a few days or weeks of schooling, more or less? From the standpoint of putting economic pressure on the employer, the loss of the right to strike in education is no loss at all. On the other hand, because teacher strikes are political—not economic— weapons, not having the right to strike actually strengthens the political effectiveness of teachers. The public is not aware of the economic ineffectiveness of teacher strikes, but it tends to be sympathetic to the argument that something should be done to help employees who cannot strike.

Because teachers typically don't have the right to strike, state legislation usually prescribes excessive time for bargaining and for impasse procedures. As a result, school management often concedes more than it would in a strike settlement. After all, the longer management is at the bargaining table, the more it gives away. The concessions management makes to avoid protracted negotiations and impasse procedures are often much greater than the concessions it would make to avoid or settle a strike.

Legislatures ought to be concerned about the fact that too much time—not too little—is devoted to public employee bargaining. Instead of providing a minimum amount of time for bargaining, legislatures should have enacted a maximum. Through the unfair labor practices mechanism, teachers unions could still be protected against any lack of time due to inadequate management preparation.

The emphasis on mediation and fact-finding in public education has been very costly to the public for another reason that is widely overlooked. As long as the alternative to settlement is an impasse procedure, teachers union persistence in unreasonable demands is only to be expected. The very existence of the impasse procedures often strengthens union determination to concede as little as possible, lest it weaken its position in the impasse procedure. Thus, in remedying a legal inequity whose practical importance is vastly overrated, the legislatures enacted impasse procedures that are more damaging to effective management than the legalization of teacher strikes would have been.

The weakness of the equity argument is dramatically illustrated in cases in which a board of education tries to discharge striking teachers after the board has bargained in good faith to impasse. In the private sector, the employer has the right to replace strikers under these circumstances; "equity" would require a similar right for school boards. Nevertheless, striking teachers have successfully argued that they can be fired only pursuant to the causes and procedures set forth in the tenure laws. These procedures typically require a board hearing for each individual teacher; the practical implications are to make it impossible to fire striking teachers in many districts. We are thus treated to the hypocritical spectacle of teachers unions lamenting the "inequitable" absence of a teacher's right to strike, at the same time urging their members to strike because it is practically impossible to discipline or fire striking teachers.

Impact of Collective Bargaining on Pupils

Let us turn next to the impact of collective bargaining upon pupils. There are at least four positions on this subject:

1. Teacher bargaining is good for pupils.

2. Teacher bargaining is bad for pupils.

3. Teacher bargaining has no visible impact on pupils one way or the other.

4. We don't really know what its impact is, and it wouldn't matter much if we did.

Theoretically, each of the four positions might have been valid at one time. In the 1960s, we probably did not know enough to draw valid conclusions about the impact of teacher bargaining. Today, however, this agnosticism is not so defensible.

The proposition that collective bargaining is good for pupils has its origins in politics, not in education. Probably the most important single difference between private and public sector bargaining is the political dimension of the latter. Essentially, it is a contest to win public favor; whoever can appear to be the defender and supporter of children has a major advantage in this struggle. For this reason, teacher union propaganda is almost invariably couched in terms of pupil welfare.

Such appeals have a certain plausibility, but only because on some issues teachers' interests appear to coincide with interests of pupils. For example, teachers want small classes, and small classes appear to be beneficial to students. Teachers want more preparation time, and who can be opposed to adequately prepared teachers? Nevertheless, even if these teacher proposals were of demonstrable benefit to pupils—and usually they are not—they would not support the conclusion that teacher bargaining is an overall benefit to pupils. For one thing, we must also look at teacher proposals on issues on which teacher interests conflict with pupil interests. For example, teachers unions typically propose that teachers be dismissed in the afternoon at the same time as the pupils. A common variant is that teachers be dismissed at the same time as the pupils on Fridays and days preceding a holiday or vacation. Such proposals are hardly in the best interests of pupils. On the contrary, they are obviously in the interest of teachers to the detriment of pupils, as are many other union proposals.

In short, teacher interests sometimes support and sometimes conflict with pupil interests. When teacher interests can be made to appear as pupil interests, the teachers union tries to persuade the community that teachers are primarily interested in pupil welfare. Nevertheless, if teacher bargaining is not harmful to pupils, it is only because school boards do not accept most union proposals.

In actuality, union proposals frequently generate more public support than they deserve. To illustrate, consider most union proposals to limit class size. A wealth of research clearly invalidates the assumption that there is an invariably positive correlation between smaller classes and student achievement; however, let us assume that the correlation exists. Assume also that teachers are successful in achieving limits on class size in negotiations. Nevertheless, it would be fallacious to conclude that bargaining has a beneficial effect upon students or upon student achievement. The practical issue is not simply whether smaller class size improves student achievement, but whether reducing class size is the optimal use of district funds. Pupils may need textbooks or physical security or a decent meal even more than smaller class size. The fact that such alternatives are typically ignored in negotiations helps to explain why most teacher arguments on the subject are merely rationalizations of positions taken in the interests of teachers. In saying this, we do not denigrate the teachers' self-interest or challenge their right to pursue it. The point is that from a union point of view, pupil welfare is a secondary or even tertiary consideration.

Realistically and practically, why should it be otherwise? How can it be? The teachers union is legally and practically the representative of *teachers*. *Pupils* did not elect teachers unions to represent *pupils*; *teachers* elected them to advance the interests of *teachers*.

Teachers frequently object to the proposition that their organizations are primarily oriented to teacher welfare. Nevertheless, this is a defensible position, even from a public policy point of view. For example, suppose a district desires to dismiss a teacher for alleged incompetence. If the teachers union were to be the judge instead of the teacher advocate, the teacher would be without effective representation. This would be an undesirable outcome, since effective representation is so important in our society.

Paradoxically, organizations of teachers would lose rather than gain support of their constituents if they adopted a public interest posture as well as in rhetoric; at a rhetorical level, there is no problem, because most teachers believe that what's good for teachers is good for the country; we have yet to hear a teachers union question whether more money for teachers, shorter hours, smaller classes, lighter loads, and more teacher benefits are in the public interest.

Alternatives to Teacher Bargaining

Assuming that the previous analysis is substantially correct, what policies or actions does it suggest? Who should do what?

Obviously, it would be virtually impossible to revert to the pre-bargaining days. For better or for worse, teacher bargaining has been institutionalized in most states. The personnel and resources available to unions of teachers and other public employees virtually ensure the continuation of collective bargaining in the public sector. Thus, the political influence of public employee unions—the same factor that gives them an undue advantage in bargaining—is also a major deterrent to remedial action at the legislative level.

Furthermore, higher education is not likely to be helpful in this matter. Many institutions of higher education have departments committed to the study and analysis of labor legislation. Unfortunately, professors in these departments frequently moonlight as mediators, arbitrators, conciliators, and fact-finders. To avoid jeopardizing their moonlighting roles, they avoid criticism of labor legislation generally, and especially of legislation that encourages and promotes the use of extended impasse procedures and grievance arbitration. On the contrary, these academics frequently promote such legislation, seeing no problem whatever in finding it in the public interest. The relationship is not necessarily conscious and deliberate; nevertheless, the philosophy that "what's good for General Motors is good for the country" lives in these departments and among teachers generally.

Although most differences between public and private sector bargaining are favorable to public employees, their practical importance varies from state to state. The arguments for public employee collective bargaining are more appealing in states—Mississippi is one—that have virtually no statutory benefits than they are in California and other states with very substantial statutory benefits. Paradoxically, however, bargaining has emerged first and foremost in the states with the most extensive statutory benefits, and it has yet to emerge in many states where these benefits are minimal. It must be emphasized, however, that most of the advantages of public employment cannot be eliminated, whatever the political jurisdiction involved. Short of disenfranchising public employees, we cannot eliminate their additional leverage on their employer through the political process. Similarly, because employment rights of public employees to due process are grounded in the U.S. Constitution, we cannot anticipate their diminution through the political process. Therefore, if equity between employment rights in the two sectors is to be achieved, it must be achieved by adjusting the representational rather than the constitutional rights of public employees. To compensate for the inherent advantages of public employment, such adjustment should provide representational rights that are different from, and significantly less than, private sector bargaining rights.

A Reply to Myron Lieberman

Albert Shanker*

In "Eggs I Have Laid: Teacher Bargaining Reconsidered," Myron Lieberman builds an interesting case. Lieberman is seldom dull, but he is often wrong. In this case, his conclusions rest on a foundation constructed of his eggshells. Poke it a little and it just doesn't hold up. Limited space prevents me from cataloging all of Lieberman's errors, so I shall confine myself to his major points.

Lieberman believes that there is an essential and major difference between collective bargaining in the public sector and in the private sector. In the private sector, employees have only one chance—collective bargaining—to get benefits. The public employee, he says, has an unfair advantage because benefits can also be gained through the political process and legislation. The public employee gets two bites of the apple, while the private employee has only one. Of course, private sector employees do try to influence and elect public officials. "The point is, however, that state officials seldom affect the context or substance of private sector bargaining," Lieberman tells us. "Political activity at the state level pays the teacher a larger dividend than it does the factory worker or farmer."

---

*Albert Shanker, A reply to Myron Lieberman, *Phi Delta Kappan* 60: 652-54 (May 1979).

This is pure nonsense, especially if we consider *all* political action—not just that at the state level. Clearly, salaries, working conditions, and job security in the private sector are also governed by political actions. Jobs in the shipping industry are completely dependent on federal legislation giving preference to American ships over foreign competition. The income of taxi drivers is regulated by the fares permitted by state and local agencies. The bargaining power of employees in banks and liquor stores depends on state banking and liquor authority regulations. The existence of entire industries depends on the imposition or absence of import duties, while jobs or unemployment in the construction industry depend on government-imposed interest rates and the way in which environmental protection standards are enforced. Most wages in the industry are determined by the Davis-Bacon Act, which requires payment of prevailing rates. The income of farmers depends on commodity price support and trade arrangements such as the Russian wheat deal—all determined by elected political officials.

Of course teachers lobby for pension protection, but private sector pensions are government-regulated too—by the Employee Retirement Income Security Act (ERISA). Private sector employees politic for laws at the state and federal levels on issues covering union organization, safety, health, minimum wages, workmen's compensation, unemployment insurance, etc. Private sector employees can be adversely affected by policy decisions at the state level: In New York City, construction of Westway, a highway on the west side of Manhattan to be built with federal funds that would provide thousands of private sector construction jobs, has thus far been stymied, largely by opposition from the state environmental agency. Governor Hugh Carey's support of Westway played no small role in his winning the endorsement of the state AFL-CIO—and the election.

Lieberman should know that there is hardly a private enterprise in the United States today that is not helped or hurt by government action. If Lieberman were right—if private sector unions got so little bang for their political buck—it wouldn't make much sense for them to become involved in political action. Then why are they so heavily involved in it? Why have they been contributing to COPE funds and campaigning for mayors, governors, members of legislatures and the Congress, presidents? Why do the unions amass war chests for political action on every governmental level? By Lieberman's lights, it's sheer folly. The fact is that everyone has a stake in political action, and for Lieberman to pretend that teachers have a bigger stake than anyone else is nonsense. In this political process, the labor movement, in addition to supporting self-interest legislation, has always been a staunch supporter of the public schools, which have provided the chance for the children of union members to improve their lot. Recently, teachers have supported the legislative programs of private sector unions in the knowledge that high employment and a healthy private sector are essential to provide an adequate tax base for public education.

Lieberman makes the point that teachers have still another advantage over private sector employees in the collective bargaining process: Teachers "in some jurisdictions" often control management. This control is so great, he says, that it "affects not only what is proposed, accepted, rejected, and modified, but the timing of concessions, the management posture toward grievances, and the extent of management support services for bargaining. Sometimes, even the choice of management negotiator is subject to an unofficial but effective teacher veto." Now somewhere in this big country there may be a situation like the one he describes, but I doubt it. (There are certainly many examples of the opposite: teacher organizations that are still controlled by the school administration.)

There is a simple test for the Lieberman theory: If teachers control both sides of the bargaining table in a substantial number of school districts, we should find many teachers with huge salaries, greatly reduced class sizes, longer holidays and vacations than ever before—you name it. The facts do not bear this out. They show that when bargaining started in the 1960s, a period of prosperity, teachers did some catching up to make up for the lean years before bargaining. In recent years, however, teachers have not even kept up with increases in the cost of living. We have all read headlines of teachers forced to strike for weeks— even months—for settlements that are below the inflation rate, but where is Lieberman's long list of fat contracts that exceed the rise in the cost of living? Surely, if teachers unions have control over school boards and their negotiators, there must be such a list.

Elsewhere in the article, Lieberman admits that teachers do *not* get what they want: "...if teacher bargaining is not harmful to pupils, it is only *because school boards do not agree to most teacher proposals at the table*" (emphasis added). Which is it: Do school boards usually cave in or do they reject most teacher proposals? Lieberman is an experienced negotiator who knows that the overwhelming majority of teacher demands are rejected.

Lieberman claims that management in the private sector, because it has a stake in greater profits, is much more likely to resist union demands than public sector management, which has no personal stake involved when public funds are given away. This, too, is simple-minded. In the private sector, management can and often does accede to labor wage and fringe benefit hikes (39% in the coal industry a year ago) because costs can be passed along to the consumer. Indeed, a wage increase can be the excuse for hiking prices so high that management adds to its profits too. This is not the case in the public sector, where the costs of settlements are watched closely by a public demanding that taxes be kept low. The public cannot throw out the management of the coal industry for raising prices, but it can oust school boards, governors, and legislators who don't bargain hard with their employees. Ask the teachers in Levittown, New York, in St. Louis, or in any school district that's recently been through a long and bitter strike whether teacher bargaining makes for school board pushovers.

Lieberman tells us that much of what teachers demand in bargaining is in the interest of teachers but to the detriment of pupils. Here again he fails to prove his case. Clearly, if teacher bargaining is bad for pupils, it should be possible to prove it. Why not compare the performance of students in school districts and states that have no teacher bargaining with the performance of students in states where teachers do bargain? Lieberman should have shown us that students in Mississippi, Alabama, Virginia, and the Carolinas do much better than students in New York, California, Connecticut, Rhode Island, Michigan, etc. Instead of presenting us with empirical evidence, Lieberman tells us only that bargaining means that teacher welfare comes first, and pupil welfare "is a secondary or even tertiary consideration" in negotiations.

"Realistically and practically," says Lieberman, "why should it be otherwise? How can it be? The teachers union is legally and practically the representative of teachers. *Pupils* did not elect teachers unions to represent *pupils*; *teachers* elected them to represent the interest of *teachers*" (emphasis in original). True enough. Did the pupils elect the school board? Or the governor or legislature? Or the state education agency? Do parents always seek what is in the best interest of their children? Parents may choose the convenient rather than the excellent. School board members may make decisions with an eye to political advancement rather than the welfare of students. Teachers may, at times, pursue their self-interest, as does everyone else in our society.

183

That everyone pursues self-interest is no condemnation of collective bargaining or of the democratic political process.

The drama of the Lieberman article does not lie in any of these arguments but rather in the fact that someone who was once a strong supporter of teacher bargaining has now reversed his position. It is as if George Washington in his later years had announced that the Revolution was a mistake and we should again become part of Mother England. Some will assert that Lieberman's conversion on the question of bargaining has its craven aspects, motivated more by his new role as negotiator for school boards than by any genuine intellectual about-face. This does Lieberman an injustice. The fact is that while he supported "collective bargaining" for teachers, he never used these words in their commonly accepted meaning. He never really believed in collective bargaining.

Let's face it—collective bargaining is a process in which employees pursue their common interests in establishing salaries, hours, and conditions of work. Lieberman saw it as something different, as a vehicle for "professionalization," defining a "profession" as being more concerned with "the service to be rendered than the economic gain to the practitioners." (Doctors, of course, go into medicine without any thought at all of the income involved, and the AMA exists solely to assure the practice of good medicine!) Lieberman never really cared for collective bargaining as an *economic* process. That's why, from the very beginning, Lieberman supported merit rating, advocated higher salaries for teachers of math and science because they were in short supply, called for the AFT to get out of the AFL-CIO, and urged teachers to exert efforts to get big salary increases for school administrators.

The teachers of America wanted *real* collective bargaining, not the new "professionalization" that Lieberman was selling. Teachers saw, and still see, collective bargaining as the legitimate democratic means for participating in decisions on their wages, hours, and working conditions. *This is the primary reason for teachers unions and teacher collective bargaining.* Although the profession and those it serves often do benefit (who can deny that talented people have come into teaching as a result of the success of collective bargaining in raising salaries and improving working conditions?), that is not the chief goal of teachers unions. Lieberman would restrict teacher bargaining because teachers haven't adopted *his* model.

Teachers do have professional concerns. Like doctors and lawyers, they are perfectly capable of holding at least two desires—the desire to practice well and the desire to earn a living commensurate with their skills—and of finding these wishes not at all in conflict. And teachers unions do address professional concerns, although not usually at the bargaining table, unless there is an identity between a working condition and a professional need. (Ironically, Lieberman has been advising school boards for years that professional issues are not subject to bargaining.) Class size is both. So is adequate preparation time. School security involves both concerns, as do sabbaticals, help for battered teachers, freedom from administrative and clerical chores, and a dozen other issues often dealt with in teacher contracts.

Standards for teachers and students, financing for schools at local, state, and federal levels, the goals of bilingual education, help for handicapped children, equal educational opportunity—these are all professional concerns of teachers that their unions have addressed in the political arena, often together with management, parents, and administrators. To the extent that the growth of teachers unions has helped teachers articulate and fight for these professional concerns, Lieberman was right in his perceptions—and wrong in his new conclusion.

Postscript From Lieberman

Any time you get into a serious discussion with Al Shanker, you learn something. In this case, I learned that the most effective defense of teacher bargaining is to distort the criticisms of it and then ridicule the distortions. Being limited to 200 words, I shall confine myself to one example.

Shanker asserts that there is a simple test for the "Lieberman theory" that teachers "control both sides of the bargaining table in a substantial number of school districts." This is not my "theory," not what I wrote, and my argument does not depend upon this atrociously inaccurate version of it. What I did say—and Shanker's rebuttal does not lay a glove on it—is that "teachers often play an important role in determining who is management" and that in bargaining "the political influence of teachers upon public management has been extremely advantageous to teachers." As my article made abundantly clear, my argument does not assume complete teacher control of the management side. It clearly points out that such control does not exist. According to the logic of Shanker's rebuttal, either teachers exert complete control over boards of education, or we can ignore the arguments that they have advantages not available to private sector employees.

12. TEACHER STRIKES

Devoted to the public policy aspects of teacher strikes, this chapter does not discuss management operations in strike situations except as a way of clarifying a public policy issue. Such a discussion would require an extensive analysis that is best left to separate books and manuals on the subject. Several state school board and school administrator organizations have published manuals on strike operations. These manuals take into account the legal and practical dimensions of teacher strikes on a state-by-state basis. A realistic discussion of strike operations must take these state factors into account; for example, whether strikes are legal or whether striking teachers still retain their tenure rights are critical practical issues in coping with strikes. In contrast, the public policy aspects of teacher strikes are essentially the same in all states, regardless of the differences between the states on their legality.

Two basic arguments are made to support legalization of teacher strikes. One is the argument that unless teacher strikes are legalized, teacher bargaining will be an exercise in futility. The teachers unions, along with other unions of public employees, contend that school boards would not bargain in good faith in the absence of a legal right to strike. Knowing that their employees were legally prohibited from striking, school boards would allegedly adopt intransigent positions in the bargaining process.

The union argument was not substantiated by experience in states that prohibited strikes by teachers. One reason was that even in the absence of a right to strike, it is feasible to ascertain whether school management is bargaining in good faith.

Furthermore, teacher strikes are a political weapon, not an economic one. Such strikes do not result in economic pressure on school boards. The fact that teacher strikes create political pressures on school boards to settle is consistent with the rationale for legalization, but it is difficult to see why state legislatures should seek or prefer this outcome. After all, the teachers unions have ample resources and opportunities to inform and persuade school boards to accommodate union demands. For example, unions frequently play a decisive role in who gets elected or appointed to school boards.

Another consideration is that teachers do not ordinarily risk loss of their jobs or even of their income by striking. The teachers who strike are typically protected by tenure laws that ensure individual tenure trials in dismissal cases. As a practical matter, it is virtually impossible to show that each individual teacher who did not work during a strike was participating in it. Needless to say, private sector employees who are absent during a strike do not enjoy any comparable immunity from loss of their jobs.

As a matter of fact, teachers typically do not risk any loss of income by going on strike. Usually, state law requires that pupils attend school for a minimum number of days in order for the district to be eligible for state aid. Consequently, school boards are forced to reschedule the days in which schools were inoperative because of a strike. The result is that teacher strikes are relatively risk-free. Even if tenure laws were abolished, in most states legalization of teacher strikes would result in situations in which the unions would be the parties lacking incentives to bargain in good faith.

The other main argument for legalization is that private sector workers can strike but teachers cannot. Supposedly, this constitutes a major inequity to the disadvantage of teachers. Several valid objections weaken—if not totally undermine—this argument. First, whether public sector employees are being treated inequitably requires an analysis of all the rights, benefits, and restrictions in both public and private sectors.

Significantly, even in states where private school teachers have the right to strike and public school teachers do not, public school teachers enjoy terms and conditions of employment far superior to those in private schools. This situation is common in public employment generally, but it is especially evident in comparisons of public to private school teachers. Unquestionably, it results from the inherent advantages of public employment. First, public employees, with an expectancy of continued employment, have constitutional rights not to be dismissed or deprived of any professional advantage without due process of law. As a practical matter, this often means that public sector employees *without* bargaining rights have more protection than private sector employees *with* bargaining rights. A second advantage is that public employers and employees frequently can shift the inefficiencies of public employment to the taxpayers, who often are unaware of the inefficiencies and seldom able to do anything to eliminate or reduce them.

The most fundamental objection to legalizing teacher strikes is that it would be inconsistent with democratic representative government. Suppose, for example, that the teachers union announces that it will strike unless an agreement is reached by a stated deadline. Suppose further that representatives of the school board and teachers union bargain around the clock in order to avert a strike. If an agreement is reached, the parties typically assert that collective bargaining "worked." Without the bargaining rhetoric, however, the parties can be said simply to have been creating public policies in the middle of the night in a process that excludes other interested parties. The necessity of school board ratification does not overcome this objection; by the time a school board votes on whether to ratify a negotiated contract, the board would usually be guilty of an unfair labor practice if it were to reject the proposed agreement.

Thus, legalizing teacher strikes creates a basic inequality, but one that favors teachers; they would become the only group that can legally prevent the delivery of a public service until a public agency adopts a public policy deemed acceptable to the teachers. No other organization or group has this right. The inequality is overlooked because the process is described in bargaining instead of political terminology; there is a tendency to overlook the fact that terms and conditions of employment for public school teachers are still public policies, just as speed limits and tax rates are public policies.

Teachers unions often urge legalization of teacher strikes because such strikes happen so infrequently. Paradoxically, the unions also urge legalization on the grounds that teacher strikes occur regardless of legalization; legalization is supposedly futile. The fact is, however, that the harm done by teacher strikes should not be assessed solely or even primarily in terms of the number of days lost. The case against legalization would be just as strong if no days were lost for this reason. Instead, the harm must be assessed in terms of the concessions made to avoid strikes, and such harm is greater than the number of days lost as a result of strikes. Second, the argument that teacher strikes will occur anyway is irrelevant. Murder and theft would occur despite legislation rendering them illegal, but no one asserts that this fact justifies eliminating their illegality.

One of the objections to legalization of teacher strikes is that educational services are essential; that is arguably the reason they are provided by government, not through a market system. The argument is that because essential services must not be interrupted, teacher strikes should not be legalized. This argument has been prominent in legislation providing state and local public employees with bargaining rights; security personnel, such as police officers and firefighters, are typically excluded from coverage in such legislation.

In our view, the essential services argument against legalization is a secondary one. In many cases, the same services are provided simultaneously by government and the private sector; education is such a service. In some situations, government services have been privatized, or privately provided services such as utilities have been taken over by government. In the latter cases, the practical consequences of strikes seem to be the same whether the service is provided by government or through the private sector. For this reason, it seems illogical to allow the strikes when the service is provided privately but not governmentally. Furthermore, even if education is "essential," it is not essential that it be provided by government. Especially if there are readily available private alternatives, the essential services argument is not very persuasive.

Paradoxically, in their efforts to legalize teacher strikes, the teachers unions find it advantageous to argue that education is not an essential service. The position adopted here, however, is that the political objections to teacher strikes pose insuperable objections to their legalization; whether or not educational services are "essential" can be debated endlessly, but the political objections are the crux of the case against legalization.[1]

---

[1] See Myron Lieberman, *Public sector bargaining* (Lexington, Mass.: Lexington Books, 1980), 107-26.

13. BINDING ARBITRATION IN PUBLIC EMPLOYMENT: A REAPPRAISAL

Arbitration is a procedure whereby an impartial third party makes a decision in a labor dispute. Arbitration may be *voluntary* (the parties have agreed to it) or *involuntary* (it is imposed upon the parties by law). Arbitration may also be *advisory* (the arbitral decision is recommended) or *binding* (the parties are bound by the decision). Binding arbitration is sometimes further divided into two additional categories: *Final* (the parties cannot appeal the decision to the courts); and *binding but not final* (the arbitral decision is binding but can be appealed to the courts).

Essentially, two kinds of disputes may be subject to arbitration. One type is commonly referred to as "interest disputes," i.e., disputes over what the terms of a labor contract should be. A situation in which the employer and union are at impasse over salaries for the coming year but agree or are required by law to turn the dispute over to an arbitrator would be an interest dispute. Suppose, however, that the employer and union already have a contract covering salaries, but a dispute arises over what X should be paid pursuant to such contract. If X files a grievance, alleging that he was not paid in accordance with the contract, and if the grievance is ultimately carried to arbitration, we have an example of "rights arbitration," i.e., arbitration over the meaning, interpretation, and/or application of a labor contract.

Interest arbitration is not particularly widespread in the private sector, although it has its uses in certain kinds of situations. Despite some increase in its use in the public sector, widespread opposition to it is not likely to diminish appreciably in the future.

One criticism of interest arbitration is that it "chills" the bargaining process. If the parties know that their dispute might be resolved by an arbitrator, they will not make many concessions, or *as* many concessions, during bargaining. The reason is that arbitrators can be expected to make concessions to both sides. Therefore, if one side has reached the bottom of the barrel before arbitration begins, the only way the arbitrator can give the other party any concession at all is to award such party a part of the barrel; that is, concessions that cannot reasonably be made.

To overcome this problem, some observers are urging the adoption of "final offer arbitration" in interest disputes. In this process, the arbitrator is limited to choosing the final offer of either the employer or the union. This limitation is expected to stimulate bargaining and to avoid the submission of extreme proposals to the arbitrator; to do so carries a heavy risk that the arbitrator will select the final offer of the other party.

Other variations and nuances of final offer arbitration and of interest arbitration in general are numerous, but interest arbitration encounters at least one major problem in the public sector that does not apply when it is used in private employment. Permitting third parties not accountable to the electorate to resolve disputes over what should be the terms and conditions of public employment is widely regarded as inconsistent with our system of government. At least it is insofar as it is assumed that public personnel policies, like public policies generally, are to be made by officials accountable to the public. It was precisely on this basis that the Connecticut Association of Boards of Education challenged the constitutionality of a 1979 Connecticut statute mandating binding arbitration of disputes over terms and conditions of public employment.

Arbitration and Public Authority

Significantly, many persons who regard binding arbitration of interest disputes as an unwise and invalid delegation of public authority nevertheless support binding arbitration of grievances in the public sector. The following discussion, however, suggests that if binding arbitration of interest disputes would be an unwise and possibly illegal delegation of public authority, so would binding arbitration of grievances. Let us see why this is so.

In the private sector, grievance arbitration is a means of resolving conflict over the interpretation and application of a contract between private parties. Obviously, disagreements over the interpretation and application of a contract arise in the public as well as the private sector.

In the public sector, however, the disagreement is one over the inter-pretation and application of a public law or a policy having the force of law. Also in the public sector, one of the parties to the dispute is the public agency that adopted the policy in dispute. What might the impli-cations of these differences be?

As in the private sector, the terminal point of the grievance proce-dure is frequently a troublesome issue. For example, public employers frequently object to grievance arbitration; their acceptance of it is often limited to advisory arbitration. On the other hand, unions of public employees typically object to advisory arbitration; in their view, advi-sory arbitration allows the public employer to decide unilaterally whether or not the contract has been violated. Some union negotiators actually prefer no contractual grievance procedure to one that provides for advisory arbitration.

Union arguments on this issue tend to regard a practical difficulty as a legal reality. Even under advisory arbitration, the public employer does not necessarily make the final decision on whether the employer has violated the contract. The union can still go to court to remedy an alleged violation. The time and expense required to do so, not the legal situation of the parties, underlies the union argument that the public employer (not the courts) is the terminal point under advisory arbitra-tion. At one time or another, most citizens have probably waived their rights in a dispute because of the time and money required to enforce them. Undeniably, such situations exist, and it makes sense to avoid them if it is reasonably possible to do so. Thus, the union argument may be correct as a practical matter, but nothing is gained, analytically at least, by treating the time and expense of litigating claims of contract violations as the absence of any legal right to such litigation.

About 95 per cent of private sector contracts provide for binding arbitration as the terminal point of the grievance procedure. Generally, public sector labor contracts are characterized by more variation on this issue. Although binding arbitration is common, the public sector also includes many contracts with advisory arbitration, no arbitration, and even no grievance procedure at all. Binding arbitration is more com-mon among larger public employers, but all sorts of variations exist among public employers of every size.

Several factors underlie the greater variation in the public sector. The private sector is covered by a single law, the National Labor Relations Act. The public sector is governed by a multiplicity of state laws. These state laws differ widely in their treatment of grievance procedures. Some merely include such procedures as a subject of bargaining. Some require grievance procedures to be included in contracts. Some specifically authorize, but do not mandate, binding arbitration of grievances, and so on.

Timing is also a factor. Binding arbitration is the exception, not the rule, in first contracts after a bargaining law is enacted. Over time, more public employers agree to the provision, and it becomes more difficult to hold out against it. Even so, because many public employers continue to be opposed to binding arbitration, there is more variation in the alternatives to it.

In retrospect, it appears that many public employers who have accepted binding arbitration of grievances have done so as a result of their uncritical acceptance of the rationale for grievance arbitration in the private sector. According to this rationale, the arbitrator does not establish or create the terms of the contract; that is the responsibility of the employer and the union in bargaining. The arbitrator's task is to apply the agreement between the parties to a given set of facts in order to decide whether or not the employer has violated the agreement.

Quite frequently, the private sector labor contract explicitly limits the arbitrator by language such as:

> The function of the arbitrator shall be to determine controversies involving the interpretation, application or alleged violation of specific provisions of this Agreement, and he shall have no power to add to, subtract from, or modify any of the terms of this Agreement, or any other terms made supplemental hereto, or to arbitrate any matter not specifically provided for by this Agreement, or to enter any new provisions into this Agreement.

As more states enacted bargaining laws, there was increasing acceptance of the rationale for binding arbitration. The public sector unions agreed that a collective bargaining contract in the public sector is public policy agreed to by the appropriate public employer. Nevertheless, they contended that an arbitrator ruling upon an alleged violation of the contract would not be making or formulating policy. The arbitrator would be merely deciding whether the public employer has acted consistently with the policy it adopted when it ratified the contract.

In the private sector, binding arbitration is usually a trade-off for a no-strike clause. Before grievance arbitration, unions had serious problems attempting to remedy alleged violations of a contract. Quite often, their only recourse was a "grievance strike"; that is, a strike during the term of a contract to force management to stop violating it. With a no-strike clause intact, this problem would be eliminated.

With encouragement from the U.S. Supreme Court, management's acceptance of binding arbitration of grievances in the private sector became the accepted trade-off for the union's agreement not to strike during the term of the contract. This quid pro quo was not as advantageous to public sector employers as it was to those in the private sector. The reason is that in most states, strikes by public employees were prohibited anyway, either by statute or judicial decision. For this reason, public employers would be giving the "quid" when they already had the "quo." Undeniably, it was to their advantage to have the union's agreement to a no-strike clause, but the private sector trade-off was clearly questionable, just on bargaining grounds, in the public sector. For the most part, however, public employers did not press the issue. Theoretically, public sector unions might have made—or have been asked to make—other concessions to justify binding arbitration, but this does not appear to have happened very often.

In any event, many public employers were (and are) very uneasy about accepting binding arbitration. It was almost as if they knew something was wrong but could not articulate their objections. Over and over again, they were beaten down by the argument that the arbitrator would only be deciding whether the employer had violated its own policies. The unions also emphasized the argument that binding arbitration was needed so that the public employer would not be the final word on its own malfeasance. Since the inception of public sector bargaining, unions have emphasized the argument that "permitting one party to a contract to be the judge of whether it has violated the contract is unfair."

Furthermore, in order to get binding arbitration, the unions were usually willing to accept contract language that restricted arbitrators, sometimes even more than was typical in the private sector. The following language from a school board agreement illustrates this point:

> The arbitrator shall limit his decision strictly to the application and interpretation of the provisions of this agreement and he shall be without power or authority to make any decision:
>
> - Contrary to, or inconsistent with or modifying or varying in any way, the terms of this agreement or of applicable law or rules or regulations having the force and effect of law

- Involving the exercise of discretion by the board under the provisions of this agreement, under its bylaws, or under applicable law

- Limiting or interfering in any way with the powers, duties, and responsibilities of the board under its bylaws, applicable law, and rules and regulations having the force and effect of law.

The Case for and against Binding Arbitration

Despite the wide acceptance of binding arbitration in the private sector, and despite union acceptance (at least initially) of restrictions upon the authority of arbitrators, something about the argument for binding arbitration in the public sector is disingenuous. Why would a public employer argue against itself? Why would an employer try to violate its own policies while the union was trying to uphold them? It is almost as if a police officer were urging a violation of the law while the culprit is demanding that the law be enforced. As paradoxical as this would be, it is very similar to the outcome of binding arbitration in the public sector. The public employee union alleges that the public employer is violating its own policies while denying paternity of the policy it allegedly adopted.

Of course, one can easily visualize situations in which a public employer deliberately wishes to deviate from its adopted policies. Management may believe that even-handed application of a policy would help an employee in disfavor, or hurt an employee whom management desires to protect. Such instances do arise and are cited by the public employee unions to justify binding arbitration of grievances. Nevertheless, such cases are not the kind typically carried to arbitration. The typical case is one in which some consequences of a clear policy were overlooked, or a situation in which the contractual policy is not clear. For one reason or another, the public employer overlooked or was unaware of the application of the policy to a particular situation. Had it been aware of the lack of clarity or of the particular situation in which the policy is deemed inappropriate, the public employer would have negotiated a different policy.

A simple example will show how this happens. Suppose a school board agrees contractually to give salary schedule credit for "five years of prior teaching experience." Let us assume that in the prebargaining years, the board always interpreted and applied this phrase to mean "public school teaching experience." Assume also that contractual language provides that the contract supersedes any past practice that conflicts or is inconsistent with the contract. Subsequently, X files a grievance that is carried to binding arbitration. The grievance is based upon board refusal to grant X five years' credit for X's teaching experience in a nonpublic school.

What are the realities of this situation? X's argument is that by refusing to grant credit for the five years of teaching in nonpublic schools, the board is violating its own adopted policy. True enough, the contract does not distinguish between public and nonpublic school experience; the board is violating the literal contractual policy by refusing to give X credit for teaching in nonpublic schools.

From a bargaining point of view, the resolution would be clear: X would get the disputed credit. From a public policy standpoint, however, the case raises some different issues. It may well be that the board should have had a more astute negotiator, or that the board was careless. Nonetheless, two things would follow from a binding arbitral award granting prior service credit for nonpublic school teaching experience:

First, the arbitrator would be establishing a public policy to which the public employer is opposed—specifically, that salary credit shall be given for nonpublic school teaching experience. It is hypocritical to argue that the arbitrator is merely interpreting but not formulating policy. Without a collective bargaining contract and binding arbitration, the board would not be forced to follow the policy that the arbitrator adopts and to which the board objects. In the absence of a contract, the board could resolve any inconsistencies or ambiguities by adopting the policy it desires instead of being forced against its wishes to adopt one promulgated by the arbitrator.

Second, it also should be noted that the grievance may arise as soon as the contract is ratified, and that the arbitrator's decision may bind the board for years to an unwanted policy. It may also happen that dozens or even hundreds of teachers will benefit from this unwanted policy for this period of time.

To us, and we suspect to many others, it seems fair to say that the arbitrator is establishing board policy in this situation. For the sake of argument, however, let us adopt a different view. We shall say that the board established a policy it did not fully understand. Had the policy been fully understood, the board would not have adopted it—but the burden is on the board, not on the arbitrator. The latter did not establish the policy; he only stated the consequences of it.

Even under this interpretation, however, it is clear that bargaining and binding arbitration of grievances result in public policies not desired by the community's duly chosen representatives responsible for them. Under normal political processes, the board at no time would have had to pay for the nonpublic school experience for any teacher. Which process, then, is to prevail? Either normal democratic political processes take precedence over public sector bargaining, or public sector bargaining takes precedence over democratic political processes.

Would it be feasible to limit binding arbitration in the public sector to factual issues? If feasible, such a limitation might be an appropriate way to avoid the policymaking dilemma otherwise inherent in binding arbitration in the public sector.

For instance, suppose a clerk at City Hall is disciplined for cursing an irate taxpayer. The clerk grieves, asserting that the alleged cursing did not happen as asserted by management. In arbitration, the issue would be one of fact, not of policy interpretation. In fact, some contracts explicitly recognize this distinction by providing that an arbitrator can overrule management on the question of whether certain actions occurred, but not over the appropriateness of disciplinary action taken if the acts did occur. Another example: An employee is fired for stealing public property. Some contracts provide that the employee can grieve over whether the theft occurred, but not over the employer's disciplinary action.

Theoretically, it would be possible to have binding arbitration while avoiding arbitral legislation by various restrictions on the arbitrator. Thus, it might be agreed that arbitration would be binding only in disputes involving the resolution of a factual issue. Whether grievances can be categorized this way is questionable, because both disputed facts and disputed policies are involved in many grievances. It would be possible to treat an arbitral decision as binding on factual issues and advisory on policy issues, but the outcome would be advisory arbitration in every case in which both elements were involved. One possibility is that the arbitrator would manipulate secondary issues to achieve an overall result desired by the arbitrator. To return to the theft example, suppose an employee with 20 years' service was fired for allegedly stealing a pencil. Under the terms of the agreement, the public employer has the right to fire employees for acts of moral turpitude. The arbitrator privately believes that the employee did steal the pencil, but that the firing was a harsh, even outrageous result.

Did the employee steal the pencil? This would be a question of fact, on which the arbitrator's decision would be binding. Was the stealing of a pencil an act of moral turpitude? This would be a question of policy, on which the arbitrator's decision would be only advisory. Obviously, the temptation would be great to rule against the city on the factual issue, thus depriving it of the right to fire the employee.

Could there be a dispute over whether an issue was factual or policymaking? As a practical matter, we doubt it, but assume this was an issue. The issue itself would need to go to arbitration; binding or advisory? Personally, we would not object to binding arbitration on this issue, but we would certainly scrap the whole idea quickly in the face of any arbitral abuse of it.

The compromise suggested above would probably be opposed by most public employee unions. For those unions that have already negotiated binding arbitration without any limitations, it would indeed be a setback, however justified on public policy grounds. At the same time, public employers that have already conceded on the issue—by not limiting binding arbitration of grievances in any way—are not likely to negotiate such a hard-to-bring-about limitation on binding arbitration. Inertia is an important factor in labor relations. Once a public employer has accepted binding arbitration—especially in more than one contract—it would be extremely difficult for that employer to insist on the limitations suggested here.

Nevertheless, the limitation might enable public employers to avoid the most serious dangers of binding arbitration even while accepting it in a form that has some genuine utility for a union; therefore, such limitation would be more palatable than a complete rejection of binding arbitration. In any case, the analysis may alert public employers that have not already agreed to binding arbitration of grievances to a valid reason for opposing or at least limiting such a concession. Needless to say, although the unions may eventually concede on this issue, they are unlikely to concede that the above analysis has any merit at all.

14. PROFESSIONAL ETHICS IN PUBLIC EDUCATION: A POSTMORTEM

Formulating and enforcing a code of ethics is one characteristic of those occupations regarded as "professions." Such a code has not emerged and never will emerge as a form of consumer protection as long as collective bargaining is the dominant form of employment relations in education.

We are not asserting that teachers, individually or collectively, are devoid of ethical principles, nor do we mean to suggest that their conduct is pervasively unethical. However, as an occupational group, teachers do not enforce a code of professional ethics. The development and enforcement of ethical standards is left to others, most notably to school administrators. In our view, this is neither deplorable nor avoidable.

Professional ethics originated in the fee-taking professions. Patients are not in a position to protect themselves from unethical conduct. For example, if a physician prescribes additional treatment, it is hardly feasible for an individual patient to make sure that the treatment is motivated by the patient's welfare rather than the physician's profit.

Historically, the occupations that took action to protect clients in such situations were deemed "professions." In other fields, the employer formulates and enforces standards of ethical conduct. For example, a school district can adopt and enforce rules prohibiting teachers from selling goods and services to students for profit. Moreover, the district is in a position to discipline teachers who violate such rules. There is no reason to rely on teachers themselves and/or teachers organizations to protect pupils from such conflicts of interest, especially when the organizations lack effective sanctions against violators.

There is some precedent, however, for teachers organizations to be involved in ethical matters. Prior to the advent of collective bargaining, the National Education Association and several state education associations had adopted codes of ethics; however, these codes were poorly drafted, and enforcement was minimal. Still, the possibility that professional ethics might someday become meaningful was alive, although not doing very well.

Practically and conceptually, however, collective bargaining was the final nail in the coffin of professional ethics in education. Under collective bargaining, unions function to protect employees; they should not exercise managerial functions. If they did, who would protect employees against capricious or discriminatory actions on the part of the union?

Indeed, as a matter of policy, we question whether unions should play any role in professional ethics other than that of protecting members against abuses of discretion by management. If teachers unions played a more active role in establishing and policing the ethical behavior of their members, two insoluble policy problems would arise. First, because the unions would not be playing their protective role, some other organization or agency would be needed to represent teachers accused of unethical conduct. Such an arrangement would not be feasible; the unions should represent teachers who have paid union dues or service fees for years for protective services.

The second problem would be accountability. Assuming that a union had powers of enforcement, what would happen if a teachers union disciplined a teacher for unethical conduct? How would union officials be held accountable for their actions? When a school administrator recommends firing a teacher (or even some lesser disciplinary action), the procedures used and the conclusions reached are rightfully regarded as part of the basis for evaluating the administrator's job performance. The administrator who does not adequately perform the role of disciplinarian is himself or herself subject to discipline.

On the other hand, no similar accountability exists when union officials or the union membership as a whole seek to discipline teachers. What penalties or sanctions do union officials or members face for inadequate performance of their role as disciplinarians? For all practical purposes, none. Such disciplinary authority without accountability would be irresponsible, regardless of the character of the union members who implement the disciplinary procedures at any given time.

Teachers unions ignore the accountability problem when they urge that union membership be made a mandatory condition of teacher employment. Such a policy gives unions the authority to discipline unethical teachers, because revoking a teacher's union membership is tantamount to termination.

Unfortunately, this "solution" would create a host of problems more serious than the one it was intended to solve. It would delegate authority over public employment to a private body, the union. The public would have no control over the procedures, standards, and safeguards involved in deciding who can teach in public schools. Competent teachers who continue to teach during a strike could be deprived of their right to teach, whereas incompetent teachers who honor picket lines could be left undisturbed. Furthermore, when a union expelled a teacher, no individual in the union would be personally responsible for that action, a consideration that would necessarily foster irresponsibility in the process.

Finally, we should not overlook the workings of internal union politics or the implications of union politics for accountability. Candidates do not win election to local, state, or national union office by advocating restrictions on teacher conduct or by emphasizing the unethical behavior of some teachers. Union elections, like elections generally, are won by emphasizing the rights and benefits of constituents, not their obligations or their failure to live up to them. Politically—and, to some extent, legally—the union cannot be both the defender of teachers' rights and interests and also the prosecutor and judge.

School administrators frequently lament this state of affairs. Periodically, someone asks when teachers unions are going to be "professional," that is, when will they assume responsibility for incompetent or unethical members? The answer is "never." School administrators undoubtedly would welcome a situation in which teachers unions exercised the most distasteful roles of management, but that isn't going to happen very often. Despite teachers who believe that "professionalism" justifies such a change and despite some naive school officials who agree, school management does not intend to delegate managerial functions to teachers unions. At least it should not do so, despite recent proposals to "empower teachers."

15.   THE NATIONAL BOARD FOR PROFESSIONAL TEACHING STANDARDS

This chapter considers two related but different sets of issues. One is the idea of national voluntary boards to certify teachers who possess a superior level of competence and the other is the way this idea is being implemented by the National Board for Professional Teaching Standards (NBPTS).

First, it would well to explain the rationale for establishing national teacher boards similar to the national medical specialty boards. The latter certify physicians as having achieved a superior level of competence in a medical specialty, such as surgery, cardiology, or anesthesiology. Board certification is not required in order to practice medicine. Instead, eligibility to practice is still the responsibility of the various state medical boards.

In education, the national board idea potentially offers the same advantages that similar boards offer in medicine as well as in accounting and a number of other professions. To appreciate this, it is necessary to understand the problems associated with "merit pay," defined here as higher pay for superior teaching performance.

At present, even if teachers are rated "outstanding" or "superior," it is still practically impossible to pay them higher salaries based on performance. In the first place, the evaluations of teachers are not reliable guides to their professional skill and competence. Both the criteria for evaluating teachers and how the criteria are applied vary widely among

---

This discussion is adapted from Myron Lieberman's article, Take the $25 million and run: The case of the National Board for Professional Teaching Standards, *Government Union Review* (Winter 1991), pp. 1-23.

districts, schools, and supervisors or principals. Sometimes, poor teachers are rated favorably in order to help them obtain employment elsewhere. Weak principals often are afraid to give unfavorable evaluations to aggressive teachers.

Despite considerable rhetoric to the contrary, school management in the United States is basically opposed to merit pay. For one thing, most administrators do not relish the prospect of drawing distinctions among teachers for salary reasons. If merit pay is substantial, more teachers will be dissatisfied than satisfied, and the principals and/or others rating teachers will need to deal with the nonrecipients. In the process, the raters themselves would be subjected to intense scrutiny that could be damaging professionally. On the other hand, because merit pay is a popular idea, school administrators tend to express support for it, all the while blaming teachers unions for its absence. At any rate, most teachers are employed under union contracts that prohibit merit pay. In most school districts, teacher salaries are based solely on years of teaching experience and extent of formal education. Years of teaching experience rated "superior" or "outstanding" receive as much salary credit as years in which teachers are rated "average" or even "poor." Actually, even in the absence of collective bargaining contracts, school districts normally do not pay higher salaries based on favorable evaluations received in or out of the district.

A Mechanism for Rewarding Teaching Excellence

Potentially, national board certification could provide an expeditious way of identifying and rewarding outstanding teachers. A school district in California could employ a board-certified teacher from New Jersey, confident that the teacher is highly competent. The reason is that the standards for board certification would be national, not local. The portability of board certification would thus benefit not only teachers but also the districts that are willing to pay higher salaries for outstanding teachers but lack a reliable way to identify them.

Another advantage of the national boards would be the way they are funded. Physicians who apply for medical board certification pay fees that cover the costs of certification. The financial benefits of board certification justify such fees as a good investment. Similarly, the teacher boards would be funded by fees paid by teacher applicants for board certification; for 1994-95, the fee has been set at $975.

The differences between board certification and conventional merit pay are critical. In conventional merit pay, school districts must invest a substantial amount of professional time paid from district funds to observing and evaluating teachers. Many districts lack the personnel to assess teacher performance effectively, at least in some fields. Furthermore, if only a small amount of district time is devoted to evaluating teachers, the procedures will be deficient. Overcoming this objection, however, requires a major investment of district resources. Inevitably, this investment will be wasted to the extent that teachers move out of the district or retire or are promoted. From a district point of view, procedures in which individual teachers pay a fee to a national board and recoup their payments from higher salaries are far more cost-effective. It should be noted, however, that school districts are not legally required to pay board-certified teachers more; that would be left to market forces and/or collective bargaining as it is in other fields.

Board certification also has the potential to help districts strengthen weak areas promptly. Retirements, transfers, pregnancies, promotions, and other factors may force districts to recruit a large number of teachers in certain fields within a relatively short time. In such situations, districts will want to recruit a nucleus of highly competent teachers. Reliance upon board certification is preferable to evaluations by unknown supervisors in other districts.

National Boards and Teachers Unions

A fundamental advantage of national boards is that they can circumvent union objections to merit pay. In a merit pay program, local school administrators decide which teachers are outstanding and how much more they should be paid for superior service. The teachers unions oppose this procedure on the grounds that it is subjective, leads to favoritism by administrators and subservience by teachers, and that high salaries for a few teachers are used as an excuse to avoid equitable salaries for all teachers.

Actually, the underlying union objection to merit pay cannot be articulated openly for political reasons. The rationale for merit pay is to encourage superior performance by rewarding it. If the rewards are not large, however, they will not overcome teacher reluctance to being scrutinized carefully. Most teachers want more pay for themselves, not high salaries for a few teachers, but the very logic of merit pay implies that relatively few teachers will receive it. If all or most receive it, the rewards cannot be very large and do not serve as incentives. If the rewards are large, relatively few teachers will receive them, and most others will object to the arrangement.

Suppose, for example, that a district employs 500 teachers and that one of every 20 receives merit pay. For every teacher who receives it, several others will feel aggrieved at not receiving it. The latter will take their grievance to union leaders, who will find themselves in an untenable position. They cannot afford to tell their dissatisfied constituents, "The merit pay plan is fair, and you did not deserve merit pay as much as the recipients of it." Such a response, even if completely justified, would be fatal to the incumbency of the union leaders, especially when the dissatisfied claimants are joined by teachers who do not claim to deserve merit pay. In other words, under conventional merit pay, the local unions have more to fear from a fair and objective plan than from one that is unfair and subjective. Of course, they cannot admit this to the public or their constituents, so they treat every merit pay plan as an unmitigated evil.[1]

Under the national board concept, determination of merit is not made by local administrators, thus there is no basis for a union to allege local bias or favoritism. Because the standards are national, the subjectivity argument also falls. The only important decision made locally is how much to pay the board-certified teachers. This would be subject to negotiations by the local teachers unions, inasmuch as they already negotiate salary differentials for advanced training, graduate degrees, onerous assignments, and extra loads, to cite just a few examples. The negotiation of salary differentials for board-certified teachers would not present unions with any problems that could not be resolved without splitting the union. Naturally, board-certified teachers would want higher salary differentials than the unions may accept in negotiations. Such an outcome, however, is common in the bargaining process. Teachers with advanced degrees want the union to negotiate higher differentials for advanced degrees, coaches want higher stipends for coaching, and so on. The critical point is that any stipends for board-certified teachers can be resolved without debilitating conflict within the teachers unions.

---

[1] For a more extensive analysis of union objections to merit pay, see Myron Lieberman, Are teachers underpaid?, *Public Interest* (Summer 1986), pp. 12-28.

Of course, if local unions do not bargain for substantial stipends for board-certified teachers, the effect will be to discredit the board idea and discourage teachers from seeking board certification. Although this may happen in some districts, it is unlikely to be a widespread problem. National Education Association (NEA) and American Federation of Teachers (AFT) leaders support the board concept. Teachers unions undoubtedly will urge school districts to establish substantial salary differentials for board-certified teachers.

Because there are more than 2.25 million public school teachers in the United States, a substantially higher salary level for all teachers is out of the question. The more sophisticated union leaders recognize this, even though their rhetoric urges that all teachers be paid as "professionals." Obviously, the salary differentials for board-certified teachers will depend in part upon the proportion of teachers who are board-certified. If half of them are certified, the costs of large salary differentials at the local level will be prohibitive. Furthermore, as the proportion of certified teachers increases, more marginal teachers will pass, thereby increasing the danger of discrediting the board idea. If, for example, the standards for certification allowed half the teachers to be certified over time, board certification would lose the credibility that is essential to its success at the local level.

In view of the potential benefits of national boards, a brief comment about the potential downside is in order. The major danger is that board certification will become easy to achieve. If this should happen, certification would no longer distinguish the superior teachers from the less qualified. Salary differentials for graduate degrees illustrate this danger. In an earlier day, a master's degree was evidence of a superior level of academic achievement. Because most school districts pay a salary differential for a master's degree, teachers are willing to bear the costs of earning one. Most universities are eager to accommodate teachers and do so in a variety of ways: easy courses, convenient schedules, elimination of residence requirements, and so on. The result is that as more teachers have been awarded master's degrees, the degree has become useless as a guide to teacher competence. And, in general, as teacher compensation was increasingly based on academic credit, the latter lost credibility as a guide to any aspect of teacher competence.

In 1993, the NBPTS set the fee for board certification at $975, a figure likely to increase if board certification appears to be a worthwhile investment. Clearly, the NBPTS has amassed an impressive list of political and educational interest groups to endorse the board idea:

    American Association of School Administrators
    American Educational Research Association
    American Federation of Teachers
    Association of Colleges and Schools of Education in State
       Universities and Land Grant Colleges and Affiliated Private
       Universities
    Association of Teacher Educators
    Council for American Private Education
    Council of Chief State School Officers
    International Reading Association
    National Association of Elementary School Principals
    National Association of Independent Colleges and Universities
    National Association of Secondary School Principals
    National Association of State Boards of Education
    National Conference of State Legislatures
    National Education Association
    National Governors' Association
    National School Boards Association

However, some basic issues remain unresolved less than a year away from the board's first test of applicants for board certification. Let us consider some of these issues briefly.

One question to be resolved is who should be eligible to apply for board certification. Initially, the NBPTS decided that any teacher with a bachelor's degree and three years of "successful" teaching experience in elementary or secondary schools would be eligible. Subsequently, however, the NEA's board of directors approved a policy declaring that eligibility to apply for board certification should require a state teaching license and graduation from an accredited program of teacher education. The NEA's position was similar to the one adopted previously by the American Association of Colleges for Teacher Education (AACTE), the major national organization of colleges and university departments of education. AACTE takes the position that applicants for board certification should be restricted to graduates from institutions accredited by AACTE and be licensed by their state.[2] This position was later supported by the Association of Teacher Educators, a national

---

[2] NEA assails national board's certification policy, *Education Week*, Jan. 17, 1990, p. 1, 11.

organization composed primarily of professors of education. It was also supported by the National Association of State Directors of Teacher Education and Certification (NASDTEC), the state officials directly responsible for administering the various state licensing requirements. Obviously, having a significant number of board-certified teachers from nonaccredited institutions would undermine the credibility of state licensing of teachers and the accreditation of teacher education.

The teachers unions have conflicting interests on the prerequisites for applying for board certification. If teachers without a state license can apply, there is a danger that a significant number of nonlicensed teachers will become board-certified. If this were to happen, state licensing of teachers would be weakened if not undermined, an outcome that the teachers unions are anxious to avoid. This outcome could be especially damaging where a state license is not required to teach in private schools. In such states, a significant number of nonlicensed teachers might become board-certified. At any rate, the NBPTS eventually adopted the NEA position on prerequisites.

In general, although little or no dispute has arisen over the potential benefits of national board certification, the potential benefits cannot be achieved unless board procedures and operations support the rationale. On these issues, several differences have emerged. Unquestionably, some are inherent in any effort to launch a significant national initiative; reasonable people often will disagree, even though they share common goals and even a common philosophy on how to achieve the goals. Other disagreements, however, raise fundamental issues about the direction and strategy adopted to implement the national board idea. The following section takes up both types of issues, although it is recognized that others may characterize them differently.

Assessment Development Laboratories

In 1989, NPBTS decided to establish board certification in 34 different fields.[3] The areas overlap but do not follow licensing requirements. Inasmuch as the number and scope of state licenses to teach vary widely among the states, it would have been practically impossible for board certification to follow the pattern of state licensure. As a matter of fact,

---

[3] NBPTS board of directors, *Policy amendment, national board of certificates* (Detroit: National Board for Professional Teaching Standards, Oct. 19, 1989).

efforts are already under way to induce the state teacher licensing agencies to adopt the NBPTS certification structure for licensing teachers. At the same time, however, the board has sought to establish certification options that would make it possible for all or most teachers to apply for certification. To put it differently, the intent was to avoid excluding any group of teachers because their teaching field was not encompassed by one of the 34 areas of certification. In announcing the areas, the board emphasized their tentative nature and the probability that additions, deletions, and modifications would be made from time to time.

The procedures and standards for various areas of board certification are to be resolved between 1994 and 1998 by means of a series of Assessment Development Laboratories (ADL). Working with the NBPTS, each ADL will:

- Specify the knowledge and skills to be assessed
- Identify appropriate methods of assessment
- Develop assessment instruments and methods
- Field test the assessment package
- Produce other needed resources, such as test manuals, instructions for candidates and examiners, and scoring keys.

In general, the certificates will relate to an age group as well as a subject. Thus, a French teacher in the elementary grades may (or may not) be required to pass the same French examinations as a secondary school French teacher, but their examinations will differ in terms of what the teachers need to know and are able to do for their students. It is not implied here that board examinations will be limited to these areas, but the examinations are expected to differ insofar as they apply to different student age ranges. Each ADL will be subject to competitive bidding in response to a request for proposal issued by the NBPTS.[4] In addition, each ADL will be subject to intensive field testing before its adoption by the NBPTS for national use.

Federal Funding of the NBPTS

In his 1987-88 annual report, NBPTS President James A. Kelly wrote:

---

[4]National Board for Professional Teaching Standards, *Draft RFP for early adolescence/English language arts assessment development laboratory* (Detroit: National Board for Professional Teaching Standards, 1990).

Following formation of the Board in May, 1987, and the naming of a President in October, the Board moved quickly to launch its work. During its first year, the Board organized its Executive, Finance, and Nominating committees, set up offices in Detroit and Washington, D.C., approved an operating budget, hired key employees, formed policy development working groups, initiated a $25 million funding proposal to Congress, held four two-day quarterly Board meetings and three regional meetings, sent Board and staff members out to meet with dozens of constituent groups, and published a brochure to explain the Board's work. It was a fast start spurred by the urgency of our mission.[5]

The NBPTS first requested $25 million in federal matching funds in 1988. The legislative vehicle was S. 2698, introduced by Sen. Christopher Dodd (D-Conn.). Although hearings were held and witnesses testified, mainly to support the bill, no action was taken before Congress adjourned. Eventually, however, Congress appropriated and/or authorized a total of $30 million in federal matching funds for research and development under NBPTS direction, and as of January 1994, $14.6 million had been received by the board and an additional $14.8 million was expected in the spring of 1994.

Conditions and Limitations

Essentially, the federal matching funds for NBPTS's research and development include the following terms and conditions:

- Funds cannot be used for board administration or operating expenses.

- Research projects to be conducted with federal funds must be widely disseminated for review and comment.

- Awards shall be made "competitively on the basis of merit."

- The board must adopt audit practices customarily applied to not-for-profit organizations.

- The board will share the results of its research with other public entities.

- The board must consult with the Fund for Development and Reform of Schools and Teaching Board on "the design and execution of its overall research and development strategy."[6]

---

[5] James A. Kelly, *President's 1987/88 annual report* (Detroit: National Board for Professional Teaching Standards, 1988), p. 5.

[6] A complete statement of the terms and conditions of the federal appropriations is contained in Public Law 102-325, July 23, 1992, Part D, especially (b) (2).

- Federal funds may be used only for "research and development activities directly related to the development of teacher assessment and certification procedures for elementary and secondary school teachers," and then only up to 50 percent of the cost of such activities.

- Congressional research and development priorities are spelled out.

- Financial assistance is not to be available unless the secretary of education determines that the funds are used for the purposes specified, and that the board has complied with the reporting and procedural requirements of the enabling legislation.

- The enabling legislation shall not be construed as establishing a national curriculum or preferred teaching methodology, infringing upon states' rights to license teachers, or providing certified individuals with legal rights related to hiring, promotion, retention, or dismissal.

- The secretary of education is not authorized to exercise "supervision or control over the research program, standards, assessment practices, administration, or staffing policies of the board."

Clearly, the prominent NEA/AFT role in the governance of national boards does raise several troublesome issues. The NEA has consistently opposed teacher testing at every stage of the employment process. While denigrating testing, it has emphasized credentialing, licensing, accreditation, and other elements of the paper curtain that shield presumed competence from any sort of testing. NEA and AFT affiliates continue to insist that academic credits and years of teaching experience are the only viable bases for compensating teachers. In view of the NEA's aggressive support for so many policies clearly inconsistent with the rationale for national boards, skepticism concerning its commitment to high standards is certainly understandable. The AFT's record on this issue is better, but not much better, as evidenced by its lack of support for maintaining examinations for would-be teachers in New York City.

Although there is some opposition to the concept of voluntary national boards for teachers, such opposition per se is not a major factor. Indeed, even the opposition is not so much to the board idea itself but to the fear that it will be the stepping stone to an involuntary national system of teacher licensing. The fear is groundless, but the rhetoric of some union leaders certainly fosters it.

Is there any objection in principle to federal support to implement voluntary national boards for teacher certification? Again, it should be emphasized that the reference here is to NBPTS certification, not licensure to practice. In opposing federal funding for NBPTS, Secretary of Education Lauro F. Cavazos argued that there would be no accountability to the secretary of education if federal appropriations were approved. In contrast, supporters insisted that the conditions provided a high degree of accountability.

The disagreement here really arises over the issue of the scope of accountability of the secretary of education regarding actions of the NBPTS. The secretary is obviously accountable in a number of areas; for example, he/she must determine that the board has complied with various procedural requirements before releasing federal funds for its use. On the other hand, the appropriation act stipulates that the secretary cannot supervise or control the research program, standards, assessment practices, administration or staffing policies of the board.

In effect, the secretary of education has the accountability of a powerful bookkeeper who is not accountable for the wisdom or effectiveness of board expenditures. On this issue, therefore, the opponents of the appropriation have the stronger argument. Essentially, the NBPTS board is accountable to no one for the quality of its programs, standards, practices, and staff. Some individuals on the board may be "accountable" to their sponsors for their actions as board members, but such accountability would be a private matter between them and their principals, if any.

As the critics of the federal appropriation have pointed out, sole source contracts, awarded without competitive bidding to organizations without a track record for unspecified research and development activities, are not sound public policy. In this connection, it should be noted that national boards in other fields were established without federal support. NBPTS supporters have attempted to counter the sole source objection by pointing to the requirement that federal funds be awarded "competitively on the basis of merit." Whether this requirement neutralizes the objection is debatable; in any event, the sight of a union-dominated organization emphasizing the importance of competition is interesting, to say the least.

In our opinion, the case for avoiding government involvement in board certification in education is much stronger than in virtually any other field. Governments are less likely to politicize technical matters if their mistakes have immediate, disastrous results. Thus, there is relatively little political controversy over the requirements for airline pilots or surgeons. In contrast, attempts to politicize the requirements to be a teacher are a common occurrence. A wide variety of special interest groups are constantly trying to change teacher licensing to their advantage, as they see it. Because the interest groups involved are often politically influential, it is often impossible to assess the changes they want; especially in the short run, they often are politically attractive even when they are or may be educationally unsound.

For that matter, the supremacy of political over technical considerations in the appropriations act is a fact, not just a potential danger to board policies. In drafting the enabling legislation, NBPTS representatives met with senatorial staff to work out the board procedures and funding estimates required for congressional approval. We know of no other professional board whose procedures and budgetary plans were established through negotiations with nontechnical political personnel. Suppose, for example, that board officials believe that a single institution or organization should receive a substantial share of the federal funds. This is simply not going to happen if prestigious institutions, especially in states represented by influential supporters of the appropriations, are shut out. The politicization of federal research and development grants is a pervasive feature of federal funding in several fields. If there were no alternative to federal funding, one might simply accept its politicization as part of cost of federally funded research and development. In this case, however, the NBPTS initiated the effort to obtain federal funds from its inception.

Board's Accountability to Secretary of Education

It was previously noted that Congress authorized $30 million and appropriated $20 million for the NBPTS. According to several senators who opposed the funding, the amount authorized was 20 percent of all the funds appropriated to the Department of Education for educational research. Despite repeated requests, the Senate sponsors had no documentation to support the amount, saying only that it relied upon NBPTS estimates that were thought to be reliable.

The actual costs of federal support will, of course, be much greater than $30 million. In order for funds to be made available to the NBPTS, the secretary of education must determine that the board will:

- Comply with federal regulations applicable to the grant

- Use federal funds only for research and development activities; its teacher assessment and certification procedures will be free from "racial, cultural, gender, or regional bias"

- "Disseminate widely for review and comment announcements of specific research funds to be conducted with Federal funds," such announcements to include "a description of the goals and focus of the specific project involved and the specific merit review procedures and evaluation criteria to be used in the competitive award process"

- Make awards of federal funds "competitively on the basis of merit... and to the extent practicably consistent with standards of excellence— a broad range of institutions associated with educational research and development"

The Federal Oversight Role

In effect, these monitoring obligations pose problems for the secretary of education. Consider, for instance, the secretary's responsibility for ensuring that the "teacher assessment and certification procedures will be free from racial, cultural, gender, or regional bias." Note that the secretary must determine this in advance of any payment. To require the secretary to examine a large number of complex testing and assessment procedures in order to confirm that they are free from racial, cultural, gender, or regional bias could easily require a substantial investment of department resources.

The list of responsibilities delegated to the secretary of education illustrates the importance of nongovernmental funding as well as operation of the boards. As we have seen, the appropriation act prohibits the secretary of education from exercising "supervision or control over the research program, standards, assessment practices, administration, or staffing policies of the Board." Actually, in view of the secretary's oversight responsibilities, this is unrealistic. Suppose, for example, any of the following events occur:

- As a result of board procedures, a disproportionately small number of female teachers pass the board exams for physics teachers. A suit is filed, alleging gender bias in the procedures.

- A disproportionately small number of African-American teachers pass the examinations in mathematics and initiate legal action to prohibit release of federal funds, alleging racial discrimination in board procedures.

- Pronounced regional variations appear in the proportions of teachers who apply for and receive board certification. Teachers from the regions (however defined) file lawsuits, alleging regional discrimination.

- A high proportion of Japanese and Chinese teachers pass the board examinations, whereas only a low proportion of Hispanic teachers do so. Would this be evidence of racial bias? Cultural bias? Neither? Quite possibly, protracted legal proceedings would be the only way to resolve these issues.

The point is that the secretary could be drawn into a host of controversies, many of which are likely to be resolved at least in part on political grounds. There is no justification for placing board procedures at risk this way, or of requiring the secretary of education to become involved in disputes over board procedures.

NBPTS Research and Development

At present, about 1,200 schools, colleges, divisions, or departments of education can be counted in the nation's institutions of higher education. These institutions employ some 35,000 professors of education, many in fields related directly to teacher competence.[7] Although not all of them do research on the subject, a substantial proportion are presumably so engaged; a large number of professors teach only 6 to 12 hours per week so that they will have time for research on teacher skills and effectiveness. This situation has existed with little change for at least several decades. In addition, scores, if not hundreds, of journals and tens of thousands of books are available on various aspects of teaching, including several aspects that presumably would be the subject of research and development conducted by the NBPTS.

Now comes the NBPTS, authorized to spend $30 million for research and development in teacher assessment and certification procedures. What Congress should be asking, along with governors, state legisla-

---

[7]Estimate provided in March 1990 by David Imig, executive director, American Association of Colleges for Teacher Education.

tures, university trustees, and taxpayers is: What is going on here? Our nation has already invested billions in research and development in the fields of teacher education and teacher effectiveness; currently, it is spending much more in one year for these purposes than the $30 million authorized for the NBPTS through 1998. Suppose that we assume that 10 percent of paid faculty time is devoted to research, as it is at most colleges and universities. On this basis, our nation is already spending $87.5 million annually on research in teacher education:

35,000	professors of education
17,500	faculty in fields involved in NBPTS research
$50,000 =	estimated annual salary plus benefits per faculty member
$875,000,000 =	total compensation
$87,500,000 =	one-tenth for research in fields of NBPTS activity

The above estimate is an extremely conservative one, inasmuch as it does not include the prorated costs of facilities, support personnel, supplies, and equipment for research on teacher assessment issues. Granted, the national board concept requires some research and development that differs from what is available, but the gap raises some hard questions. For example, why is so much money required to stimulate the research needed to implement the board concept? What research are these professors conducting that is more important than the research needed to implement the board concept? What effort has been made to use the research time currently available, for which professors are being paid, on NBPTS issues? In this connection, the NEA and the American Educational Research Association (AERA) set forth an interesting qualification to their support for the federal appropriations for the NBPTS. The qualification was that the funds not be taken from the other appropriations by the Department of Education. The obvious question is: Why not? If the NBPTS can achieve all the good things that the NEA and AERA and others claim for it, why shouldn't departmental priorities be rearranged to make these things possible? Indeed, why shouldn't the priorities of the NEA Foundation also be rearranged if the board concept is as promising as NEA leaders assert?

Implications of NBPTS Strategy For Research Costs

When national boards were first proposed in 1960, the strategic plan envisaged was very different from the one adopted by the NBPTS. The original proposal was to establish national boards in fields demonstrating the greatest need to raise teacher salaries, and then build upon the experience gained to add new areas of certification. In contrast, the NBPTS is trying to establish approximately 34 boards by 1998.

Any schedule for establishing boards must recognize the fact that implementation is likely to generate several important but unforeseeable problems. This is especially true of the first few boards. Later, as experience is gained from the early boards, the creation of subsequent ones should be a more expeditious process. A critical issue: What are the implications for the NBPTS funding? The NBPTS approach emphasizes the certainty of unforeseen problems, including inability at this early stage to predict the savings, if any, as more boards are established.

Conceptually, a different approach is possible. Defense contractors often conduct research and development in situations in which it is impossible to develop realistic estimates of the costs of completing the project. In these situations, the work proceeds to the point at which future costs can be estimated. In our view, it was neither necessary nor desirable that the federal government underwrite research and development for the NBPTS. Those objections aside, government might fund or help to fund the complete process for a few boards, but future funding, if any, would be contingent and based upon the experience gained from the first board certificates to be implemented.

One could hardly object if private sources were willing to support the NBPTS on a long-range basis before any one board certificate is operative; however, the case for such commitments from public funds is not persuasive. Of course, teacher union leaders are eager to avoid situations in which some teachers enjoy the possibility of board certification and others do not, but a federal appropriation is not the solution to this problem. The critical point is that the NBPTS had sufficient funding without federal assistance to launch five to eight national board certificates. If $50 million is required to establish 34 national boards, the $30 million NBPTS is committed to raise from private sources should be more than sufficient to implement five to eight board certificates. Once five to eight certificates are established and operating effectively, a large-scale effort to set up the others would be in order, and funding for them would not be a major problem.

Union Issues in National Board Certification

The roles of the NEA and the AFT in national board certification is a frequent topic of discussion. Because much of the discussion is inaccurate and appears to overlook the critical issues, some clarification of the roles of these organizations is in order.

NBPTS bylaws provide for a board of directors of 63 members and the president ex officio. Two-thirds (42 members) must be Teaching Professional Members. Of these 42 members, "one third shall be people who hold, or within the past 10 years have held, local state, or national office in the two national teacher unions. Of this group, equal numbers shall be from each union." Beginning in 1994, however, at such time as the board has issued at least 5,000 certificates, board-certified teachers will begin to elect the Teaching Professional Members as vacancies occur; because directors can serve for only two consecutive three-year terms, board-certified teachers themselves eventually will elect the 42 Teaching Professional Members of the board. It should be noted, however, that the rate at which this happens is tied to the rate at which the board certifies teachers, and the latter is a matter of conjecture at this time. Consequently, the existing arrangements for choosing directors may be operative through the mid 1990s.

Putting aside the obvious discrimination against nonunion teachers in a matter in which union membership should be irrelevant, the bylaws thus require that 14 of the 63 board members be NEA or AFT leaders. In addition, however, NEA/AFT leaders may become directors by meeting the requirements for other categories of board membership. Thus, although only 14 of the 63 board members must be NEA/AFT leaders, the majority of NBPTS directors are NEA or AFT members; only a handful of the 42 Teaching Professional Members are not members of either the NEA or the AFT.

Without attempting to delve into every nuance, it should be apparent that the AFT/NEA contingent can veto any board action to which they are opposed. Within rather broad limits, they also can achieve adoption of any policy they regard as important to union interests. These conclusions are in no way negated by the fact that the union members do not always vote as a unified bloc, or the fact that the NEA and the AFT appear to have different positions on some board issues. Regardless of the arithmetic of board membership, full-time union leaders with access to tremendous organizational resources, more time to devote to pursuing union interests, and a large stake in doing so, are bound to exert more influence than directors *pro bono* who are not affected occupationally by the outcome of board activities. This is only one reason why the union interests will be dominant. Another is that union leaders are more influential than unaffiliated board members in the appointment of other board members and staff.

Realistically, the issue is not whether the NEA/AFT will dominate the board; it is whether such domination will erode the board's integrity. Clearly, the possibility that it will has a basis in union dynamics. For instance, consider the question of which fields will be board-certified. Obviously, if teachers of driver education, cosmetology, and typing can be certified, the practice will tend to discredit the board concept. The unions, however, will come under strong pressure to extend the concept to every subject, grade level, or activity. Teachers for whom it is not available will view this fact as an inequity and demand that their union remedy the situation. They will complain about "elitism" or second-class citizenship; inevitably, charges of racism will emerge, especially if ethnic differences exist in the proportion of teachers in fields not certified.

How will union leaders react to these charges? Surely not by asserting that content in the field in question is insufficient to justify board certification. On the contrary, they will urge that teachers of all subjects be eligible for board certification.

Union dynamics will also affect the proportion of teachers who apply for board certification and the proportion in various fields eventually certified. If the boards are to be self-sustaining, an adequate number of teachers must be induced to apply and pay for the examination procedures. As the number increases, however, the level of expertise and the salary differentials paid to board-certified teachers inevitably will decrease. Thus far, the NBPTS has not come to grips with this basic issue. Instead, it is being deferred until some of the ADLs have submitted their recommendations on requirements for a board-certified teacher. At that point, policy decisions on the proportion of board-certified teachers will need to be made.

The question of whether to allow substantial differences in the proportion of board-certified teachers from field to field is very important. For example, should the pass rates in fields in which the supply of teachers is ample be the same as in such fields as mathematics and science, which are characterized by pervasive shortages?

A basic problem arises out of differences in the talent pool and from one field of certification to another. Suppose, for example, that all high school teachers, regardless of field, must achieve a certain level of proficiency in the core examination taken by all high school teachers seeking board certification. Suppose also that cutoff point X would enable 20 percent of the physical education teachers to be certified but might allow 60 percent of the physics teachers to pass. Conversely, suppose a cutoff point that allows 20 percent of the physics teachers to pass is adopted. In that case, a much lower proportion of physical education teachers will pass. In the first scenario, some ill-qualified physics teachers will pass; in the second scenario, very few physical education teachers will become board-certified.

Professional football illustrates both the difficulty and the importance of the issues. Quarterbacks are paid more than offensive linemen. The top 10 percent of the quarterbacks are paid much more than the top 10 percent of the offensive linemen. On the other hand, because there are more offensive linemen than quarterbacks, the former are in a stronger position to control union policies on compensation. In practice, the players union tries to reduce the disparities by such policies as higher minimum salaries for all players and equal fringe benefits. Currently, there is discussion about placing all players on a salary schedule for a certain number of years, with the right to negotiate an unlimited amount afterward. Such proposals are intended to shift more of the salaries to the lower-paid positions; instead of paying huge bonuses to outstanding college players, the owners could pay more to players in the lesser-paid positions.

The point here is simple but fundamental. If employees at lower salary levels outnumber those at higher levels, the union will seek to reduce the disparities, not maintain or expand them. Evidence to this effect is overwhelming, in and out of education. Teachers unions illustrate the principle in scores of ways. One is their insistence that mathematics and science teachers be paid the same as others. Another is the puny differentials paid for a doctoral degree; inasmuch as few teachers have an earned doctorate, the differentials for them are very small. Still another is the union emphasis on the same health benefits for all employees.

At first glance, experience with the medical specialty boards does not support this argument. Physicians in the United States number about 600,000; about 400,000 of them have been certified by one or more of the 23 medical specialty societies. Today, most medical school graduates expect eventually to apply for board certification. About 75 percent of the graduates in American and Canadian medical schools pass their board examinations on their first try; ultimately, about 85 percent pass. About 23 percent of the licensed physicians in the United States are graduates of other foreign medical schools; of these, about 35 percent pass their board examinations on their first try, and about 40 percent eventually pass.[8] Even though this pattern is acceptable in the medical field, it would be disastrous for the educational boards to allow a comparable proportion of teachers to become board-certified. In the first place, admission standards for medical schools and for passing the state medical examinations are much higher than those for becoming a licensed teacher. Second, as the number of persons in any given profession increases, it becomes more difficult to maintain high entry standards. For these and other reasons, standards for board certification that allow even a third of all teachers to become board-certified eventually will not distinguish superior teachers from others

The underlying problem is that a fundamental tension exists between a union dedicated to advancing the welfare of all teachers and an organization whose purpose is to identify and reward a minority of them. This is not to say that every issue will be resolved to accommodate the unions instead of the national boards. Secondary union interests may well be subordinated to fundamental national board interests. Still, on critical issues that affect basic union and basic national board interests, the former are certain to prevail. The only way to avoid this is to separate control of the national boards from control by teachers unions; unfortunately, union control of the NBPTS has been institutionalized with little prospect of change.

Subject Matter Tests and Board Eligibility

This concluding section is devoted to a different approach to solving some of the difficult problems inherent in national board certification

---

[8]Information on medical specialty boards was provided in 1990 by the Council of Medical Specialty Societies.

for teachers. The suggestion is based on an analogy to board certification of physicians. Such certification occurs at two levels after physicians meet the requirements to take board examinations. A physician who passes the first level becomes "board-eligible," meaning that he/she is eligible to take the remaining tests to become "board-certified." Board-eligible thus refers to eligibility to complete the process, not to initiate it. It therefore differs from the issue of what should be the prerequisites to apply for board certification. The suggestion made here is that achieving a certain level of proficiency in the subjects taught might be treated as the way to become board-eligible—eligible to complete the process of board certification. This suggestion is based partly on the costs of assessing teachers in action. On this issue especially, the economics of board certification will be extremely important. If board procedures include the observation of all teachers who apply for board certification, the costs of the procedures could be prohibitive. On the other hand, board procedures without assessment of teachers in action will not be widely accepted.

Among other things, the suggestion offered here is intended to help resolve this dilemma. Everyone agrees that good teachers must know the subject they teach. Also, there is unanimous agreement that it is possible to test a teacher's knowledge of a subject. In order to keep the costs of observing teachers within reasonable limits, subject matter tests could be used to screen out teachers who lack outstanding knowledge of their subject. The more expensive board procedures could then be limited to teachers who have demonstrated such knowledge. These teachers could be board-eligible, meaning that they are qualified to take the remaining tests required to be board-certified.

As matters stand, it is impossible to tell how much teachers know about their subject. The teachers may have a certain number of credits in a subject, but the standards for passing courses vary among different institutions, subjects, and professors. Even the same professor may use different standards for various courses or students. Consequently, it is practically impossible for school districts to determine how well their teachers know the subjects they teach. National board examinations would not solve this problem completely, but they could be a big step toward its resolution.

Subject matter tests for teachers seeking board certification should be instituted with an explicit statement that knowledge of a subject is only one of the qualifications of a good teacher. The board position should be that although knowledge of the subject is only one component of good teaching, it is a critical one that can be measured. Such an approach would greatly facilitate the accountability of institutions of higher education. If teachers seeking board certification are tested in the subjects they teach, colleges that allow credit for inferior academic achievement would be quickly exposed.

Currently, NBPTS publications concede that knowledge of subject matter should be an important requirement for board certification. Unfortunately, there is no corresponding recognition of its strategic importance. The teachers unions will negotiate the terms and conditions of employment for board-certified teachers, but their domination of board governance and procedures is undesirable. Unfortunately, political leaders and media personnel are ill-equipped to raise any hard questions about the enterprise.

16.   ARE TEACHERS UNDERPAID?

Many proposed educational reforms would adversely affect terms and conditions of teacher employment. A longer school day and school year are obvious examples, but many others could be cited. Naturally, teachers do not regard such proposals as "reform." In their eyes, such proposals are merely a means to exploit teachers. Justified or not, this attitude cannot be ignored in view of the fact that public school teaching is one of the most highly unionized occupations. About three of every four public school teachers in the United States are represented by a union and almost as many are union members.

Teachers unions are in business to achieve more—not less—favorable terms and conditions of employment for teachers. In other occupations, unions have accepted adverse changes ("givebacks," in union terminology) only in the face of highly visible threats to the job security of their members. The concessions made by the United Auto Workers to enable U.S. automobile manufacturers to compete with Japanese companies illustrate this point. In education, however, a quantum increase in the number of private schools is the only potential threat to the livelihood of public school teachers.

Whether or not such an increase may take place, terms and conditions of teacher employment have not been affected thus far by the possibility. On the contrary, the reform reports unanimously support a substantial increase in teacher salaries. Teachers understandably view such proposals as "real" or "genuine" reforms, not "fads" or "quick fixes."

A substantially similar version of this essay appeared as an article by Myron Lieberman under the same title in *Public Interest*, Summer 1986, pp. 12-28.

Therefore, let us consider the reforms most strongly supported by teachers. After all, if their opposition is a major roadblock to reform, perhaps reforms that they enthusiastically support have a better chance to succeed.

How Teachers Are Paid

Unquestionably, most teachers are paid solely according to their training and years of experience. Salary schedules differ primarily in the number of years that receive salary credit and in the kind and amount of higher education credits required for salary increases. Also, some variation is seen in the stipends paid for coaching, class advising, bandleading, and other extracurricular activities, and in whether additional amounts are paid for advanced degrees (as distinguished from mere accumulation of credit).

Most teacher salary schedules do not provide salary differentials according to the subject or grade level. It is not unusual, however, to pay school psychologists, counselors, special education teachers, and a few other groups a stipend above the schedule for most teachers. Even in these cases, however, additional training is the major factor considered.

It was not always thus. In the early 1900s, the common practice was to pay secondary school teachers more than those in elementary schools. The differentials were both cause and result of the fact that elementary school teachers were overwhelmingly female, whereas high school teachers were more evenly divided between the sexes. The movement toward a single schedule covering kindergarten to grade 12 resulted from the fact that there are twice as many elementary as secondary school teachers. It became impossible to achieve a leadership position in teachers organizations without supporting a single schedule covering all grades.

Actually, a different pattern might have materialized in the early 1960s. Today, it is widely agreed that the 1961 collective bargaining election among New York City's teachers was the single most important stimulus to teacher bargaining and teachers unions in the 1960s. One of the critical issues in the New York City election was whether all teachers should be in the same bargaining unit. For tactical reasons, the National Education Association (NEA) supported the idea that elementary, junior high, and senior high school teachers should separately choose unions to represent their grade levels. If the NEA position had prevailed, it is virtually certain that many school districts would have reverted to the practice of paying secondary more than elementary school teachers.

The NEA position did not prevail, however, and today the issue is moot. For political reasons, the elimination of salary differentials for higher grade levels could not be publicly ascribed to the fact that elementary school teachers outnumbered secondary teachers in teachers unions by a two-to-one margin. Instead, it was rationalized by the alleged importance of the first few years of schooling and by the fact that elementary school teachers usually worked as many days as teachers in secondary schools. Neither reason is very impressive. We do not pay high school mathematics teachers as much as university professors of the subject, even though we could make the same argument about the importance of the early years. The fact is that salaries are influenced less by the importance of the work than by the availability of the skills needed. In general, we pay enough to get the job done adequately, no more. Nor is the fact that elementary teachers work as many school days particularly important. So do school custodians and secretaries, but no one contends they should be paid as much as teachers for this reason.

How much are teachers paid? Perhaps the most accurate as well as the most surprising answer is that nobody knows. A wealth of data on the subject exists, but it is incomplete on certain critical points. Significantly, the NEA, the largest of the two national teachers unions, is the primary source of data on teacher salaries; even federal agencies rely upon the NEA for information on teacher salaries and salary trends.

As we shall see, the missing data would show significantly higher levels of compensation than those disseminated in U.S. Department of Education statistics. Not surprisingly, the missing data would weaken union claims that teachers are underpaid. In conducting its salary surveys, the NEA uses two categories: "classroom teachers" and "instructional staff." The latter includes supervisors of instruction, librarians, guidance counselors, psychologists, and principals, and its average wage is significantly higher than the average for classroom teachers.

A Nation At Risk, the report of the National Commission on Excellence in Education,[1] is widely regarded as the leading reform manifesto. Like most reform reports, the document says nothing about

---

[1] National Commission on Excellence in Education, *A nation at risk* (Washington, D.C.: U.S. Government Printing Office, 1983).

the fringe benefits paid to teachers. Our reference here is not to their shorter work year and workday (which will be discussed later) but to payment made for teacher retirement; health and welfare benefits; leave benefits; extra duty pay (for example, coaching); unemployment insurance; and worker's compensation.

As in the private sector, health and welfare benefits—primarily medical and hospital insurance—have become major components of teacher compensation. Additionally, the data on teacher salaries do not ordinarily include the amounts paid by boards and state governments for retirement.

Nevertheless, these important elements of total compensation were ignored by the national commission, as they are generally in discussion of teacher salaries. Obviously, these omissions result in significant understatements of compensation.

Like public employee pension systems generally, benefits in teacher retirement systems tend to be much more generous than those available to most private sector employees. Nationally, expenditures for all teacher fringe benefits are almost certain to be 10 to 20 percent higher than the comparable figure for all workers outside of teaching. It is highly probable that teacher fringe benefits increased even more rapidly than private sector benefits in the 1980s and 1990s. Some states emphasized higher pension benefits instead of direct salary increases in the 1970s; in these states, substantially greater school district and state contributions were required as teacher retirements increased.

Aside from state contributions to teacher retirement, teachers frequently opt for increases in fringe benefits instead of increases in salaries. This often occurs because the fringe benefits are not taxable to the teachers; the additional income to teachers would be taxed if the funds for health and welfare benefits were added to teacher salaries. Typically, teachers ignore fringe benefits in their efforts to persuade the public that they should be paid more. Teachers invariably allege that their salaries have lagged behind the cost of living, at the same time ignoring school board payments for medical and dental costs, which have escalated more than any other component of the cost of living.

Like the administration that preceded it, the Clinton administration introduced legislation to eliminate the tax-sheltered status of health insurance benefits, an initiative that has aroused intense union opposition in the past. Nevertheless, in addition to providing a much-needed brake on the costs of health care, the change would clearly be consistent with economic realities.

227

Like fringe benefits, the amount of time teachers work is usually ignored in discussions of teacher salaries. It is understandable why teachers should ignore this issue, but not why others should. The number of teacher workdays varies, but 180 days is a reasonably accurate national average. Serious controversy exists, however, with respect to the length of the teacher workday. Most teachers work a defined school day, usually 6 to 7.5 hours, including lunch and preparation periods. The lunch period is usually at least 30 minutes, but it is not always duty-free, even when this is mandated by state law. On the other hand, preparation periods often are not used for preparation; occasionally, they are used for personal tasks, or simply for rest during the day.

The major issue is how much time teachers devote to their work outside the regular school day. A 1990 NEA report asserted categorically that, "teachers average 46 hours of work a week."[2] This conclusion was based upon teachers' subjective judgments and recollections of how much time they devoted to school tasks.

Given the self-serving nature of the study and the procedures used, a healthy skepticism seems warranted. No doubt some teachers average 46 hours a week, despite union efforts to discourage voluntary work because it weakens union efforts to have it compensated. Still, teachers unions have never shown any interest in a 40- or 35-hour workweek that would encompass the work teachers allegedly perform outside the regular school day. Regardless, the NEA's claim that teachers average 46 hours of work per week appears to be a substantial exaggeration.

To summarize, both the rate and the amount of teacher compensation are typically understated, whereas their hours of work are overstated. In addition, teachers typically enjoy certain benefits, such as tenure, which have financial value even if they are not regarded as part of the compensation package. Let us put aside these considerations, however, and turn to the contention that it is imperative to raise the economic status of teachers if one is to improve public schooling.

The Case for and Against Higher Teacher Salaries

Precisely why is it imperative—or even desirable—to raise average teacher salaries? The reasons most often cited are that (1) teaching is

---

[2]NEA News press release, Estimates of school statistics, 1989-90, April 30, 1990.

not as high quality as it should be because teachers are recruited largely from lower ranks of high school and college graduates, and (2) it is impossible to attract teachers to certain fields because salaries in those fields are too low. As *A Nation at Risk* observed, "Too many teachers are being drawn from the bottom quarter of graduating high school and college students." The report went on to point out: "The shortage of teachers in mathematics and science is particularly severe. A 1981 survey of forty-five states revealed a shortage of mathematics teachers in thirty states, and of physics teachers everywhere." To remedy those problems, *A Nation at Risk* recommended that "Salaries for the teaching profession should be increased and should be professionally competitive, market-sensitive, and performance-based."

The commission did not say how large an increase would be required to achieve these objectives. Generally, however, reform proposals emphasize the fact that teaching is not economically competitive with other professions. Supposedly, low salaries also force teachers to moonlight extensively, thus reducing the time that should be devoted to their teaching positions or to professional improvement. Despite differences in language and emphasis, these are the major arguments for increasing teacher salaries.

These arguments are expressed as if their validity were self-evident; unfortunately, none demonstrates a causal relationship between the decline in scholastic aptitude among beginning teachers and the actual decline in student achievement. The causal relationship is assumed without question. Nevertheless, if one assumes that the decline in student achievement has multiple causes, then we should have at least a rough idea of how it is affected by the talent level of teachers. But no one seems to have any idea how much additional teacher talent would be attracted by increases in teacher compensation, or how much more students would learn if teachers were paid more.

The more one considers the matter, the less impressive is the argument that calls for a significant increase in the level of teacher compensation. The critical point is the absence of any concrete idea of what, where, when, and how educational benefits would accrue from increasing teacher salaries. Instead, there are only general appeals to raise teacher salaries, without the slightest indication of what levels of improvement would result. To put it bluntly, there is an extremely weak empirical basis for raising teacher salaries generally.

Private Schools and Merit Pay

There is widespread belief and considerable evidence that private schools educate at least as well as public schools. Unquestionably, however, teachers in private schools are paid less and receive fewer fringe benefits than teachers in public schools. Of course, the differences vary from area to area and from school to school, but most private school teachers probably earn only two-thirds to three-quarters as much as public school teachers.

How can this be? That is, how can it be argued that higher salaries for public school teachers are essential, while teachers in private schools are paid considerably less but presumably perform as well or better? Clearly, the lower average salaries in private schools cannot be explained by the presence of a small number of teachers who are members of religious orders; the differentials apply to lay teachers, who comprise the vast majority anyway. It is often asserted that private school teachers have more autonomy, more freedom from bureaucratic demands, and more input into professional decisions, such as the textbook selection. These claims, however, have not been substantiated on a systematic basis.

In any event, proposals to raise the economic status of teachers generally are wishful thinking, a conclusion that is conceded even by some teacher union leaders. Along with other reformers, they are showing more interest in proposals that call for substantial salary increases for one or more subgroups of teachers. These subgroups would be differentiated from other teachers by their function, their subject matter specialization, and/or their superior teaching performance.

Although all three kinds of salary proposals are often labeled "merit pay," important differences are seen among them. Incentives, costs, ease of administration, and other consequences are considerations that need to be addressed. Differentials based upon subject matter require minimal administrative judgment, are relatively easy to administer, and probably would have more immediate effects than merit pay. A college senior majoring in mathematics is more likely to become a teacher because of a subject differential than one based on merit pay. The student would realize that the subject matter differential would be available immediately, whereas the merit pay differential would be uncertain, involve a great deal of judgment, require a multiyear evaluation period, and would likely be resented by more experienced teachers.

These comments are not intended to endorse one approach or criticize another, but rather to underscore the need to examine each on its own merits.

Because these three approaches are often confused, let us begin by illustrating the differences:

1. A is a "master teacher" who helps to train new teachers. B is an excellent teacher who doesn't want to be bothered by training duties and isn't concerned about the salary differential for doing so. If the district pays A more than B because of A's role in training teachers, we have a salary differential based upon different functions. Such proposals are often referred to as "differentiated staffing."

2. C is a mathematics teacher; D is a history teacher. Both are excellent teachers. Both do everything expected of teachers, in and out of the classroom. Nevertheless, because of the tremendous shortage of mathematics teachers, C is paid $5,000 annually more than D. In this case, the salary differential is based upon subject matter specialization.

3. E is an outstanding mathematics teacher; F is an average mathematics teacher. They are the same age, have the same training and experience, and perform the same tasks throughout the day. Nevertheless, the district pays E more than F because it wishes to pay outstanding teachers more than average ones. In this case, the salary differential is based upon differences in the quality of performance.

We shall refer only to the third group of salary proposals as "merit pay"; proposals to pay teachers more based upon functional differentiation or subject matter specialization do not involve merit pay as defined here.

Educational reformers repeatedly have noted the severe teacher shortages in certain fields, such as mathematics and science. The cause of the shortages is simple enough. Persons who have the abilities and aptitudes to be competent teachers of these subjects can earn substantially more in private sector positions. According to the folklore of education, concern for young people is the primary and common characteristic of teachers. In the real world, however, a mathematics teacher has more in common with other people having mathematical skills and aptitudes than with other teachers. There is a strong nonschool demand for mathematics teachers and for students who are potential mathematics teachers. No such strong nonschool demand exists for persons who would make good history teachers. This is why it is imprudent to pay both the same salaries.

Suppose a university decided that professors of surgery and professors of English literature should be paid the same. In that case, the university either would overpay professors of English literature, perhaps by as much as $75,000 per year, or it would be unable to hire professors of surgery. Even surgeons not qualified to teach surgery would not teach for the salaries paid to professors of English literature. As absurd as this self-imposed dilemma would be, it is precisely the dilemma facing school districts that pay mathematics teachers the same as history teachers; the districts end up without mathematics teachers.

Teacher bargaining plays a critical role in perpetuating this short-sighted policy. Teachers unions try to avoid wage differentials; such differentials lead to internal strife, something the unions don't want. Furthermore, the lower the differential, the less likely it will achieve its purpose; the higher the differential, the more opposition to it among the teachers who do not receive it. The differential is offered because the supply of teachers in the subject receiving the differential is very limited. However, unions seldom negotiate hard for large gains for a few constituents. The union negotiates for gains for most if not all of its constituents. The union negotiator responds to what most members want—and what they want is more money for themselves, not concessions that indicate their services are not as valuable as someone else's.

Although single salary schedules do not necessarily eliminate interunion conflict over salaries, they do tend to minimize it. However, that is seldom given as the reason unions negotiate them. Reasons usually given are that all teachers love children, all are members of the same profession, and all have the same amount of training. Furthermore, unions view the shortages in specific fields as leverage to achieve salary increases for all teachers.

Additionally, salary differentials for fields experiencing severe shortages could be a disastrous precedent. Once one concedes that market factors are a legitimate concern in salaries for mathematics teachers, why stop there? Why not go on to say that if the school district has several competent applicants for teaching history, it should lower the salary offered for history teachers? Actually, overpayment of some teachers is as serious a problem as underpayment of others; in fact, reducing the overpayment may be essential to resolving the problems of underpayment.

School boards lament their inability to compete for people who would be competent mathematics or science teachers. Still, if boards would stop overpaying teachers in fields that could be competently staffed at lower salaries, they could pay the higher salaries needed to recruit teachers in fields of shortage. Realistically, however, teachers unions could not survive the interunion conflicts that would emerge if salaries were geared even in part to grade level or subject.

In past years, salary differentials based on different functions have been the subject of widespread discussion and some legislation. Several governors and legislative leaders have indicated their willingness to increase the salaries of some, but not all, teachers. Typically, state-mandated merit rating is neither politically nor administratively feasible. Consequently, political leaders have relied more and more on functional differentiation as a basis for additional compensation.

The 'Team Teaching' Fiasco

Past experience with differentiated staffing among teachers demonstrates the problems associated with the team teaching approach, one of the most celebrated flops promoted by the Ford Foundation in the 1950s. It was essentially an effort to pay teachers more by differentiating their roles. The advocates of team teaching were impressed by functional differentiation in medicine. Medical occupations include physicians, nurses, laboratory technicians, nutritionists, physical therapists, and so on. Physicians perform the most highly specialized functions that require the most training. The other occupations are subordinate to the physicians and command less pay. Physicians do not spend their time performing work that can be performed by their subordinates. To do so would escalate the costs of the services involved; it would also reduce the time physicians could use their professional skills. The more work that professionals do that could be performed by less qualified workers, the less time they have to concentrate on doing work they alone are qualified to do.

In principle, the concept makes good sense. It was applied to education initially by adding teacher's aides to regular classrooms. In elementary grades, aides carried out such tasks as meeting buses, helping children take off or put on coats, and collecting or distributing assignments. In secondary schools, the concept of differentiated staffing was

233

tied to instruction of large groups. It is just as easy to lecture to 250 students as to 25. Instead of 10 classes, each with 25 students, why not have one teacher lecture to 250? This teacher could be the most qualified to teach the particular assignment; furthermore, the teacher would have more time to prepare the lecture because of the overall savings in time involved. Instead of requiring 10 teachers to prepare the same lesson, one teacher could do so. The other teachers could use time saved to work with individual students or on some other topic. Thus the "team" could be of varying size and composition.

Educators sought to introduce team teaching in selected districts across the country. Most "lighthouse" districts—that is, affluent suburban districts that confused wealth with leadership—jumped on the team teaching bandwagon. Like most educational reforms, team teaching started with enormous fanfare; not long afterward, however, it was buried in a shallow unmarked grave.

'Master Teachers' and Merit Pay

"Master teacher" plans reflect a different approach. In these plans, districts designate a certain proportion of teachers as "master teachers." The state then allocates a certain amount of money each year for them; in this way, districts are able to pay more to their outstanding teachers. Master teachers are then released from teaching for part of the day to help new teachers, work on curriculum, or perform other such duties. Master teacher plans vary considerably, but the following requirements appear frequently:

- Master teachers will be released from teaching for part of the day to help new teachers, work on curriculum, and/or perform other duties as may be negotiated or agreed upon. In other words, to avoid having state-mandated "merit pay," the legislation provides for some functional differentiation between master teachers and others. The most common belief is that the master teacher will work with new teachers or teachers who are having difficulties.

- Master teachers must carry a specified proportion of a full teaching load (usually 50 to 80 percent).

- Master teachers cannot supervise or evaluate other teachers. The real reason for this is that teachers who supervise or evaluate other teachers are usually excluded from teacher bargaining units by the state bargaining laws. Consequently, if master teachers supervised or evaluated other teachers, the unions would frequently lose them as dues-paying members. (Of course, this reason is not articulated publicly.)

In practice, master teacher plans are usually counterproductive. Clearly, the additional stipend is irrelevant to keeping talented teachers in the profession. Teachers receiving it are usually at the top of the salary schedule and have no plans to retire or take a nonteaching job. Frequently, their spouses have settled occupations in the area. In fact, many master teachers would continue to teach even if their salaries were reduced instead of increased.

Although enacted to keep good teachers in the classroom, the master teacher programs have had precisely the opposite effect. To maintain the fiction of functional specialization, the master teachers are assigned nonteaching tasks outside the classroom. Neither the school district nor the teachers really care what these tasks are, inasmuch as they are only a means of avoiding the implication that the master teachers are receiving merit pay. In practice, master teacher legislation typically encourages good teachers to get out of the classroom to perform duties that the districts are unwilling to pay for themselves.

This brings us to merit pay. As we have defined it, merit pay exists if and only if teacher A is paid more than teacher B for performing the same kind of work, i.e., teaching the same grade or subject. Clearly, paying teachers on the basis of merit is not a common practice in the United States; it is doubtful whether one percent of the nation's school districts have merit pay, even under an expansive definition of it.

Why, despite widespread public support for merit pay, do such a minuscule number of school districts provide merit pay? One widely overlooked reason is that most school administrators do not want the task of identifying the teachers who are to receive merit pay. Such action usually generates intense scrutiny of administration judgments. Inasmuch as most teachers do not receive merit pay, many dissatisfied teachers will criticize every award; the typical administrator can do without this headache.

Nevertheless, merit pay has widespread public support, and administrators need some other reason to explain its absence. Teachers unions meet this need. Their opposition to merit pay provides the excuse administrators need to explain their failure to implement it.

Significantly, merit pay is about as rare where unions are weak as where they are strong. In most districts, union opposition to merit pay is simply an additional reason that it does not happen. As with administrators, however, the real reasons unions are opposed to merit pay are not the reasons given in public. The unions emphasize the "subjectivity" of merit pay and the alleged likelihood that it will be used to reward lackeys of the school administration.

Actually, unions have more to fear from fair than from unfair administration of merit pay. No matter how fair and objective the administration of merit pay, many teachers will feel they were erroneously passed over for it. If they approach the union for help, the union is in a no-win situation. It cannot afford to get involved in controversies over whether union members A, B, and C are more deserving of merit pay than union member X; such controversies would divide and weaken the union. Nor can it say to the As, Bs, and Cs (who will always outnumber the Xs) that "you don't deserve merit pay as much as X." The only way the unions can avoid this dilemma is to avoid merit pay, preferably by emphasizing objections that ignore union dynamics.

For these and other reasons, merit pay plans in which the determinations of merit are made by local school administrators are unlikely to be adopted widely in public education. In contrast, proposals to implement merit pay through national board certification are currently under development, and may be operational in 1995. The issues raised by national board certification are covered in chapter 15.

The Likely Future for Teacher Salaries

Where does this leave us? In the 1990s, teacher salaries will be affected more by changes outside than within the field of education. Some changes will be conducive to an increase in the relative economic position of teachers. For example, the number of teachers needed must be recruited from a smaller population base than would normally be available. In addition, opportunities for talented women outside education have increased considerably in recent years. As a result, many women who formerly would have entered teaching are going into other occupations. Supply side factors such as these will tend to strengthen teacher salaries in the years ahead. At the same time, other demographic data suggest that teachers will have a difficult time maintaining their present economic status.

In 1983, the median age of our population was 30.9 and there were twice as many persons under 18 as there were over 65. Sometime in the twenty-first century, the median age will be over 40 and more persons will be over 65 than under 18. Significantly, elderly recipients of federal assistance receive about 10 times as much per recipient as child beneficiaries of such assistance. Furthermore, public opinion polls show that the elderly are much less willing to be taxed for education than are parents and younger citizens. In short, the graying of the population will not only increase the demand for noneducational services but will help to create a social and political context that is less supportive of higher teacher salaries.

It is difficult to say whether external factors favorable to higher salaries will be more influential than the factors keeping salaries down. The important conclusion is that the structure and relative economic ranking of teacher salaries are not likely to change significantly in the near future. Whether these things will change for at least a decade is doubtful; the most that can be expected are some showcase examples of higher salaries. If high elementary/secondary salaries are paid, they are much more likely to materialize in the private sector. Although this is an intriguing possibility, a thorough analysis of it would take us too far afield in this book.

17.   AGENCY SHOP FEES

One of the most important public policy and practical issues in teacher bargaining relates to compulsory payment of fees by nonmembers of the union. Such fees are widely referred to as "agency shop" or "fair share" fees; the first term will be used here.

The basic public policy problem can be stated as follows: Should public policy require, tolerate, or prohibit agency shop fees? State legislators might adopt any of these divergent answers. Where the states allow but do not mandate agency shop fees, the public policy question is also a bargaining issue. In effect, state legislatures have referred the public policy issue to local school boards, which must then decide what to do about it.

The importance of the issue stems from the fact that dues and agency shop fees are the main source of union revenues. It is very difficult, however, to ascertain how much union revenue comes from agency shop clauses. In the 21 right-to-work states, agency shop fees are not allowed. In the states allowing them, the fees vary with the state and among districts within states. As a matter of fact, even the unions might have difficulty determining how much union revenue comes from agency shop clauses. Teachers who pay agency shop fees are not union members and do not participate in union affairs; for instance, they cannot vote on whether to accept proposed contracts with the school board. When the agency shop fee is nearly as much as union dues, some teachers decide to join the union. Thus, some union income from members is actually due to the existence of agency shop clauses in the contract. In states that allow agency shop fees, we estimate that 5 to 7 percent of union revenues results from agency shop fees, directly or indirectly.

The union rationale for agency shop is that members of the bargaining unit should not receive the benefits of representation without paying their "fair share" of its costs. This rationale is based on the fact that when a union becomes the exclusive representative, it must represent everyone in the bargaining unit, whether or not the individuals are members of the union. Thus, it is in the interests of the employees to be "free riders"; that is, to receive the benefits of representation without paying for union services that supposedly were responsible for them.

Objections to this rationale are several. Obviously, if a union did not need exclusive representation, it would have no right to force nonmembers to pay for the its services. In practice, the unions demanded the right to represent everyone, and then, having achieved this right, cited it to force nonmembers to pay the service fee. It is as if someone painted a house against the owner's wishes, then demanded to be paid for the service so that the owner would not be a "free rider."

The most basic objection to agency shop is also an objection to collective bargaining: It violates the rights of individuals to contract for their labor. Instead, collective bargaining forces individuals to accept representation they may not want and conditions of employment that may not be as good as those that could be negotiated individually. Unquestionably, many individuals are made worse off by union representation; for example, mathematics and science teachers could often negotiate higher salaries for themselves if they were not tied to the salary schedule for all teachers. In any event, most people would strenuously object to being compelled to buy a service because the vendor insisted that the benefits outweighed the costs. Benefits are supposed to be evaluated by the buyer, not by the party who compels the alleged beneficiary to pay for them.

During bargaining, school boards face strong temptations to agree to agency shop fees. The teachers unions accord such clauses a high priority and typically will offer valuable concessions in exchange for board agreement to an agency shop clause. Such trade-offs are very attractive to school boards because individual teachers, not the boards, pay for the concession. Furthermore, by agreeing to an agency shop clause, the board is discouraging support for a rival union that might challenge the incumbent union for not extracting enough concessions from the board. With an agency shop clause, incumbent unions need not fear defections so much if they agree to board proposals that are highly unpopular among the teachers. If teachers must pay a service fee regardless of other considerations, the union does not lose as much revenue by agreeing to unpopular board proposals.

In states that do not mandate or prohibit agency shop fees, the public policy issues must be faced at the district level. The local district is faced with a dilemma: It can protect the rights of individual teachers, or it can sacrifice them for union concessions on other matters. Whatever one's view of the dilemma, many boards have opted for the concessions from the union instead of protections for all teachers in the bargaining unit.

School boards that accept agency shop clauses face complex problems of implementation. One is the amount of the agency shop fee. The U.S. Supreme Court has held that the fee must be the individual's prorated share of the costs of bargaining and processing grievances: In theory, nonmembers cannot be assessed for other union activities. Logically, this means that the agency shop fees must be less than regular union dues and assessments, but teachers unions still try to collect regular dues and assessments as a "service fee" from nonmembers. The unions have a very expansive view of how much they spend for bargaining and grievance handling; opponents of agency shop fees have a more restrictive view. Understandably, litigation over this issue is widespread, especially since the proportion of union expenditures for bargaining and grievance handling can vary widely from one time to another and from district to district.

Implementation of agency shop clauses raises several other issues that cannot be discussed here. Among them:

- Procedures for assessing the amount of the agency shop fees

- Procedures for challenging the fees and seeking review of fees already paid

- The use that can be made of fees that have been paid but challenged

- Who bears the cost of challenges to agency shop fees

- School board liability for agency shop payments that violate employees' constitutional rights

- Information unions must provide on request to payers of agency shop fees

- Whether the agency shop fees apply only to the local union that is the exclusive representative or may also include the teacher's share of the costs of the state and national affiliates that provide bargaining assistance to the local unions

- Who has the burden of proof on what issues in litigation involving agency shop fees.

To illustrate the unpredictability of these matters, the U.S. Supreme Court has held that the costs of preparation for an illegal strike can be counted as expenditures requiring payment of a "fair share" by nonmembers under an agency shop clause. Given such decisions, it is hardly any wonder that agency shop fees are a source of continuing confusion and litigation among all parties interested in the issue.[1]

---

[1] For a more extensive analysis of agency shop issues, see Charles W. Baird, The permissible use of forced union dues from Hanson to Beck, *Government Union Review* (Summer 1992), pp. 1-55; and Edwin Vierira Jr. and Lehnert Ferriss, Faculty association: The U.S. Supreme Court hands out another stone instead of a fish, *Government Union Review* (Winter 1993), pp. 1-36.

18.   ACADEMIC BIAS IN PUBLIC
SECTOR LABOR RELATIONS

The thesis in this discussion is that the leading academic centers for labor relations in the United States are characterized by a pronounced bias in favor of public sector bargaining. By "bias," we mean that these centers do not raise questions or conduct research that would challenge the major assumptions of, or the rationale for, public sector bargaining. Additionally, academic research on public sector bargaining generally avoids critical issues concerning the implementation of state bargaining laws. In our opinion, a major reason for this situation is the fact that the professors who teach and conduct research on public sector labor relations frequently have strong professional and financial incentives for avoiding such issues.

In this chapter, we make no claim to demonstrating the validity of this opinion. Instead, our primary objective is to suggest the basis for it, and perhaps to shift the burden of proof to the academic groups involved to provide data (if they can) that invalidate the argument. Admittedly, our argument is an impressionistic one, but the impressions are based upon a considerable body of experience with public sector bargaining and with leading personalities and academic institutions, as well as considerable familiarity with the literature on the subject.

First of all, let us delineate the academic groups that could be expected to conduct research on public sector bargaining. Professors of labor relations, regardless of institutional title or department, constitute the largest category of academicians in this group. In some institutions, they are found in departments or institutes of labor relations. In others, they are part of the faculty in economics, political science, law, public administration, educational administration, personnel administration, sociology, and/or management. In larger institutions, courses on public sector labor relations are often offered in several departments; for example, a course in labor law may emphasize the legal framework of collective bargaining; a course in labor economics is likely to devote more attention to the union movement; and courses in public administration or educational administration are likely to emphasize state bargaining laws. Other variations could be mentioned.

In addition to teaching labor relations or labor law or collective bargaining, many professors teach subject matter that cannot be fully understood without some understanding of public sector bargaining. For example, courses in local government, which are usually offered in political science departments, would be seriously deficient if they did not consider the impact of public sector bargaining on local governments. Nevertheless, professors who teach courses in educational administration advocate "shared decision making" without considering the negative impact mutual decision clauses have on management's ability to operate schools. To the extent that public sector bargaining has an impact on other disciplines, we should expect appropriate attention to it in courses that are not labeled "collective bargaining," "labor relations," or "labor law."

Although professors generally have ignored public sector bargaining, even as a public policy option, one academic group (professors of labor law/labor relations/labor economics, hereinafter referred to as "professors of labor relations") has played an important role in generating public and legislative support for it. This came about as a result of the participation of this group in legislative study committees on public sector labor relations. One outstanding example from New York in the 1960s was the 1965 *Report of the Governor's Committee on Public Employee Relations*, widely known as the "Taylor Report" because of the prestige of the committee chairman, Prof. George Taylor of the University of Pennsylvania. The report was prepared by five nationally known arbitrators, four of whom were prestigious academics in the field of labor relations. The report, which embraced public sector bargaining, became the basis for the public sector bargaining legislation enacted in 1965 in New York. The prestige of the committee and the fact that the report was used as the basis of legislation in the nation's most populous state were important factors in the explosive growth of public sector bargaining after 1964. The same pattern was followed in other states, most notably California, where a council appointed by the California Assembly and chaired by the dean of the Institute of Labor and Industrial Relations at UCLA unanimously recommended that California enact public sector bargaining for state and local public employees.

Although public sector bargaining did not come about in every state in the same way, the pattern in New York and California is illustrative of several important factors in many other states. First, public sector unions, especially those active in education, were able to focus legislative attention on the issue. In this respect, the academics were more ratifiers or legitimizers than innovators. Their advice on the details of state legislation was more influential than their recommendation in favor of public sector bargaining, which was more or less inevitable. For example, in 1961, George Taylor had recommended that the New York City Board of Education adopt collective bargaining and had proposed a plan of implementation that was adopted by the board. It was this plan that led to the stunning victory of the United Federation of Teachers (UFT) over the National Education Association (NEA) affiliates in New York City in 1961 and provided the major stimulus for teacher bargaining in the 1960s. (UFT is the New York City affiliate of the American Federation of Teachers.)

Academic Base of Public Sector Bargaining

Another noteworthy fact about academic involvement in public sector bargaining at the policy level was its narrow academic base. For most practical purposes, it was confined to academics whose field of expertise was predominantly collective bargaining under the National Labor Relations Act (NLRA). Professors in public administration, educational administration, and other disciplines affected by public sector bargaining were seldom involved. Most of them knew very little about collective bargaining and were slow to grasp the implications and consequences of public sector bargaining. Professors whose subject matter included public sector labor relations were civil service–oriented and typically did not realize that public sector bargaining would result in the demise of traditional civil service systems. Had their advice been sought, it probably would have been less supportive of public sector bargaining, but their opposition would have been uninformed and probably unpersuasive in the legislatures. Thus, for all practical purposes, academic involvement in public sector bargaining was dominated by labor relations professors oriented to collective bargaining under the NLRA. For the most part, their concern was not whether to have public sector bargaining but how to implement it. Thus, a major change in public policy, in public sector labor relations, in public administration (including several specialized fields therein, such as educational and hospital administration), in the labor movement, and in political science took place with the blessing of one group of academics while the others were seldom involved.

We expect professors to regard their subject matter as important. Nevertheless, regarding a subject matter as important is different from regarding the state of affairs it reveals as desirable. Professors who study wars or pollution or disease believe in the importance of these subjects, but do not contend that these things are desirable. Analogously, professors of labor relations might regard public sector bargaining or collective bargaining as important but not necessarily desirable. Any such supposition, however, founders on the stake that the labor relations professoriat has in collective bargaining. A substantial number of professors of labor relations moonlight as impartial third parties, especially as arbitrators. For this reason, they have a significant interest in expanding the demand for labor arbitration services.

Professorial reaction to this point is predictable enough. It will be indignation, or resignation, over the implication that many professors would support public sector bargaining because they might earn more outside income. In fact, the better known and more established professor/arbitrators already have more arbitration business than they can handle; the suggestion that they would be influenced by the potential expansion of arbitral services seems to be a weak argument indeed.

Granted, the reaction is valid as applied to some professor/arbitrators. How many professors have all the arbitration business they can handle would be a very interesting datum that is badly needed. In any case, if every professor/arbitrator had more private sector business than he/she could accept, that fact would strengthen, not weaken, the argument of this discussion. Let us see why this is so.

Typically, arbitrators are called upon to decide whether an employer has violated a collective bargaining agreement and what the remedy should be if a violation is found. Employment as an arbitrator is usually arranged through the procedures of the American Arbitration

Association (AAA). Under AAA procedures, the employer and union are sent a list of arbitrators. Each party strikes unacceptable names until agreement is reached. In its review of a list of arbitrators, a union is hardly likely to accept someone on record as opposed to, or highly critical of, public sector bargaining. Certainly, opposition to private sector bargaining would destroy a professor's acceptability to unions. Although it is possible for a professor to support private sector bargaining while opposing it in the public sector, this does not seem to have happened very often. Even if it has or will, opposition to public sector bargaining is likely to damage a professor's moonlighting prospects in the private sector. Why should a union bother to analyze the reasoning of an arbitrator opposed to public sector bargaining when it can choose from among a host of arbitrators known to be enthusiastic supporters of it? In this connection, it should be noted that many national unions have local affiliates in both sectors. In their private sector cases, can such unions be expected to select arbitrators opposed to public sector bargaining? Any such expectation would be unrealistic.

In other words, the labor relations professor/arbitrator has a larger stake in supporting public sector bargaining than the expansion of the market for his moonlighting services. Not that the issue is perceived this way: as the Italian economist Vilfredo Pareto once observed, men find it easy to convert their interests into their convictions. Professor/arbitrators are not as likely as nonarbitrators to perceive public policy objections to the extension of arbitral procedures to the public sector. The reason is that they don't search as much for such objections—and they don't search as much because it is not in their interest to do so.

One must also consider the dynamics of the academic personnel ladder. A scholar may wish to research several issues that challenge the desirability of collective bargaining, but academic departments that offer programs or receive contracts and/or grants that require union cooperation are hardly likely to welcome such an initiative or its advocate.

Professorial reactions frequently emphasize the value of arbitral experience. Undoubtedly, such experience is helpful to anyone teaching courses in labor relations or collective bargaining. The issue is whether the emphasis on arbitral experience is conducive to the avoidance of issues that would challenge the desirability of public sector bargaining.

In broad perspective, the basic problem is not confined to labor relations. It is similar to the situation of a journalist who needs access to political leaders but wishes to maintain journalistic independence. The access problem becomes unresolvable if the journalist writes articles critical of his subject. Similarly, the price of professorial access to unions through arbitration is avoidance of the critical function of the labor relations professoriat.

To state the matter bluntly, the "objectivity" of the impartial third party industry is a myth, and a self-serving myth at that. Unfortunately, the myth has had adverse effects upon public sector labor relations. One is the all but unanimous recommendation to establish public sector bargaining whenever these academics dominated advisory bodies on the issue. The fallacy in allowing members of the labor relations community to dominate such advisory bodies was the assumption that individuals who are impartial third parties in specific disputes between labor and management are impartial concerning the procedures to resolve such disputes. This is like asking football referees if the National Football League should expand. Clearly, their interest lies in expansion, regardless of their impartiality in games between teams who differ on the expansion issue. Similarly, professors who arbitrate specific disputes between private sector employees and unions are not disinterested parties on the issue of whether public employers and unions should adopt procedures that increase the need for arbitral services.

Impasse Procedures and the Democratic Process

The impact of the labor relations community was reflected in several ways in addition to its uncritical encouragement of public sector bargaining. For instance, this influence was reflected in the emphasis placed upon protracted impasse procedures and specific legislation that maximized the use of impartial third parties. In the 1960s, most professors of labor relations probably accepted the view that public management would act arbitrarily and capriciously in the absence of a public employee's right to strike. As a result, their legislative recommendations included heavy emphasis upon mediation and fact-finding and, occasionally, even interest arbitration. Unfortunately, however, the impairment of democratic representative government that results from this approach was largely ignored. Let us consider three examples of such impairment.

In the ordinary collective bargaining situation, an employer is prohibited from making unilateral changes in terms and conditions of employment without giving the union a chance to bargain on the changes. For example, suppose the collective bargaining contract does not say anything about hours of work, but the employer must reduce the hours for various reasons. In this situation, the employer cannot make the change without allowing the union to bargain over it.

In the private sector, this requirement is not especially troublesome. The employer gives notice, the parties bargain promptly if the union so requests, and within a relatively short time, agreement is reached or the employer can act unilaterally. The employer's obligation is to bargain in good faith; it can act unilaterally, even in the absence of an agreement, within a relatively short time.

This is not the case, however, in public sector bargaining. To illustrate, consider the situations that arose in California when many school districts learned in late summer of 1982 that their state aid for 1982-83 was to be reduced. In many districts, this information necessitated a reduction in hours to be worked by nonteacher employees, such as custodians, bus drivers, secretaries, and teacher aides. Under California law, enacted before its public sector bargaining law, a reduction of hours of classified school employees required 30 days' notice. For this reason, many districts were forced to send out such notices immediately so that the reductions would take effect at the beginning of the 1982-83 school year.

Consequently, the unions representing support personnel filed unfair labor practice charges, arguing that school boards could not reduce hours of employment without first bargaining upon the proposed reductions. The position was upheld by the state's Public Employment Relations Board (PERB). When did a district fulfill its obligation to bargain so that it could act unilaterally if agreement was not reached? The answer, according to the PERB, was at the time the school district and employee union had completed the statutorily mandated impasse procedure. Unfortunately for the school district, the full procedure can and often does require several months. In fact, it was commonplace for impasse procedures to take six to nine months. Obviously, if a school district intended to reduce hours, the unions had a vested interest in extending the impasse procedure as long as possible, inasmuch as the district could not implement the reductions until the impasse procedure was completed. Significantly, the districts could not act to reduce the hours of employment until they knew their income, yet they were frequently not informed of their income until just a few days or weeks before they had to act on this information.

The upshot of the situation is this: By imposing collective bargaining procedures on public legislative bodies, the state bargaining law gives private interest groups a veto power over policymaking by such bodies. The fact that personnel policies are involved is irrelevant. In effect, an interest group with a stake in frustrating sound public policy has a veto power over it, at least for a fairly lengthy period.

The point here is not that union veto power over changes in public personnel policy is undesirable public policy. Instead, the point is that the issue was ignored in academic discussions of public sector bargaining. In the situation just discussed, the public sector unions simply delay bargaining and completion of impasse procedures. Inasmuch as the unions maintain the hours of work by such tactics, school boards are forced to make many undesirable concessions in order to get them to agree to the reductions.

For all practical purposes, the fact that the state statutory impasse procedures preclude unilateral action by public employers for much longer than for private employers has been widely ignored. At least on this issue, the application of private sector principles of collective bargaining has been extremely disadvantageous to public employers.

The 'Scope of Bargaining' Issue

The "scope of bargaining" issue presents an even more dramatic example of how readily professors of labor relations have subordinated democratic representative government to public sector bargaining. Scope of bargaining refers to matters that are subject to bargaining. In conventional private sector labor relations, items fall into one of the following categories relating to the scope of bargaining: (1) mandatory subjects, (2) permissive subjects, and (3) prohibited subjects.

Conceptually, these categories are clear enough, even though in practical terms it is often difficult to categorize a particular item. Wages are an example of a mandatory subject of bargaining; a party must bargain on this subject if requested to do so. Retiree benefits is a permissive subject; it is not illegal to request bargaining or to bargain on this issue, but it is an unfair practice to insist upon such bargaining to the point of impasse. An example of a prohibited subject is a proposal to discriminate against a particular ethnic or religious group or the opponents of union leaders.

In public sector bargaining, however, these categories apply to public policies. A mandatory subject of public sector bargaining is a public policy to be negotiated with one special-interest group. A permissive subject of bargaining is a public policy that may be negotiated with one interest group. Thus, in the public sector, the broader the scope, the greater the range of public policies that are negotiated bilaterally instead of being subject to the normal legislative processes in which no interest group has a preferred legal position, whatever its practical advantages may be.

For the most part, professors of labor relations have supported a broad scope of public sector bargaining. Consider the recommendations made in 1973 by the Assembly Advisory Council in California. The council was chaired by Dr. Benjamin Aaron, dean of the School of Labor and Industrial Relations at UCLA and a nationally known arbitrator. Concerning the scope of bargaining, the council report recommended that the scope itself be resolved by the bargaining process. This recommendation would have legitimized whatever policies are negotiated bilaterally between a public agency and a public employee union, at least as far as their subject matter is concerned. The council made this recommendation despite its recognition that "by its very nature, bilateral determination in labor relations excludes third-party groups from the decision-making process." The council also recommended legalizing the right to strike, opposed inclusion of a management rights clause in the bargaining law, and recommended that bargaining agreements take precedence over statutes, regulations, and/or ordinances that conflict with bargaining agreements.

Preliminarily, if one proposed that a public agency be authorized to negotiate all public policies with one interest group, the proposal would probably be dismissed as a crackpot suggestion by someone with no understanding of or no sympathy for democratic representative government. Yet, absurd as such a proposal would be, it is essentially no different from the recommendation of the Aaron Committee. A recommendation that there be no statutory limits on the scope of public sector bargaining is tantamount to allowing the issue to be resolved through the bargaining power of the parties. Undoubtedly, in many situations the public employer would be able to dictate an extremely narrow scope of bargaining. In many other situations, it is equally certain that the public sector union would be able to negotiate many policies only peripherally related—or not at all related—to terms and conditions of employment.

It is difficult to imagine that such latitude would be offered to any other interest group. Indeed, the position on the scope of bargaining recommended by the Aaron Committee is antidemocratic to an extreme. Bilateral negotiations to establish a particular public policy necessarily require the exclusion of other groups from the policymaking process, as the Aaron Committee itself recognized. If a school board is going to negotiate the school calendar with the teachers union, it cannot extend the same privilege to any other group, including any other union; to do so would vitiate the agreement reached with the teachers union. This point illustrates the basic philosophical fallacy of public sector bargaining. It is hailed as "democratic" by its supporters, who view the issue in terms of the public employees. The impact of public sector bargaining on those who are excluded from, or severely disadvantaged in, the policymaking process is ignored or minimized.

In addition to the fact that labor relations professors have a vested interest in the impartial third-party industry, many have acquired a vested interest in public sector bargaining in their role as public employees. This was not a major factor in the emergence of public sector bargaining, but it is an important obstacle to subsequent academic criticism of it. Such criticism requires professors to challenge their own privileges, a challenge to which few professors are equal.

In the late 1960s, there was not as much bargaining by professorial unions as there is today. Over time, many faculties became dependent on the benefits of public sector bargaining on their own campus. The professorial unions may have averted cutbacks, achieved wage increases, and/or made it all but impossible to dismiss marginal or incompetent faculty. Regrettably, the professors who benefit from public sector bargaining tend to regard such benefits as the logical outcome of enlightened public policy. Under these circumstances, academics have little incentive to question the public policy justification for public sector bargaining. Indeed, given the fact that wage increases and promotions often depend on approval by faculty committees, a critic of public sector bargaining faces a significant risk in adopting positions that challenge the benefits as well as the professional integrity of his colleagues.

Realistically, what department of labor relations would employ someone who believes that the moonlighting arbitral activities of his colleagues constitutes a serious research and policy problem?

One point especially needs to be stressed. The most harmful consequences of academic bias are not the overt manifestations of support for public sector bargaining. The problem is the uncritical support accorded public sector bargaining and the continuing neglect of critical research issues by academics paid to provide analytical and policy leadership in this area. If issues such as the staggering costs of public sector bargaining had been raised by academics, there would be less reason to be concerned about the bias and outside activities of the labor relations professoriat.

Furthermore, just as critical issues bearing on the desirability of public sector bargaining were not raised, neither were (nor are) important issues that could be embarrassing to unions. The lack of attention accorded the political use of unfair labor practice charges illustrates this point. In the public sector, bargaining is a contest for public favor. In impasse situations, the public sector union tries to cast the public management group as villains who "don't care about kids," or "union busters," or whatever pejorative term is calculated to gain public support. Such efforts are much less frequent in the private sector, where economic power is typically the key to union success.

In the public sector, job actions are typically preceded by a propaganda barrage intended to persuade the public that the public employer is responsible for the dispute and interruption of services. In this context, unfair labor practice charges are primarily propaganda weapons. The charges cost very little to file and are almost invariably reported in the local media. The union need only submit some forms, which take only a few minutes to complete, in order to achieve media coverage that can damage management politically. Most of these charges are washed out in the eventual settlement; the fact that they are dropped with prejudice receives little or no attention in the media.

Although such charges require minimal union resources, they consume a significant amount of public resources. The charges must be reviewed and answered, typically by legal counsel. One or more management representatives, often including an attorney, must attend an informal conference on the charges. If the matter is not resolved, a date is set for a formal hearing. Usually, however, an agreement that includes dropping the charges is reached before the date set for the formal hearing. Thus, the union squeezes whatever propaganda value it can out of the charges, but subsequently avoids a hearing on their merits.

Admittedly, these assertions about unfair labor practice charges in the public sector are based on other experience, not data or documentation. We believe that an objective study would substantiate our conclusions concerning the public relations use of unfair labor practice charges (and by implication, the waste of public resources resulting therefrom). The important point, however, is the absence of studies dealing with this issue and others like it. Here again, we encounter the same problem: The professors who are in the best position to recognize the problem are not interested in pursuing it.

Public Sector Bargaining Reconsidered

What can be done to remedy the situation? There are academic opponents of public sector bargaining, but understandably, they seldom are experienced as arbitrators. Partly for this reason, many of their objections are based upon erroneous or irrelevant assumptions that render the objections highly vulnerable.

For instance, consider the objections that public sector bargaining forces public employees to become union members, or that public employees are worse off as a result of public sector bargaining. Arguments such as these are counterproductive. It is possible to have public sector bargaining without compulsory union membership; in fact, such is the case everywhere. Granted, public sector unions tend to press for compulsory membership, but this tendency is not a decisive objection to public sector bargaining. Nevertheless, this kind of criticism is prominent among some academic critics of public sector bargaining. Because this line of reasoning can be easily refuted, it should not be a basis for opposition to public sector bargaining.

Similarly, one frequently hears that public employees generally are worse off under public sector bargaining than would otherwise be the case. This criticism is typically based upon data showing that nonunion public employees receive larger percentage wage increases than unionized ones. Typically, there are several technical problems with such data; for example, they fail to take into account the impact of unionization upon nonunionized employees or account for such benefits as greater job security. The most serious problem, however, is that with one exception to be noted below, the argument is inherently unrealistic. Even if public employees are acting like lemmings in embracing public sector bargaining, one wonders why public management is not more active in promoting it, if employees receive less—not more—benefits under it. Of course, both workers and management can be mistaken as to where their interests lie, but the argument that employees are typically worse off under unionization is not persuasive, despite the number of individual instances in which it is valid.

The argument against public sector bargaining would be more persuasive if it took into account all of the real costs as well as the benefits of public sector bargaining. When this is done, the costs may not be equal to the increased benefits. Employees may achieve gains that would not occur in the absence of unionization, but they may still be worse off overall as a result of the costs. An analogy here is a firm that sells more widgets because of advertising but is worse off overall because the increased sales do not offset advertising costs.

The first thing to be done is to ascertain the facts about the involvement of academics in arbitration—fact-finding, training programs for union and management, speaking engagements, grants, consultancies, the whole picture. Obviously, generating and disseminating such data will encounter fierce academic opposition, and not solely from the labor relations community. Professors will perceive—and rightly so— that a request for such data constitutes a threat to their freedom to use their full-time positions to advance their moonlighting interests.

Academic opposition to such disclosure will take many forms. It will be charged that requiring professors to disclose their financial relationships to employers and/or unions would jeopardize academic freedom. This is true—but not in the way its apologists have in mind. Such disclosure jeopardizes academic freedom to mask professorial support for an interest group as objective research. Disclosure does not constitute a restraint on what a professor can write or teach; it provides helpful data in assessing professorial selection of research issues and research publications.

Another frequent but invalid argument will be as follows: A professor should be evaluated on the basis of his teaching and research. If such teaching and research is inadequate because of the time devoted to outside activities, the inadequacies would have been noted in the evaluations of the professor's teaching, research, and/or publications. Inadequate performance should not be assumed or inferred from outside activities when it is possible to evaluate a professor's full-time activities directly.

Initially, it should be noted that public employees often are precluded from accepting compensation from outside sources, without regard to any showing of actual partiality. Candidates for public office are required to disclose contributions and their source: We do not wait until a public official has demonstrated partiality before requiring disclosure. Similarly, at all levels of government, there are disclosure requirements that are not subject to a showing of actual bias or favoritism.

The logic of these requirements applies to professors in private as well as in public institutions. The former assert the validity and objectivity of their research, and their research and publications are evaluated in the same forums and according to the same standards as those of their colleagues in public institutions. Furthermore, just as public officials have a common stake in avoiding restrictions on their ability to conceal certain relationships, so do professors. Legislators are much more lenient than the public in judging other legislators; after all, adherence to strict standards could boomerang on them. For the same reason, the notion that a professor should be evaluated only by his peers is not a guarantee of objectivity; quite the reverse. The common academic desire for a privileged sanctuary from which to moonlight and manipulate a subject matter for a variety of private entrepreneurial motives will ordinarily weaken, if not stifle, criticism of fellow academics for abuse of their freedom.

Again, it must be emphasized that the selection of research issues is critical. A professor may have conducted competent objective research for 25 years and still be vulnerable to criticism that his professional activities have been subordinated to his moonlighting interests. This would be the case if the professor had avoided research issues more important than those actually pursued. Avoiding such issues avoids the dilemma of either having to say something anathema to a moonlighting client or becoming professionally vulnerable for not saying it.

Admittedly, some important issues are not even potentially threatening to academic moonlighting opportunities. An individual professor can easily justify avoidance of any specific issue, but the upshot is a collective avoidance for which no one is responsible. In such situations, the appropriate remedy is to reduce the total funds to the academic group involved. In other words, trustees and legislatures need not pinpoint individual responsibility; if an academic department consistently ignores basic issues that jeopardize the moonlighting opportunities of professors (and even if they do not!) the remedy is to reduce the department as a whole.

It must also be noted that many professors, including some who oppose public sector bargaining, will oppose disclosure of their outside activities for reasons that have nothing to do with academic competence or bias. Beyond any doubt, some are involved in more outside employment than is permitted by their institutional policy. Some may be embarrassed by the fact that their research is primarily supportive of moonlighting interest, such as a consulting firm. Some will be unable to withstand disclosure about their activities while on sabbatical leave, and so on. We are not proposing that the outside activities of labor relations professors be prohibited; only that they be fully disclosed.

Finally, it is essential to develop a research agenda geared to public policy needs, not to the private or institutional needs of professors of labor relations. In this connection, public management could be much more effective in generating useful research. A state school board organization, or state association of local governments, could draw up and disseminate a research agenda. Fair consideration of this agenda could be a consideration in selecting institutions for training programs, recruitment, and so on. In other words, public management has the collective leverage to remedy research gaps to some extent. The problem is one of leadership, especially at the state level.

Public sector bargaining is not the only disaster area shielded by the academic mystique, but it is time to clean up the wreckage. We can no longer afford to allow ritual invocations of "academic freedom" to thwart a critical review of the interests and activities of professors of labor relations.

19. EDUCATIONAL REFORM AND TEACHER BARGAINING

In this chapter, which is devoted to a discussion of the relationships between educational reform and teacher bargaining, some of the analysis and recommendations are applicable to state and local governments generally, but the discussion will be confined to education.

A few basic facts about our educational situation should be noted. Teacher salaries constitute the largest single expenditure in school district budgets. In most districts, 50 to 70 percent of district expenditures go for teacher salaries and fringe benefits. At the same time, collective bargaining has become the most common procedure for establishing, revising, eliminating, and implementing personnel policies applicable to teachers. Since the enactment of public sector bargaining (PSB) statutes in Ohio and Illinois in 1983, every major Northern state has had legislation that authorizes and regulates collective bargaining by teacher unions. In conjunction with the other states that have enacted such legislation and the school districts where teacher bargaining takes place in the absence of a PSB statute, most of the nation's public school teachers work pursuant to a labor contract negotiated by their union. For this reason, the prospects for educational reform must be assessed in terms of their implications for teacher bargaining. Is bargaining likely to foster, retard, or have no effect upon educational reform?

Most proposed public school reforms involve matters subject to teacher bargaining. Merit pay for outstanding teachers is one example. As matters stand, merit pay cannot be implemented in PSB states without first negotiating on it. Similarly, the length of the school day and school year are normally subject to bargaining; therefore, proposals to increase instructional time are subject to bargaining. Reforms that would make it easier to dismiss incompetent teachers are still another item subject to bargaining.

Even proposals to pay teachers higher salaries must be negotiated with the unions. Although the unions are not likely to oppose such proposals, they are virtually certain to oppose most of the reforms currently being discussed. For example, unions are in business to shorten, not lengthen, the school day and school year for teachers. Their role is to protect teachers against dismissal, not to make it easier for school management to dismiss them. Managerial discretion and flexibility in layoffs, transfers, and assignments is anathema to most teachers unions. They typically strive to have seniority serve as the criterion for personnel decisions sought by teachers and reverse seniority serve as the criterion for adverse decisions, such as which teachers are to be laid off or involuntarily reassigned. These examples suggest that most educational reforms will face hostile treatment in teacher bargaining.

If experience in the private sector is any guide, we can expect teacher bargaining to have negative consequences for educational reform and productivity. It is now recognized that our industries in deepest economic trouble are also the ones most heavily unionized. The reasons are clear enough. The unions in these industries have had a negative impact upon productivity by limiting managerial flexibility in employment and deployment of staff—restrictions on outside contracting; emphasis on pay for work not done (leaves, holdups, vacations, callback and call-in time, etc.); seniority in layoffs—and by striving to achieve other policies and practices that, regardless of motivation, require more pay for less work.

There is no valid reason to assume that the impact of collective bargaining on productivity is or would be different in public than in private employment. On the contrary, bargaining has an even greater negative impact on productivity in the public than in the private sector. In both sectors, the unions try to restrict or even eliminate managerial flexibility in layoffs, transfers, reassignments, part-time employment, outside contracting for unit work, work out of classification, and other personnel decisions. Nevertheless, although union objectives are similar in the two sectors, bargaining is more damaging to productivity in the public sector for at least two reasons. First, the costs of union demands in the public sector are borne by taxpayers, not the owners of the enterprise. Generally, shareholders monitor the performance of companies in which they own stock more effectively than citizens monitor the performance of government. A shareholder of a company has a direct stake in the performance of the company and can respond immediately to what he or she perceives as bad management decisions—by selling the stock, for example. On the other hand, it would not be worthwhile for most citizens to devote much of their own time to evaluating public officials with major managerial responsibilities; there is no feasible way for most citizens to use this information to their own advantage. As a result, there is less pressure on public managers than on private sector managers to oppose excessive settlements.

In fact, public management often has a strong political incentive to support excessive union demands. The increased costs to each taxpayer may be an irritant, but may be subordinate to positions on other issues that are more important to individual taxpayers. At the same time, the benefits achieved by public sector unions and public employees may gain political support for board members. Paying school secretaries more than the going rate in private employment would not be a major item in a school board budget, but the secretaries would probably support the board for reelection. In other words, where elected public management is concerned, a decision that is utterly indefensible on managerial or bargaining grounds may still be made on political grounds.

The Politicization of Managerial Decisions

Public sector bargaining inevitably lends to the politicization of managerial decisions that should be made on nonpolitical grounds. The manager of a private enterprise is not likely to retain an incompetent employee because of political pressure. On the other hand, public agencies are frequently pressured to do so, and frequently yield to such pressure.

The successful union campaigns opposing merit pay for outstanding teachers are frequent examples of their power to block desirable changes. From a union point of view, merit pay is extremely dangerous, albeit not because merit pay would be too subjective and would lead to favoritism. Needless to say, merit pay would not always be implemented properly. However, the policy option is not between a perfect system (no merit pay) and an imperfect system (merit pay). It is between alternative compensation policies, each of which has advantages and disadvantages. Each can be implemented in ways that render the alternative approach much more attractive as a public policy option.

The union opposition to merit pay, however, does not rest upon a calculation of its advantages and disadvantages to *teachers*. Instead, such opposition is based upon its advantages and disadvantages to *unions*. Here, the disadvantages clearly outweigh the advantages. Merit pay is a threat—or is at least perceived as a threat—to the unions themselves. The stability of unions depends upon their ability to eliminate or to minimize conflict among members of the bargaining unit. The ideal union contract has just enough in it to satisfy everyone. It avoids giving any subgroup benefits deemed disproportionate to what others are getting. Merit pay, to be meaningful—or at least consistent with its avowed rationale—must provide substantial rewards to a minority of teachers. Most teachers who do not receive merit pay will tend to feel or to claim that the district is overpaying the "merit" teachers. Yet, if the amount is not substantial, the rationale for merit pay loses force and the plan is not worth the time and trouble of implementation.

Let us assume that a union agrees to a merit pay system. How is a union representative going to respond to a grievance alleging that the grievant was erroneously passed over for merit pay? The claim will be that the grievant is more deserving than another teacher who is to receive merit pay. Such a claim places the union in a no-win situation. For the union to support the grievance would mean assisting a union member, but only at the expense of another union member. To refuse to support the grievance will antagonize the grievant. Either way, the union may be confronted by charges that it has violated its duty to represent all union members fairly. These problems would exist even if the union itself completely controlled the designation of merit teachers. Indeed, such control would exacerbate some of the union problems associated with merit pay.

Understandably, unions want no such dilemmas. They cannot give management a free hand in designating merit pay recipients. But, the deeper the union gets involved in the process, the greater the danger that it will antagonize a portion of its constituency. The only way to avoid such dilemmas is to oppose merit pay.

Of course, outright opposition to merit pay may not be politically expedient. For this reason, unions may propose merit pay under conditions that advance union interests. One can easily imagine union representatives agreeing to accept merit pay if the public employer will accept compulsory payment of union dues. The union argument could be stated along these lines:

> We don't like merit pay, but we are willing to accept it under certain conditions. One such condition is that it not be used as a union-busting device. This will happen if the merit teachers happen not to be members of the union. We're not saying that you intend to use merit pay this way, but we can't avoid taking the necessary precautions. On the other hand, if every teacher has to pay dues, we will withdraw our opposition because we know it can't be used to bust the union.

Whatever the scenario, the unions will try to use merit pay to maximize union power. Whether or not good teachers are rewarded in the process will be secondary to union interests. For example, most unions will insist on teacher involvement in setting the criteria for designation of merit teachers. This may take the form of an advisory group that includes teachers. How will teacher members be selected? The union will contend that teacher representatives should be designated by teachers themselves; formally or informally, this means that they will be designated by the union. If an election is involved, teachers without union support will be unable to compete with teachers supported by the union. Will union-supported candidates recommend that antiunion—or even nonunion—teachers receive substantial salary increments ahead of their union-oriented colleagues? It could happen, but it won't, at least not often enough to justify the experiment.

Anyone with experience in teacher bargaining soon becomes aware that teacher negotiating teams frequently emphasize benefits that go to the bargaining team. Shop teachers on negotiating teams negotiate for preparation periods for shop teachers. Teachers with large families negotiate more vigorously for health insurance for dependents. Senior teachers want more longevity pay. Quite frequently, teachers seek to be on the negotiating team to redress some perceived inequity. If the coaches believe they are underpaid, they may attempt to place a coach on the negotiating team to make sure the problem, as they see it, is resolved.

Realistically, the same dynamics must be expected with respect to merit pay. The union negotiating team is likely to negotiate hard for criteria likely to enhance the prospect of merit pay for team members. Teachers who don't receive merit pay will try to change the criteria, the selection process, or whatever was deemed responsible for this injustice.

To the extent that a union is willing to consider merit pay at all, its internal politics will dominate its approach to the issue. Management negotiators will come under increasing pressure to accommodate these internal union needs. This way, the management team that refuses to compromise a viable plan will be portrayed as refusing to bargain in good faith, adopting a take-it-or-leave-it attitude, showing no consideration for teacher views, or being deficient in other ways. School boards cannot be expected to be immune from these tactics—not after a wealth of experience has revealed their vulnerability to them on one issue after another.

Are teachers unions wrong in perceiving a threat to the union in merit pay? Given the fact that unions generally oppose differentials based upon merit, opposition to merit pay by teachers unions is not an aberration from a union point of view. Nonetheless, the perceptions of union leaders and their posture are what local school boards will have to confront. How many school boards will insist upon merit pay over the adamant opposition of teachers unions? Given the virtually complete absence of merit pay, even in states without a PSB statute, and its absence in other areas of public employment generally, the underlying problem may be the lack of commitment by public management, not the opposition of teacher unions. This lack of commitment may be only an excuse to conceal the actual state of affairs from the public. For what it may be worth, our guess is that merit pay will not be implemented on a significant scale in the bargaining states for many years to come, if at all. It will be interesting to see whether implementation is more frequent in the states with PSB statutes.

The preceding discussion is not an exhaustive analysis of the obstacles to reform posed by teacher bargaining. For that matter, it is not even an exhaustive analysis of the bargaining problems associated with merit pay. Our purpose was simply to illustrate a point: Unless careful thought is given to the bargaining implications of educational reform, the reformers will end up advocating unrealistic and unattainable solutions to real problems. In this connection, the unionization of higher education must also be regarded as a significant barrier to reform in elementary and secondary education. Suppose, for example, that it becomes advisable to initiate a different program of teacher education. Such a program cannot simply be superimposed upon existing programs. Some displacement of courses and staff is likely to be essential. It is unrealistic to expect a professorial union to accept layoffs while new staff members are being added. Similarly, changes in certification requirements (or their abolition) are opposed by faculty unions if they threaten faculty jobs, as they always do. Excessive certification of public school personnel is widespread in the United States, but professorial unions exacerbate the problem everywhere. The more courses that can be legally required for teacher certification, the greater the demand for, and security of, the professors who teach these courses.

A Perspective on Educational Reform

Although it is essential to assess the bargaining implications of each specific education reform, educational reformers must also develop a broader perspective on teacher bargaining. Otherwise, the reform movement in education may devote its energies to winning battles while the war is being lost on a wider front. To avoid such an outcome, the educational reform movement will need to become involved in activities intended to eliminate or reduce the obstacles to reform posed by teacher bargaining. Inevitably, serious proponents of reform will find themselves on a collision course with teacher bargaining as we have known it. Strategically, the reformers will find it necessary to form coalitions with other groups seeking limits on public sector bargaining, sometimes for very different, although not conflicting, reasons.

What can be done?

First of all, we must distinguish between short- and long-range goals. Although precision here is not possible, five years can be used as a rough dividing line. On this basis, we do not believe that any rollback of teacher bargaining on a broad scale is feasible in the short run for three reasons. The first is that teacher bargaining is usually encompassed in statutes affecting local government employees generally. It would usually be impossible to enact an amendment affecting education only. It has been done occasionally, but the fate of teacher bargaining is usually tied to the fate of public sector bargaining generally.

The second reason is that public sector bargaining invariably strengthens unions politically. The influence that led to the enactment of PSB statutes increases as bargaining leads to more members and more dues income. Although the data are not available, the proportion of public employees generally (including teachers) who pay dues is certain to be much higher after a PSB statute has been enacted. One obvious reason is that PSB legislation is usually required to legitimize agency shop clauses; once a legislation has authorized such provisions, an increasing number of teachers unions negotiate them.

A third factor is that the kind of program required for any rollback does not exist, and at least a few years would be required to develop one. In the next five to 10 years, any rollback, if it happened at all, would be the result of judicial decisions. On this score, the U.S. Supreme Court played a critical, probably decisive, role in the 1980s. Because the next few appointees may be the swing vote on the critical issues in PSB, the 1996 presidential election might well be the most important single event shaping the future of public sector bargaining for decades to come.

On the other hand, and despite the enactment of PSB statutes in Ohio and Illinois in 1983, we believe it is feasible to halt the expansion of PSB to more states in the future. The programs required to achieve this objective are also not in place, but time is not as important as is an understanding of what has to be done and why.

Popular Arguments Versus Realities

Twenty years of experience with the political/legislative controversies over PSB has convinced us that the popular arguments for and against PSB have little or nothing to do with reality. To us, this is an important fact with significant implications for any strategy intended to contain its negative consequences.

Space limits the discussion of this factor to a few examples. One typical argument for PSB is that it is necessary to end "second-class citizenship" for public employees. This inequity supposedly grows out of the fact that private sector employees have bargaining rights under the National Labor Relations Act (NLRA). Allegedly, in the absence of bargaining rights, public employees are inequitably disadvantaged in the pursuit of their interests.

At the outset, it should be noted that the equity argument ignores the private sector employees who do not have bargaining rights under the NLRA; for example, an enterprise must be a certain size to come under NLRA jurisdiction. PSB statutes, however, require school boards to bargain, even though a private employer with the same number of employees would not be required to do so.

As we have noted elsewhere, the equity argument focuses on a single alleged inequity while ignoring the advantages of public employment.

The upshot is that while public sector unions are lobbying for PSB statutes in order to eliminate "second-class citizenship," public employees actually are enjoying higher wages, more generous fringe benefits, a less onerous workload, and—in some respects, at least—more job protection than private sector employees with bargaining rights.

Controversies over the agency shop also illustrate the gulf between the rhetoric and the reality. Public sector unions seek legislation mandating compulsory payment of service fees as a condition of employment. When this is not achievable, they seek legislation authorizing the negotiation of such clauses in public sector contracts. Such clauses are commonly referred to as "agency shop" clauses.

The rationale is that because everyone in the bargaining unit benefits from union representation, everyone should be obligated to pay. This rationale is maintained—even is unchallenged—in the face of the most obvious evidence refuting it. For example, when layoffs are necessary, school boards usually prefer to retain an outstanding but less senior teacher rather than a marginal teacher with greater seniority. On the other hand, unions demand that school boards apply seniority in layoffs. Indisputably, the actual teachers to be laid off will be different, depending upon which criteria are used.

How can it be argued that a teacher who will lose his or her job if seniority prevails "benefits" from union representation that will be directly responsible for the loss of the position? The point is not whether seniority is good or bad, but rather that the union's position is clearly detrimental to the basic interests of some teachers. This conclusion would be valid regardless of the union's position.

Whatever position the union takes will be detrimental to some teachers (i.e., those laid off due to application of the criteria advocated by the union). This fact is fatal to the rationale for the agency shop. This rationale is that *all* teachers "benefit from union representation." The fact is that some teachers are typically disadvantaged, often to the point of losing their jobs, by union representation. Layoffs are only one of many examples that can be cited to demonstrate the absurdity of the rationale for agency shop. Nevertheless, its absurdity has little or nothing to do with the debate over the issue.

In fact, the political/legal controversies over the agency shop ignore the most fundamental facts about the issue. In the private sector, several lawsuits have challenged the union's right to use dues income for political purposes, such as supporting candidates for public office. As result of these lawsuits, the U.S. Supreme Court has held that employees in the private sector may be forced to pay dues as a condition of employment, but only to the extent that the dues are devoted to negotiation and the administration of the contract, including processing grievances.

In the public sector, however, it is practically and logically impossible to maintain the distinction between "negotiations" and "political action" (even though the Supreme Court has done just that!). The function of the union is to negotiate an agreement with a board of education, a city government, or an agency of the state government. These agreements are public policies. Usually, they must be ratified by the appropriate legislative body (school board, city council, etc.). Before PSB, matters covered by public sector contracts were resolved through legislative action. For example, teachers organizations tried to get legislatures and school boards to adopt minimum salary laws, leave and retirement benefits, and protections against layoffs and arbitrary dismissals. In fact, these efforts continue under PSB.

Similarly, before public sector bargaining, local teachers organizations tried to elect candidates deemed supportive of their interests. In addition, the organizations lobbied school board members and sought to influence board actions in presentations at board meetings. When conditions of public employment are negotiated, the union tries to achieve the same benefits it formerly sought through political action. The critical point, however, is that the negotiating activities of the teachers union are also *inherently* political—not because of their content but because they are an effort to change the policies of public officials who are usually elected. To try to distinguish between the political and nonpolitical activities of any public sector union is an exercise in futility. Public personnel policies are still public policies, a fact that is conveniently ignored by those who distinguish between the "negotiating" and the "political" activities of public employee unions.

Semantic distinctions notwithstanding, the public sector union is in effect a political party—an organization formed to influence public policy. The difference between conventional political parties and public sector unions lies in (1) the range of public policies they seek to shape or influence and (2) their membership and financial base. These differences are important from certain standpoints, but they do not affect the conclusion that public sector unions are inherently political organizations, in any reasonable definition of the term.

Perhaps the most important gap between the rhetoric and the reality of teacher bargaining is the claim that it is only a procedural requirement. According to the rhetoric, PSB does not require that the employer agree to a proposal or make a concession. Typically, language to this effect is included in PSB statutes, as it is in the NLRA. Thus, it is argued that PSB merely lets employees be heard. The public employer, like its counterpart in the private sector, can always reject a union proposal without violating the law. Based on this rationale, PSB is portrayed as the most innocuous of policies, merely affording public employees the right to be heard on matters that affect them. But the rationale is immediately suspect. If a school board is considering a school calendar or bus routes, concerned parents or community residents can express their views on the issue to board members or at a school board meeting before action is taken. The parties affected would have a right to be heard that cannot be taken from them even if the school board wished to do so. Of course, teachers have the same right, even on matters that do not affect them. The notion that PSB is essential for this purpose is completely unwarranted.

In any event, the argument that PSB imposes only procedural obligations on public employers is unrealistic. To see why, consider the argument that the right to veto legislation accords the president of the United States no control over the substance of congressional legislation. Members of Congress know that such a claim would be extremely unrealistic, even though Congress can legally override a veto. The practical difficulties of overcoming the veto are usually so great that Congress accords considerable deference to the president's views, even if a congressional majority disagrees with them.

Unfortunately, it is not widely understood that PSB provides teachers unions with a legal veto power over changes in teacher personnel policies. The reason is that the school board may not change terms and conditions of employment until it has fulfilled its bargaining obligations. This point in time can vary enormously, depending upon the provisions in the PSB statute. Usually, the school board cannot act unilaterally until impasse procedures, which may take a year or more, are completed.

It is true, therefore, that a school board can reject union proposals. It is not true, however, that the employer is therefore free to act as it wishes with respect to the issues in dispute. To say that school boards "merely" have to reject union proposals is like saying that Congress "merely" has to override a presidential veto if it wishes to maintain its position on a legislative issue unchanged by presidential views on the issue.

In our personal and professional lives, we are often faced with the question of whether continued adherence to a position is worth the costs. Where public agencies are concerned, bargaining adds a great deal to the costs. School boards often modify their positions in bargaining for this reason. The teachers union points to such changes as evidence that under bargaining, the board must thoughtfully consider teachers' views and can no longer merely go through the motions of consideration. In reality, for every board concession that comes about this way, dozens of others result from a board decision that continued rejection of the union's position is not worth the time and trouble involved.

Public sector bargaining is a union initiative, so it is not surprising that its rhetoric serves union needs and interests. The success of this rhetoric can be measured by the fact that even the opponents of PSB do not understand the basic inconsistency between PSB and democratic representative government. This mistake explains why and how states have legitimated the establishment of public policies through negotiations with one interest group from which other interest groups are excluded. Similarly, legislation that accords a private organization— the public sector union—veto power over changes in public policy would not be enacted if the underlying issues were broadly understood.

Ordinarily, citizens would be offended if public policy were made by strikes or threats of strikes, or by negotiations that excluded everyone but the one interest group with the largest stake in the outcome. However, by referring to "negotiated contracts" instead of "public policies," even the opponents of PSB have accepted the formulation of the issue in the terms most favorable to the unions. As a result, the debate over PSB is focused on whether public employees should have the same rights as private sector employees. Instead, the issue should be framed as whether public agencies should negotiate public policies with one interest group that has the sole right to suspend public services or to hold up changes in public policies until its demands are met.

If citizens were asked whether public employees should have the same bargaining rights as private sector employees, a majority would probably respond in the affirmative. If they were asked whether public policies should be negotiated with the interest group with the biggest stake in the outcome, while others are excluded from the process, most would be likely to respond in the negative. Opponents of PSB could be much more effective if they formulated the issues in terms of procedures for establishing public policy instead of allowing them to be viewed inaccurately, and more narrowly, as issues related solely to terms and conditions of employment for public employees.

The Objectives of Public Sector Bargaining

We hope that this analysis has not been unduly pessimistic or has exaggerated the adverse effects of teacher bargaining upon educational reform. The fact is, however, that PSB statutes have created an institution and a process intended primarily to advance teacher welfare. There is no reason to be surprised, because other objectives are subordinate to it; on the contrary—and legislative preambles notwithstanding—the union's function is to advance the compensation and benefits of its constituency. Some of us may doubt whether the long-range interests of teachers are best served by PSB, but it will take the educational equivalent of imported Japanese automobiles to convince the teachers themselves of this fact.

Consider for a moment some typical union demands in bargaining:

- Parental complaints about teachers must be in writing.
- Teachers are entitled to union representation in meetings with parents who have complaints.
- Teachers may leave when their students are permitted to leave.
- Teachers shall not be required to attend functions outside of regular school hours unless they are paid extra for doing so.
- There shall be no discrimination against any teacher on account of sexual preference or life-style.
- No teacher shall be assigned an aide without the teacher's consent.
- Any observation of a teacher's performance shall be arranged in advance with the teacher.
- Teachers shall have the unlimited right to expel pupils, and pupils may not be readmitted to class unless the teacher so agrees.
- Teachers shall have three days' leave annually for personal business, without having to give reasons.
- Any negative information placed in a teacher's personnel file shall be removed and destroyed after two years.

What would happen if school boards accepted these proposals and countless others like them submitted over and over again by teachers unions? We believe that one of the consequences would be a significant acceleration of the growth of private schools. In conjunction with the other factors leading in this direction, bargaining is already adding an impetus of its own. As this happens, the political base of private schools is also expanding. Like the United Auto Workers, the National Education Association and the American Federation of Teachers may have to learn the hard way that both unions and employees suffer in the long run when the employer is losing its market share to employers not restricted by union contracts. A direct attack on teacher bargaining may be futile, but its proponents may do more to hasten its demise than its opponents ever could.

20. ALTERNATIVES TO TEACHERS UNIONS

The purpose of this concluding chapter is to discuss the prospects for a national nonbargaining teachers organization. We shall discuss what such an organization should stand for and how it might be established on a large scale.

The basic issues raised must be resolved from a public policy as well as teacher's perspective. These perspectives are related, but they do not necessarily lead to identical conclusions. What is good (or bad) for teachers is not necessarily good (or bad) for our society. For this reason, we propose to discuss the public policy dimension first and then try to analyze the issues from a teacher's point of view.

Regardless of the content of public policy, our system of government is supposed to ensure that no organization has any special procedural advantages in the policymaking process. Of course, every organization is more interested and more active with respect to some policies than with others. Such differences, however, do not necessarily result from advantages conferred by law but from the voluntary actions of organizations. A teachers organization may be the only one represented at meetings of the school board, but in such a case, any problems that result from this fact are not due to a breakdown in the policymaking process, but rather to the way other organizations voluntarily relate— or choose not to relate—to the process.

With teacher bargaining, however, we have institutionalized an anti-democratic system of formulating, adopting, and revising public policies in the field of education. For instance, a teacher salary schedule is a public policy. It is no less a public policy because it is a salary or a personnel policy. Indeed, it is common practice for teachers unions to propose that the collective bargaining contracts include language such as: "The Board of Education agrees that the provisions of this contract constitute board policy for the duration of this agreement, and the board agrees that it will not adopt any change in policy that violates or is inconsistent with this agreement."

The underlying public policy objection to teacher bargaining over salary policy, as with other terms and conditions of teacher employment, is that it constitutes the adoption of public policy through negotiations with one interest group, the unions. As a legal and practical matter, other individuals and groups are excluded from the policymaking process. Thus, salary schedules and a wide range of items such as the school calendar and beginning and ending times of the school day are "terms and conditions of employment," hence items subject to bargaining. Nevertheless, parents, businessmen, and farmers (among others) may also have a strong interest in these and other policies subject to bargaining. A policymaking process that denies equal procedural rights to such other groups is indefensible.

We regard many National Education Association (NEA) and American Federation of Teachers (AFT) policies as bad for teachers, bad for education, and bad for our nation. Nevertheless, disagreement with NEA/AFT policies does not necessarily constitute justification for another organization. These unions can always say, "If you don't like the union's policies, become active and change them." There is some merit in this argument, but it does not invalidate the rationale for a non-bargaining teachers organization. Essentially, the reason is that the bargaining process results in an organizational infrastructure that has a vital stake in bargaining per se. The upshot is that any effort to change NEA/AFT probargaining policies will meet with overwhelming and probably insuperable resistance from the union bureaucracy. This is not true, or is less true, of other policies supported by both the NEA and AFT. In both unions, one occasionally finds strong internal divisions, but such divisions do not arise with respect to policies that underlie union status.

To appreciate the importance of this point, suppose one wants to change the policies of a local organization of teachers. One sees other teachers in a building and in various meetings within the school, neighborhood, and school district. It is, therefore, possible for one to assess the level of support for the policies supported. Thus, although one still has no volunteer time and resources to bring about organizational change, if an appropriate level of support exists, one may have a realistic chance to succeed.

The dynamics are drastically different at the state and national levels. How can one work effectively to change the policies of a national union? One must be elected a delegate, attend conferences all over the country year after year, and devote a significant share of time and disposable income to the process. For most issues, one might be willing to do this. After all, one's opponent presumably has the same problem. But, as we have said, this is not the case with teacher bargaining. The opposition will include the union bureaucracy, and the latter will be campaigning as part of their regular jobs against the nonbargaining policies one seeks to establish. An attack on bargaining, after all, is an attack upon the system that provides thousands of union employees and bureaucrats an excellent livelihood. Because they control the agenda, the conferences, the public relations, and the communications, an internal assault upon existing policy in the existing system has no real chance to succeed. To be successful, opponents of the bargaining system must have access to organizational resources they control. It is not feasible to seek control of a national teachers union in order to de-unionize it.

One other aspect of this problem deserves comment. In any large organization, one must be willing to get into the arena and outwork and outthink the opposition. Otherwise, organizational resources and influence go by default to the opposition. At the same time, it must be emphasized that many NEA and AFT policies, in addition to support for bargaining, are dictated by union, not educational needs. Indeed, NEA and AFT consistently support policies that are deemed to be good for the unions but have adverse effects upon pupils, parents, family, and society in general. Union positions on day care, minimum wage laws, compulsory education, and home schooling illustrate union tendencies along this line. In many cases, the union stake in these issues is not apparent to most teachers. Nevertheless, efforts to change union policies on these issues would also encounter the entrenched opposition of the union bureaucracy. Also for this reason, it would be futile to attempt to change NEA/AFT policies by working within these unions.

It must be emphasized that opposition to unionization, although critically important, is not in itself a sufficient condition to establish a competitive organization. Logically and politically, an alternative organization must have an effective answer to the question of what it stands for—"effective" in terms of teacher and administrator as well as public support. We shall not try to present here a comprehensive program for an alternative organization. Let us try instead to illustrate the kind of programmatic and policy difference that would strengthen the image of an alternative organization in both public and professional opinion. As an example, we shall use minimum wage laws. Both NEA and AFT support these laws. Beyond any reasonable doubt, minimum wage laws have adverse effects upon youth employment, especially minority youth. The reason is obvious. If we make any factor of production more expensive to use, employers will do their utmost to use less of it. Obviously, disadvantaged minorities include larger proportions of unskilled labor of the type squeezed out of the labor market by minimum wage laws. Consequently, our entire society suffers from the inability of many young people to find entry level jobs and to learn the habits and attitudes essential to future occupational success.

One writer makes this point by noting that white trade unions in South Africa were a moving force behind the apartheid system.[1] These unions were afraid of competition from black workers. To discourage employers from hiring less educated blacks, the unions established standard rates for the job and sought to add a host of legal and educational requirements that would discourage employers from using unskilled black labor. If employers must pay a standard rate to both black and white workers, they are more likely to choose whites, sometimes for economically justifiable reasons, sometimes not. If employers are allowed to choose among competing employees, they will often choose black workers. Thus, the imposition of minimum wage laws and standard rates tends to weaken the ability of black workers to compete effectively for jobs. Although American minimum wage laws are not racist in intent, they clearly have a greater adverse effect upon blacks and Hispanics than upon whites.

This example demonstrates three important things:

- How NEA/AFT policies generally are oriented to union considerations, not to the long-range interests of pupils or teachers.
- A potential programmatic difference that would be advantageous to a nonunion organization. No teacher would need be concerned about losing a job because young people are working, not wasting their time in school or on the streets.

---

[1] Charles W. Baird, The varieties of "right-to-work": An essay in honor of W.H. Hutt, *Government Union Review* (Spring 1988), pp. 1-22.

- How an alternative organization might have a special appeal to minority communities and minority teachers.

Much remains to be said on all of these matters, but one distinction is absolutely crucial: the difference between the unions' interest and the teachers' interest. The unions assert that these interests are identical. "How else," they ask, "could the union support a policy if most of its members were opposed to it?" It is a fair question that deserves a realistic answer. And the answer is this: The fact that most union members do not support a union policy is no guarantee that the union will adopt the majority position. Most Americans have supported gun control for decades, yet until recently it has made little headway in Congress. The reason is that support for gun control must be mobilized and directed to specific legislative objectives. Such action requires resources and political direction. Inasmuch as the opponents of gun control would benefit only as citizens from such control, they do not provide the resources required to capitalize upon the widespread support for gun control. By the same token, even though most teachers oppose a union policy, they may find it too costly to allocate the time and resources required to ensure that the majority view prevails. In any political contest between a minority with a major stake in a policy and a diffuse majority, the minority is likely to prevail. Furthermore, the larger the organization, the more difficult it is to oppose organizational policies with private funds. This fact explains why national union leadership can adopt positions that are inconsistent with majority sentiment in the union.

Teachers' Stake in an Organizational Alternative

Let us turn next to why and how an alternative organization might enroll a very substantial number of teachers. Teachers need and are entitled to an organization devoted to their interests. Perhaps the most difficult problem confronting a teachers organization opposed to bargaining is how to avoid the perception that it is administrator-dominated and not truly devoted to teacher interests. If, for example, a teachers organization explicitly accepts the early NEA/AFT position that teachers should not have the right to strike, how would the organization avoid the criticism that it is a mere patsy for management?

Intellectually, the question is easily answered. Outside of the labor context, disagreement with duly enacted public policies does not justify disrupting a public service. Likewise, a commitment to obey the law does not imply that the organization is dominated by the government that enacted the law. When unions obey labor laws to which they are opposed, that fact is not deemed evidence that unions are dominated by government. There is a difference between government domination of an organization and respect for laws.

Intellectually, therefore, a teachers organization should not be regarded as dominated by government (i.e., management) merely because it abides by the outcomes of representative government or does not assert the right to disrupt a public service if its demands are not met. Politically, however, the outcome is problematic. As for most people generally, it is very easy for teachers to regard themselves as justified exceptions to general rules. Thus, most teachers recognize that anarchy would result if every interest group could shut down a government service until it achieved its demands. Nevertheless, many teachers who accept the general principle that public service should not be disrupted also support a teacher's right to strike. The conclusion to be drawn from this is that a successful alternative to teachers unions must first appeal to the self-interest of teachers and second to broad public policy objectives.

The problem of creating an alternative teachers organization is compounded by the absence of competition in education. On this issue, the nation's recent experiences in industries that face international competition are instructive. In such industries, unions have been forced to give up inefficient practices or face a further decline in the company and the union's membership and resources. Public education faces no such competition. To the contrary, teachers unions are the major opposition to vouchers or any program that would foster competition in the education field. Teachers benefit from competition outside of education but have developed a rationale to avoid it in their own field. To say the least, it would be difficult to persuade most public school teachers to support policies that foster competition with public schools. Because teachers unions have been able to block the arrival of competition, they are able to avoid the pressure to eliminate inefficiencies resulting from teacher bargaining. Even the opponents of teacher bargaining probably would oppose competition in education, despite the fact that competition is usually necessary to eliminate bargaining or mitigate its adverse effects.

From the standpoint of teacher welfare, why should teachers seek to avoid or to replace collective bargaining? And what should they propose in its stead? These are the critical issues; the very reasons that bargaining is undesirable from a public policy standpoint seem to strengthen its appeal to teachers.

It is easier to avoid bargaining than to get rid of it. For this reason, the membership base of a nonbargaining organization must initially come from the nonbargaining states. A national organization composed predominantly of teachers in nonbargaining states would be preferable to the status quo, but let us consider a possible approach to teachers in the bargaining states.

At the outset, we do not believe efforts to repeal the bargaining laws would be successful in these states. Instead, the effort would need to provide teachers with an alternative local organization that they would be free to join. Under this alternative, policies on conditions of employment would be resolved pursuant to normal school board policymaking procedures. In addition, however, teachers would be given a package of statutory benefits and protections that most school boards as well as teachers would prefer to collective bargaining. Inasmuch as such a package would be the key to the success of this approach, let us discuss it briefly.

Let us assume the average teacher pays $300 a year in local, state, and national union dues. For this, the teacher receives certain benefits: representation in collective bargaining and in tenure cases, some seniority advantages, and a number of contractual protections whose importance varies widely. We must also consider the costs of the bargaining process. If we add up the total costs of bargaining, most teachers would probably prefer receiving a prorated share of the costs rather than receiving the "benefits" of bargaining. Most teachers do not need tenure protection. Civil rights laws protect against racial, religious, and/or sexual discrimination. Market factors also provide teachers with some protection. In other words, some of the basic benefits of bargaining are secondary or available in the absence of bargaining or are of no consequence to most teachers. We would hazard a guess that the total costs of teacher bargaining in the United States are about $2 billion annually. This estimate refers only to the costs of the process. It includes both teacher and school board costs, as well as the costs to the judicial system and administrative agencies such as the state employment relations boards. To be sure, some of these costs would exist under any defensible system of employment relations in public education, but we believe a better system for teachers as well as public agencies could be established for a great deal less than the costs of the bargaining system.

Let us discuss the approach in terms of job security. Teachers have a major interest in not being fired, and they are willing to pay to protect this interest. Is it possible to offer them a better deal in the nonbargaining mode than they are getting? When we say "better deal," we do not necessarily mean stronger legal protection; the phrase is more likely to mean equivalent protection at a much lower cost to the teachers.

Suppose that instead of teachers paying union dues, school boards contributed a per capita amount to a teacher defense fund. A teacher challenging dismissal could draw upon this fund up to a stipulated amount for whatever representation the teacher desired. The amount available to individual teachers might be geared to their years of service. It might also be feasible to treat the benefit like unemployment insurance or worker's compensation, with teachers receiving more if their school system pays out less. At any rate, given the enormous costs of the existing system, it should be feasible to offer reasonable job security, with financial support for contested dismissals, for teachers choosing the nonbargaining alternative.

We have not worked out the details of such an arrangement, and closer analysis may demonstrate that it is not feasible. The example is merely intended to suggest a general approach, not a specific plan. To enact such a plan, it would be essential to achieve the support of school management organizations. They must recognize the appalling inefficiencies of bargaining and be willing to share the savings with teachers willing to scrap the process. Such sharing would be statutorily essential because of the bargaining laws. Let us try to explain this critical but neglected point.

In states with bargaining laws, it is an unfair labor practice either to threaten teachers or promise them benefits for voting against union representation. A school board cannot legally say to its teachers, "If you vote against teacher union representation, we will pay you half of what it would cost us to bargain with the union."

For years, one of the authors represented a small California school board that employs 50 teachers and about 30 classified employees. He was paid just over $4,000 a year to negotiate for the board, about $50 per employee. It would be illegal for the school board to offer the employees $50 each if they voted against union representation, thus rendering his employment unnecessary.

In states without bargaining laws, this offer could legally be made. In time, teachers would raise the price of voting against union representation, but that is another matter. The critical point is that in the bargaining states, it is not legally possible for school boards to offer teachers a share of the savings that would result from a teacher vote against union representation. Suppose, however, that state statutes gave teachers an option. If they voted against union representation, they would automatically receive certain statutory benefits. Because teachers would have the option statutorily, local school boards would not have to offer it. On what basis could the unions argue that teachers should not have the option, especially when they could always revert to the bargaining mode if they wished to do so? It seems to us that the unions would be forced to argue that teachers could not choose what was in their best interests. Such an approach assumes that one can devise a statutory package of benefits that school boards as well as teachers would sometimes prefer to the bargaining option. We believe that it is feasible to develop such a package. The savings in union dues, teacher time devoted to the union, and board expenses for bargaining, plus the statutory advantages of the nonbargaining option, might be attractive on a broad scale. No one really knows, because the approach has never been tried. Surely, it could and would be supported by school management. The alternative teachers association should work with school management organizations to develop such a package. If successful, it might transform the self-interest of teachers into a strategic weapon instead of a strategic obstacle to growth in membership.

At least one other alternative merits consideration: establishing an organization that includes both public and private school teachers. Such an organization would have to avoid intransigent opposition to public support for private education. That is, it could succeed only if private school teachers viewed it as supportive of their interest and if a sizable number of public school teachers supported it. One danger is that if the organization initially enrolled many private school teachers, it might not be attractive to public school teachers. Interestingly enough, the percentage of public school teachers who send their own children to private schools is much higher than the average for all parents. The critical point, however, is that aid to private schools is a threat to the national labor organizations, not to the teachers they represent. Realistically, it is unlikely that individual public school teachers would be adversely affected if we increased support for private schools. In fact, it is possible that such an approach could benefit public school teachers. Currently, parents of pupils in private schools have no reason to support larger appropriations for public education. Under a voucher system, parents of children in private schools would have reason to support increasing the amount of the voucher. As this happens, public and private schools would have to compete for teachers by offering higher salaries and benefits.

The advantage of such an approach is the possibility of establishing a large organization within a very short period of time. This would be helpful in many ways, such as increasing the benefit package that could be made available to members. The major difficulties would be the organizational platform, the modus operandi, and the difficulty of attracting public school teachers to join an organization that enrolls a substantial proportion of teachers in private schools. We do not regard this approach as the most promising one, but simply mention it as a possibility if other approaches are unsuccessful.

Dual Membership

A critical policy issue involves the status of teachers who are either NEA or AFT members or who hold membership in both unions—a common occurrence during the rise of the AFT to prominence. Our view is that it would be essential to continue to allow dual membership; that is, membership in the NEA or AFT organizations and in the alternative organization. Perhaps the alternative organization could establish a reduced rate for such teachers. Whether teachers who pay the reduced rate should be entitled to the full rights, benefits, and privileges of members paying the full rate is a matter for discussion.

First of all, logic and experience indicate that teachers do not like to pay full dues to two competing organizations. Efforts to merge the NEA and AFT at the local level illustrate this point. If a dual dues structure is adopted, what would NEA/AFT members who elected to join an alternative organization get for their money? For $10 to $25 a year, such teachers should get a publication devoted to criticizing perceived deficiencies and inconsistencies in NEA/AFT operations, information that would not be found in their own publications. Additionally, such teachers should also receive some benefits not available through the NEA or AFT. Essentially, the reduced dues rate would serve to support a caucus within NEA or AFT. Paradoxically, such a caucus might conservatize these unions to some degree, thereby rendering them more acceptable to teachers inclined to joining an alternative organization.

A dual membership structure is essential for several other reasons. Individual teachers may see little to gain by being forced to drop their union membership in order to establish membership in another organization. However, the prospect of joining a new organization with a substantial number of fellow teachers is another matter. Furthermore, it is important to gain the resources of the existing organizations whenever possible. For this reason, the strategy should be aimed at winning over local NEA or AFT leaders and local organizations en masse, and it is impossible to do this unless dual membership is accepted. Instead of persuading individual teachers to join the alternative organization, strategy should also seek to persuade teacher leaders to bring their entire organization into the alternative organization. Such a strategy requires intensive efforts to persuade local union leaders to make the change and to prepare them for union efforts to block it.

Over the years, one of the authors has given considerable thought to problems of this kind. One reason is that he was interested in a merger of the NEA and AFT and gave much thought to how to achieve it. Although the issues in this context would be different, some of the strategic considerations would not be. If prior experience is any guide, the critical issues in organizational mergers are not policy issues. They are the distribution of power, positions, and resources in the merged organization. To persuade NEA or AFT leaders to lead their local unions into another organization, the leaders in the alternative organization would need to be prepared to share leadership. Leadership opportunities would need to be made available to NEA or AFT leaders and members of their organization.

Obviously, the foregoing strategy requires an intimate knowledge of the day-to-day operations of the NEA/AFT. This is another reason that the concept of dual membership is essential; it would often be impossible to get the information needed without the teachers entitled to it as NEA/AFT members. In addition, it would be essential to understand every dimension and aspect of NEA and AFT policies, operations, and membership.

Prospects for an Alternative Organization

Obviously, we have not covered all of the important issues involved in looking toward an alternative organization. Without minimizing what we have not discussed, let us conclude with a few comments about the prospects for an alternative organization.

First of all, a statutory alternative to bargaining would be essential in the bargaining states. In both the private and public sectors, the growth and strength of unions is closely related to the statutory framework found in various state laws. Teacher bargaining is no exception. Just as teachers unions were able to expand because of favorable legislation, it is essential to enact legislation that provides realistic alternatives to it.

People who want change generally underestimate the difficulties of achieving it. For this reason—and to guard against naive optimism—we have tried to address some of the real problems facing an alternative organization. Fortunately, there are also some favorable factors that could be used to good advantage in such an effort. Let us comment briefly on a few.

There is some evidence that teachers are becoming more dissatisfied with their unions. Feistritzer's study of teachers showed that although 75 percent of teachers with 25-29 years of experience are NEA members, only 55 percent of hires in the last five years are members.[2] Thirty-eight percent of teachers with less than five years of experience were not members of either NEA or AFT, whereas only 14 percent of teachers with 24-29 years of teaching were not union members. In a 1986 poll, one-third of the teachers were dissatisfied with their national union, 27 percent with their state union, and 21 percent with their local union. These data mirror a widespread national decline in private sector union membership, from an all-time high of 36 percent of the private nonfarm labor force in 1945 to less than 11 percent in 1992. The unions themselves are deeply concerned about the decline in their membership and influence. For many years, public sector unions increased rapidly while private sector unions were declining, but it appears that public sector unionization has also crested in the United States. An alternative teacher organization would compete with unions

---

[2] See Emily Feistritzer, *Profiles of teachers in the U.S.* (Washington, D.C.: National Center for Education Information, 1986.)

that are defenders of the status quo—not an advantageous position in the field of education.

In our opinion, a practical alternative to collective bargaining would be supported by school management. More precisely, school board members and school administrators and their state and national organizations could be persuaded to support efforts to replace the bargaining system. Such support would not happen automatically, but it is achievable within a reasonable period of time.

Furthermore, both the NEA and AFT are extremely vulnerable if one knows where to look for the vulnerabilities. For example, few NEA members have any idea of the enormous salaries and fringe benefits paid to NEA officers and staff. One obvious reason is that it would be impossible to raise the dues if the rank and file realized how many union staff members are receiving $50,000-$125,000 a year in salaries and fringe benefits—and how many elected officers are receiving a great deal more, much of it concealed in budget lines that are designed to conceal more than to reveal.[3]

Teachers may be spending $1 billion a year in local, state, and national dues. This is a staggering estimate but, we believe, a realistic one. The national offices of NEA and AFT alone have incomes of about $250 million. It is inevitable that the rank and file of membership will begin to question the way these vast amounts are being spent.

Paradoxically, the failures of the two organizations are partly responsible for the absence of a competing national nonunion organization. Especially in the South, many teachers are unwilling to join any national teachers organization as a result of their experience with the NEA or AFT. This experience should have led to efforts to bring about change within these national organizations; instead, it has often led to an antipathy toward support for any national organization.

In conclusion, let us suggest that the situation does not justify either optimism or pessimism. Developing a competitive national nonunion organization would be difficult, but not necessarily more difficult than the development of the AFT into a major organization. The future of nonunion organizations does not depend upon their existing numbers but on how they relate to existing circumstances and those

---

[3] See Myron Lieberman, Charlene Haar, and Leo Troy, *The NEA and AFT: Teacher unions in power and politics* (Rockport, Me.: Pro-Active Publishers, 1994).

that will exist in the future. In fact, it may be easier to bring about a major change in their prospects than to induce incremental ones.

As it happened, the AFT did not replace, take over, or merge with the NEA, as was once expected. Instead, the emergence of the AFT into a competitive organization transformed the NEA into a union. It could well be that the emergence of a strong nonbargaining teacher organization would have profound effects upon the NEA/AFT. In any event, teacher unionization has yet to face a credible challenge. We do not really know what would happen if and when such a challenge arose. Nevertheless, mounting such a challenge would be a worthwhile effort, especially if there is wider appreciation of the contradictions between public sector bargaining and democratic government.

Conclusions

The adversarial nature of collective bargaining creates animosities between teachers and administrators at a time when closer working relationships are being promoted as a model for school improvement. Unfortunately, more open and decentralized models of decision making are not likely to be implemented as long as traditional methods of collective bargaining remain in effect. The threat of union interference in the operation of schools is real, and school boards will rightly remain cautious whenever suggestions of mutual decision making are raised. Furthermore, the restrictive language found in many contracts makes change and competition—competition that has as its objective a more open and flexible school governance system—difficult if not impossible to achieve.

The time has come for a reassessment of collective bargaining in public education. The need for the development of alternative methods of receiving and addressing employee concerns is at hand. As we have pointed out, this reassessment is not likely to be generated by the leadership of the national teachers unions. These leaders have a vested interest in the status quo. The fact is, however, that teachers embraced collective bargaining just as it was beginning a precipitous decline in the private sector. In the light of contemporary concerns for school reorganization and 30 years of experience with public sector bargaining, perhaps the time has come to reassess the laws that foster and protect collective bargaining in public education.

INDEX